SKATEBOARDING LA

£4.99

⑬

ω39

ALTERNATIVE CRIMINOLOGY SERIES

General Editor: Jeff Ferrell

Skateboarding LA

Inside Professional Street Skateboarding

Gregory J. Snyder

NEW YORK UNIVERSITY PRESS

New York

NEW YORK UNIVERSITY PRESS
New York
www.nyupress.org

References to Internet websites (URLs) were accurate at the time of writing. Neither the author nor New York University Press is responsible for URLs that may have expired or changed since the manuscript was prepared.

Library of Congress Cataloging-in-Publication Data
Names: Snyder, Gregory J., author.
Title: Skateboarding LA : inside professional street skateboarding / Gregory J. Snyder.
Description: New York : New York University Press, [2017] |
Includes bibliographical references and index.
Identifiers: LCCN 2017010913 | ISBN 9780814769867 (cl : alk. paper) |
ISBN 9780814737910 (pb : alk. paper)
Subjects: LCSH: Skateboarding—California—Los Angeles.
Classification: LCC GV859.8 .S595 2017 | DDC 796.2209794/94—dc23
LC record available at https://lccn.loc.gov/2017010913

New York University Press books are printed on acid-free paper, and their binding materials are chosen for strength and durability. We strive to use environmentally responsible suppliers and materials to the greatest extent possible in publishing our books.

Manufactured in the United States of America

10 9 8 7 6 5 4 3 2 1

Also available as an ebook

For Luna, I'm over the moon.

—Love Daddy

CONTENTS

ACKNOWLEDGMENTS

So much has changed since I started this book; we've moved, survived a hurricane, and had a beautiful daughter, Luna Jayne (5), who provides constant joy and inspiration, along with many challenges. To that end it would have been impossible to write this book without the support and so many sacrifices made by my beautiful and talented wife Alma. Thank you so much for putting up with my research and writing schedule.

Our extended family has also changed as I now have two amazing sisters-in-law, Maria (Brian's wife) and Michelle (Boo's wife), who are extremely supportive. Special thanks to Michelle for tolerating my presence on the air mattress in their living room every summer. Brian and Maria also have a son, Ian Charles (2); he rips. Brother Brian also gave me the idea for the opening story of our failure to build a ramp.

Thanks to Mom and Dad for limitless support and generosity. For helping out with Luna while I was away, and Dad for reading everything I sent and responding with notes almost immediately.

Aaron, there is no way to calculate the debt I owe you. This book obviously would not be what it is without your enduring presence; but beyond this book, I have been inspired by your commitment to skating since you were 9 and I feel that helped me to find my path as an ethnographer. Thank you for your patience, your caring, and your joy in my learning. It has been an honor to be your student. Thanks also for reading every draft of this manuscript, offering insight, and fact-checking my skate knowledge.

Ilene Kalish, for 10 years you have been my editor, and for the last 6 you've been my colleague, my (very strict) writing coach, and my friend. You believed in this project when it was just a table of contents. It has been an intellectual thrill to work with you, and you have forced me to make this book as good as it can be (though any shortfalls are completely my own). Also, tons of thanks go to Caelyn Cobb for all of her hard work.

Late in this project Pete Lehman came on board. What started as a simple email question quickly turned into a full-on critical review of the whole book from a person who is both a skater and a scholar. I could not have been luckier; thank you so much for all the work you did.

Matt Gottwig very early expressed real interest in this project and offered to help beyond just showing me skating; he assisted with some data gathering, and let me witness firsthand some amazing skating. Thanks Gotty.

Nick Tucker, thank you for your enthusiasm, for your inspiring skating, and for letting me share in the story of your success.

Aquil Brathwaite, thank you for so many great conversations and thank you for your continued curiosity about things outside of skating. You allowed me to participate in your world as an equal, and I consider that to be a great gift. Thanks also for inviting me to the Diamond House. Thanks to Jeron Wilson, who was incredibly hospitable and generous with his time. Shout-out to Torey Pudwill, Boo Johnson, and Jamie Foy.

Corey White was also extremely helpful and schooled me on the ways of digital media.

RB Umali was a constant sounding board, responding to every email and text almost immediately, and was always down to talk skating despite his hectic schedule.

Thanks to Atiba Jefferson, who gave me his time and energy, despite the fact that he is the hardest working dude in the game.

Troy Turner, it has been a joy having you help out with this project. Huge thanks to Kelly Hart, Diego Najera, Sebo Walker, Cody McEntire, Bill Weiss, Gabe Clement, Eric Sorenson, Mike Guffey, Sean McNulty, Robbie McKinley, Alec Beck, Hoops (Mike Adalpe), Dave Mayhew, Kimathi Smith, Jaime Reyes, Yuto Kojima, Shad Lambert, Brian Emmers, Billy Roper, Brian Jones, Alex Corporan, Mark Razo, Neftali Williams, and Bryan Paternoster.

To my colleagues at Baruch, thank you for your mentorship and your belief in me. Glenn Petersen, your advocacy for me during my tenure ride was incredible and made the process bearable. Much love to Carolle Charles, Ken Guest, Michael Plekon, Robin Root, Carla Bellamy, Angie Beeman, Barbara Katz Rothman, Susan Chambre, and Ted Hencken.

Special thanks to Shelley Watson, for all you do and for the love you give.

To my many criminology colleagues, thanks for all of your advice and support. Tons of love go to brother Keith Hayward and uncle Jeff Ferrell; you dudes are always on point and keep me in check. Much love to Tony Jefferson, Paul Willis, Avi Brisman, Carla Barrett, Travis Linnemen, Stabislav (Stas) Vysotsky, Bobby Weide, Mark Hamm, Frank Wilson, Harold Henderson, Eamonn Carrabine, Dave Brotherton, Jayne Mooney, Jock Young (RIP—we lost a giant). Also, Johnny Illan, James Pitts, Carl Root, Eddy Green, and Jeffery Ian Ross.

Shout-out to the Greek Squad, Kostas Avramidis, and Myrto Tsilimpounidi who showed a couple graffiti heads (me and Jeff) the best damn walking tour of Athens anyone could possibly imagine.

Thanks to my New York family for all the love and support. Des and Maria, Adam and Kathleen, Rachel and Efrain, Fred and Courtney. Much love and thanks to Kareem Bunton, Jaleel Bunton, Torbitt and Virginia Schwartz, Wilder Zoby, George Duvoe, Niels Alpert, Brian Freeman, Quindell Willis, Shannon Moore, Cervantes Ramirez, Sergio Hernandez, Scotty Hard, Konstance Patton, Dave Smith (Smoota) and Amy Touchette, Aaron Landsman, Timmy and Margaret, Gabe Banner, and Steve Powers.

Special thanks to Mickey Duzyj, who also read portions of the text and offered amazing feedback.

Shout-out to the Red Hook Parents for fostering a great community for our children.

Finally, this book is also dedicated to Bob Kanuri, a dear, dear friend whom we lost way too early. Bob you would have loved this book, and I look forward to long discussions on the other side. We love you and we miss you.

Thank you skateboarding; keep up the good work.

In service.

Greg
Red Hook, Brooklyn
10.20.16

Prologue

It is a sunny Sunday in Los Angeles and Matt Gottwig, a skater who one day hopes to become a pro, is attempting to perform a trick on a ledge on Hollywood Boulevard. Matt fails to land his "back tailslide" on the first attempt, but on his second try he nails it. A security guard approaches us, but we gather our things and quickly leave before he can say anything.

Now there's talk of the next spot. Marko Jazbinsec, pro skater and owner of Goldstar Skateboards, announces that there is a " 'bump over a hydrant,' on Orange between Hollywood and Franklin."

Our crew of six, which includes two skaters, two "filmers," my brother Aaron, and myself, head over to the next spot. The "spot" is in front of the Biltmore Hotel and across from the back of the Kodak Theater, which will host the Oscars in two weeks. The hydrant is yellow with a red top, flanked by red curb cutouts, which the skaters will use as a ramp, or "bump," to launch themselves into the air and over the hydrant. When we arrive the filmers, the photographers, and myself quickly take our positions and the session begins. (I'm shooting video, but there is an understanding that my video will be used only for my research.)

Billy Roper, a veteran skater, flies down the sidewalk and knocks out a clean "ollie" over the hydrant for a warm-up trick. Matt however is the focus of this spot, and after a quick look he decides on a "heelflip," a trick where he will ollie, or pop the board into the air and use the heel of his front foot to flip the board one time on its horizontal axis. And even though a heelflip is not the most difficult trick, it is, as skaters say, "a legit trick," meaning of publishable quality, especially considering the time constraints of the spot.

This is a fairly difficult spot to skate, and it will take a few tries to overcome the myriad tiny challenges that the surface presents. We are also right in the center of Hollywood, and we won't go unnoticed for long, which adds to the pressure to perform.

Matt flies down the sidewalk, wheels whirring over the concrete, ollies into the air, and attempts his heelflip. On the first few tries he fails badly. In between takes, Matt looks at the digital photo on Aaron's camera to confirm that he's lined up properly.

Matt is starting to get a feel for the space and is getting closer to landing the heelflip. However, a person from the Biltmore Hotel, with STAFF written on the back of his shirt, comes out and tells us we have to leave. Marko walks over to the man, and politely tells him that we'll be done in a few minutes. But STAFF insists we leave now, and whips out his cell phone and tells us he's "calling the cops." Nobody seems deterred by this threat. Marko returns to his filming position and signals to Matt to try again.

The tension increases. All of the crew (except me) have been in this situation before, and they know it takes a while for the cops to actually arrive, but now the pressure is mounting. If Matt cannot land the

Matt Gottwig, heelflip over fire hydrant. Photo: Aaron Snyder.

trick before the cops come, he will lose the opportunity to get "a clip"—documented video evidence of a skateboard trick—and all this effort will be for naught. I take my cues from the others who are doing nothing, but I also begin to develop a slow rage towards STAFF.

This is public space. We are not on the grounds of the hotel, we are on the sidewalk and in the street, and we are doing nothing destructive to the property or disruptive to traffic, and not only are the hotel guests not complaining, some have even stopped to watch. It is however, surprisingly loud.

Matt stays focused. Though aware of the situation, he is concentrating on his skating. STAFF however is increasing his rhetoric. On Matt's ninth attempt, he comes cruising down the sidewalk heading for the hydrant, in clear defiance of our accuser, and pops into the air, just missing landing the trick. Thinking that maybe the guy now understands a little bit better that Matt is trying to achieve something creative, dangerous, and possibly even interesting, Billy goes over to STAFF and tries to reason with him. Hell no.

Matt flies down again for the tenth attempt. He gets close but has to bail out at the last second. He screams in frustration. The pressure is mounting; he's likely got only one or two more tries before the cops arrive and send us away, leaving Matt's work unfinished. On the eleventh attempt, Matt rides down the sidewalk, pops into the air, and executes a perfect heelflip; he lands cleanly on the board and rolls away down the street. The crew lets out a cheer, and in seconds we are gone, leaving STAFF standing there with his jaw open, phone to his ear, on hold with the police, looking silly.

Not only did Matt land the trick, but because he did it so quickly after being told to leave, he has also spared us any unwanted stress of dealing with the cops. There is an outpouring of collective joy, and because I witnessed and documented the feat, I feel part of it. We walk around the corner, and Marko flips the screen on his camera so we can see the finished product. Everyone agrees it looks great and gives Matt praise for his trick. No mention is made of the cops, or STAFF, or that we got away with one; skateboarding is illegal in most American cities, and eluding the law is just part of the process of being a professional street skater.

Introduction

I got my first and only skateboard, a used Alva, in 1980, the summer between sixth and seventh grades. This was the summer when Peter Hoeffel introduced my middle brother Brian and me to the Sex Pistols, Devo, and the Clash. Peter was also a skater, and he made it clear that in order to be "punk" we had to build a skateboard ramp in our backyard, so we too could become skate punks. At the time there was no such thing as street skating and no skate parks in our hometown, Green Bay, Wisconsin, so building a ramp was our only option.

We were young and dumb, and we built our ramp with no help from adults or anyone who had ever built one before, but we were very excited when we finally finished it. That is until Peter took the first run, and shouted out, "it suuuuucks" and we discovered immediately how poorly designed our ramp was. (For skate nerds, it sucked because we had 10 feet on the deck side and 12 feet on the other, with 4 feet of vert and only 8 feet of flat. Oops.)

Soon the summer was over and I started junior high and the ramp sat there unused until Brian and Peter dismantled it and turned it into a quarter pipe for their BMX bikes. They got really good on their bikes, and our skateboards collected dust in the garage. My skating officially came to a close when I left my board in the path of my mom's car and she ran over it, snapping it in two.

My youngest brother, Aaron, was between three and five years old during this time, and although he never got to skateboard on the ramp, he says that it had a big impact on him when skateboarding began to increase in popularity in the late 1980s with the advent of street skateboarding.

While my interest in skating waned rather quickly, Aaron soon became obsessed. He began skating when he was nine, just around the time I left for college, and soon thereafter announced that skating was his life's purpose. He began skateboarding in Green Bay and kept at it when my family moved to Madison, Wisconsin, in 1988. In 1995, when he was 18 years old, he moved to San Diego, California, to try to become a professional skateboarder.

In 2001 he turned pro for Darkstar Skateboards, but by 2004 he was no longer a sponsored professional. Aaron moved to Los Angeles and continued to skate, but he was having a difficult time growing up and out of skateboarding. By 2008, at the beginning of this project, Aaron

Aaron Snyder with his Christmas gift. Photo: Maureen Snyder.

Aaron Snyder, judo air, age 12. Photo: Maureen Snyder.

was very much an outsider in skating, the very thing he loved the most. Looking back, I remember vividly a moment in 2009 when Aaron, on the verge of tears, pulled the car over so he could vent and express the frustration and depression that accompanied no longer being a part of skating.

It took some time, but today much of this has changed, and I can't help but feel like working on this project helped to make a difference. Aaron has become something else, and yet, mostly he's still just a skater. He is still searching for his ideal career, but he works as a freelance video editor for reality television as well as skate-related content. He has found a crew of skaters in West Los Angeles who provide inspiration and ca-maraderie, and he is well respected for both his skills and his knowledge of the culture. In 2010 he was hired as a judge for the Street League Skateboarding competition, which allowed him to develop relationships with some of the best skateboarders in the world, and I was included.

He has also surprisingly become an activist and was part of the team that successfully lobbied local LA politicians to unlock his favorite skate

Aaron Snyder, backside tailslide to fakie. Photo: Kimathi Smith.

Aaron Snyder's pro board. Photo: Aaron Snyder.

spot in the world, the Courthouse in West Los Angeles, which I will have a lot to say about later in the book. He has thus become the de facto liaison between City Council members and skaters. He's organized cleanups, developed a relationship with the chair of the West LA Neighborhood Council, and even worked briefly with Nike executives to sponsor future renovations to the Courthouse. He is also working on his own short documentary about skateboard activism and the attempt to "free" public skate spots.

Professional Street Skateboarding

This book is about professional street skateboarding, a highly refined, athletic, and aesthetic pursuit, from which a large number of people profit, not recreational skateboarding as a mode of transportation, resistance, or ritual. (Skateboarding has been estimated to be a $5 billion a year industry.)[1] Street skateboarders see the world differently, because they are skating on it, and to do so they creatively interpret architectural features—ledges, banks, gaps, stairs, and handrails—to perform their tricks. The tricks they perform are filmed and photographed and then disseminated to numerous platforms—videos, magazines, social media, websites. Skaters do this to increase their reputations, and hence their earnings. This model is similar in some ways to the academy, where professors publish original research articles (tricks) in the most prestigious journals (magazines), and from these published feats, money and other rewards follow.

Skateable stairs, SAMO 14, Santa Monica High School. Photo: Gregory Snyder.

The careers of skateboarders have been advanced by their own media efforts in which they document and disseminate skateboarding feats to a global audience of consumers and producers of skateboarding content, that is, tricks performed on street obstacles. As a result, there are numerous support careers within the industry, which come from the need to document, disseminate, design, and distribute skateboarding content and products. This means that what I refer to as the "skateboarding subculture" supports the career aims of not only highly talented skateboarders, but also "filmers," photographers, video editors, writers, journalists, shoe designers, clothing designers, graphic artists, team managers, web designers, and company owners, to name just a few. Importantly, all of the participants in this industry have one thing in common—they are skaters. (Except of course for the major athletic apparel corporations, like Nike, Adidas, Converse, and New Balance, whose "action sports directors," I have found, are usually not skaters.)

Despite this professionalism and its worldwide popularity, skateboarding in much of the United States is illegal. Skaters therefore are enmeshed in a constant battle with security guards and police to skate in public spaces. The result is that they are always getting kicked out of spots and constantly have to be on the lookout for police. But for the most part the consequences of illegality are merely a nuisance; skaters are often ticketed and forced to pay a nominal fine (which pro skaters can easily afford), but they are usually not arrested or sentenced to jail, just simply forced to leave. But they always come back.

It is tempting to interpret skateboarding in and on public space as small acts of spatial transformation with potential political resistance, as sociologist Francisco Vivoni and architecture historian Iain Borden have done superbly.[2] However, I will show that the politics of professional skateboarding come less from the types of activities that skaters engage in and more from the camaraderie that comes from sharing a passion with like-minded others. Skaters are constantly getting kicked out of spots and being reminded that skating is illegal and that they are a public nuisance. But skaters' persistent transformation of spots, while not directly political, informs their interpretation of public space. This has created strong bonds of social cohesion among skaters, bonds that, combined with a deft use of social media, have translated into small but significant collective actions.[3] This is to say that the politics of many

No skateboarding, Los Angeles. Photo: Gregory Snyder.

subcultures lie not in spectacular acts of symbolic resistance but in the way subcultural solidarity fosters a community.[4]

In my previous research on graffiti writers in New York City, the idea of what I called a "subculture career" emerged out of my protracted study. As the graffiti writers aged, they found ways to turn their skills and connections within their subculture into careers. This is not the case with my research on skateboarding, which has had a fully formed, and ever-expanding, subculture industry for more than two decades. Instead I found that a large number of skaters have subculture careers, and as they have gained economic and social power, they have translated this into political power, especially in issues related to their use of public space. The politics of subculture, therefore, lie not in the content of subcultural activity manifesting as abstract resistance, but in the community that accrues from social interaction with people who share a worldview. This means that the politics of skateboarding, and subcultures in general, are less about the form of activity and more about the community and solidarity that come from participating in the subculture.

An additional lesson of this study, and one that skaters have been trying to convince me of for a long time, is that skateboarders believe they can do anything. I first heard photographer Giovani Reda proclaim that "skateboarders can change the world" at a contest he was hosting that also raised money for a sick kid. Nowadays, Reda, who produced and directed the 2016 video with over 667,000 views on YouTube in which Brian Anderson comes out as a gay man, signs all of his Instagram posts with the hashtag #skatersruletheworld.[5] Skaters believe that they can change the world, or at least how the world views skateboarding. For a long time I resisted this notion, dismissing it as simple bluster, but having spent time with skaters, I'm starting to believe them.[6]

Subculture and Self-Preservation

The Contemporary Centre for Cultural Studies in England, which later came to be known as the Birmingham School, gained prominence in the late 1960s and early 1970s under the direction of Stuart Hall. With an energetic crew of young graduate students including Tony Jefferson, John Clarke, Dick Hebdige, and Brian Roberts, the CCCS began to focus their critical gaze toward elements of pop and working-class culture, specifically the spectacular styles of working-class youth cultures. These scholars emphasized that it was important for investigators of culture to focus not only on so-called "high culture" but also on youth, pop, and working-class cultures. Their initial interest was piqued by the so-called teddy boys, whose dress was a riff on the Edwardian suits of the period, marketed toward the upper class. The teddy boys put together a look that shocked mainstream sensibilities, and most closely resembled what today we would call rockabilly culture. The teds spawned other groups, like the mods (think the Who, with crisp suits, skinny ties, amphetamines, and tricked-out Vespas) and the rockers, who wore leather jackets and were inspired by early Elvis Presley, culminating most importantly with the punks, who wore ripped clothes safety pinned together, with spiked and dyed hair, all the while snarling a giant "fuck off" to everything that England held sacred, like the Beatles, Pink Floyd, and most famously in the case of the Sex Pistols, the queen.

Birmingham School cultural studies used a theoretical model that led them to interpret working-class youths' style as an act of symbolic resistance that hoped to momentarily "win space" from the larger society. Subculturalists did this, these scholars argued, by mocking, reshaping, and resisting capitalism's attempt to impose an identity upon them. Working-class youth "bricolaged" together a pastiche of styles, which shocked mainstream sensibilities and amounted to an act of symbolic political resistance.

In their most famous book, *Resistance through Rituals*, Hall and Jefferson write: "There is no 'subcultural career' for the working class lad, no 'solution' in the subcultural milieu, for problems posed by the key structuring experiences of the class."[7] The ideological foundations of the Birmingham School were firmly rooted in Marxism (and semiotics), which meant that they dismissed as pure co-optation any attempt by young people to survive by selling commodities. On this last point they were simply wrong.

When British sociologist Angela McRobbie, a second-generation Birmingham scholar, wrote about what she called "subcultural entrepreneurialism" in the 1980s, many of her Birmingham colleagues rejected her ideas. However, McRobbie understood that subculture participants are interested not as much in radical politics as in the survival of themselves and their culture. McRobbie argued therefore that they come up with creative ways to persist and subsist. McRobbie, it turned out, was right all along. She writes:

> The presence of the entrepreneurial dynamic has rarely been acknowledged in most subcultural analysis. Those points at which subcultures offered the prospect of a career through the magical exchange of the commodity have warranted little attention. . . . Selling goods and commodities came too close to "selling out."[8]

Kara-Jane Lombard is one of the few contemporary scholars not seduced by the call of resistance. In her research on skateboarding in Australia, she argues that skateboarding is so diverse that to view it as "pure resistance is problematic."[9] This is to say that while skaters subscribe to an antiestablishment worldview, it is not necessarily resistant in terms of politics or economics. Skaters are passionate about skateboarding, and so they go to great lengths to use public space for their own purposes. While this can be interpreted as a form of politics, very often at least part of the motivation for these performances is profit. This does not mean that they are compromised, as much as it means that skaters engage in a complex negotiation between personal and cultural survival and capitalism.

Despite all of the interest that the Birmingham School generated toward resistant subcultures, it is important to remember that the resistance that they described was merely symbolic. While the Birmingham School taught us to take seriously subcultural style, that symbols matter, and that commodification was imminent, it needs to be remembered that their argument was also that symbolic politics were largely ineffective. They argued that symbolic resistance is likely to remain so, while the aesthetics of that resistance become repackaged and sold to a wider audience.[10] This should not deter scholars from their interest in subcultures, but rather encourage them to attempt to understand how subcultures seek to negotiate and avoid this trap. Skating's eventual mainstreaming can lead to more money and more problems; for example, none of the executives at Nike actually understand the real language of skateboarding. This means that they can't tell a kickflip from a heelflip, or a feeble grind from a smith grind (a skill that every

15-year-old skater in the world can accomplish). On the plus side, this also suggests that skaters will still be able to retain some amount of control over the commodification of their subculture. Skaters (and graffiti writers and others) are involved in a day-to-day process where the need to profit from their accomplishments, in order to continue to do the thing that they love, compromises the very thing that they have created, making them individually and culturally more vulnerable. This negotiation will be played out in this book.

Skating is resistant in that it offers an alternative career path, and one that requires no assistance whatsoever from state educational institutions. It can offer a life and a career almost entirely within the confines of the subculture.

Very few skaters, even those who have fairly successful professional careers, will be able to retire off of skateboarding. Many however are more likely to make a career in the skateboarding industry. Skaters, like professional athletes, have a very limited time frame in which to make an income from their physicality; however, the entrepreneurial spirit of the subculture makes it so that kids who are successful on some level at skateboarding can find a way to participate in the skateboarding industry, which for the past three decades has primarily been skater-owned or skater-run.

This phenomenon is currently under strain. As skateboarding becomes more popular (and hence more lucrative for skaters and for those who capitalize on it), the tendency for skaters to give up a little bit of control for a little extra money is real. In stark terms skaters are currently engaged in a culture-wide debate over whether or not their subculture is being co-opted, at the same time that they are profiting off of its mainstreaming. The ultimate end result of this move is difficult to predict, but skaters will not give up without a fight, and will likely negotiate for themselves a coalition that they can live with between skater-owned and corporate-owned companies. That said skateboarding will be an Olympic sport in Tokyo in 2020.

On a theoretical level in this book I look specifically at the literature on subculture, space, and the city. In doing so I will apply urban sociologists' notion of the "ethnic enclave" to show that distinct subcultural enclaves exist in major cities across the world. This book shows that in places where subcultures exist and persist, like graffiti writing in New York City or skateboarding in Los Angeles, subcultural enclaves create and sustain subculture careers.

This is the first ethnographic study of skateboarding, and my main goal is to produce thick cultural description that will provide outsiders some insight into the process of this complex, but mostly misunderstood subculture. This does not mean that I'm not going to make an argument about skateboarding. The themes of this research revolve around the idea of subculture careers, subculture media, subculture enclaves, and subculture community, all of which call for a reassessment of much of the existing literature surrounding the sociological and political significance of subcultures.

This book is a detailed study of the subculture of skateboarding and of the collective impact that skateboarding careers have on cities. I show that more than petty vandalism and exaggerated claims of destruction, skateboarding creates opportunities for skaters the world over and draws highly talented people to cities like Los Angeles.

Skateboarding and Urban Space

Almost as important as how skateboarding happens is where skateboarding happens. This book also explores the manner by which professional street skateboarders choose skateboarding spots, and the processes of skateboard documentation and production, which turn these spots into landmarks. These urban spaces, which include ledges, banks, gaps, handrails, and stairs, are generally architectural happy accidents that meet specific criteria such as the size of an obstacle and the smoothness of the approach; however, just as important is the subcultural history of a spot, which makes it a litmus test for skaters from different parts of the world, and from different generations. Any place that meets these criteria skaters say is "skateable," and they refer to it simply as a "spot."[11]

For over 30 years, skateboarders have sought and found tens of thousands of skateboarding spaces and performed courageous and original tricks on them, thus investing a spot with personal and subcultural meaning. In this book I address the significance of these famous "skate spots" as well as the role these spots play in providing potential career opportunities and drawing future generations of skaters to California.

DWP Ledges, Department of Water and Power, Los Angeles. Photo: Gregory Snyder.

In urban sociology, the focus on space has become one of the dominant themes over the past decade, and research has shown that space, like class, race, and gender, is one of the key structuring elements of social life.[12] Some city spaces curtail opportunities, exacerbate poverty, limit quality health care, provide inadequate education, and prevent access to quality food.[13] The spatially disadvantaged are born into city spaces of environmental toxicity and are cut off from public transportation, social services, and quality schools, while the upper and middle classes continue to benefit from spaces that drastically reinforce their privilege. And like racial privilege, spatial privilege is seemingly invisible to those who benefit from it.[14]

Professional street skateboarders' unique relationship to urban space helps to further the numerous academic discussions surrounding space. French social theorist Henri Lefebvre argued in *The Production of Space* that everyday life was the site of future resistance and that citizens had a "right to the city."[15] Lefebvre initiated what some have called

Hollywood 16, Hollywood High School, Los Angeles. Photo: Aaron Snyder.

the "spatial turn," which culminated in the idea that all social life is "emplaced," or as urban sociologist Herbert Gans puts it, "natural space becomes a social phenomenon, or social space, once people begin to use it."[16]

This interest in space and capital, often called the spatial turn, cuts across a wide range of disciplines from sociology to geography, architectural design, and urban planning. Within these groups there is an emerging consensus that space is critical for understanding life chances; however, many argue that public spaces, where citizens are free to relax, congregate, play, and protest, are becoming less and less inclusive as capitalism attempts to turn public spaces into sites for consumption and profit. Many critics have therefore focused attention, theoretically and empirically, on groups, from guerilla gardeners to those who customize "lowrider" cars, whose activities appropriate, resist, critique, and otherwise highlight "everyday practices" as acts of lived resistance.[17]

As sociologist Karen Malone and others have shown, the spaces of young people tend to be less gendered than adult spaces, and youth, in an effort to escape the prying eyes of parents, tend to favor public spaces.[18] Unable to congregate at bars or clubs, and possessing little disposable income, young men and women spend a majority of their non-school and non-home time on the streets, which the adult world generally interprets as unproductive, sometimes criminal, mischief. As MacDonald and Shildrick write, "The age-old impulse of respectable, adult society to corral and control those engaged in apparently unproductive, street-based leisure . . . has culminated of late in the increasing imposition of 'Anti-Social Orders' and night-time street curfews on British youth."[19]

Despite the general negativity associated with youth skateboarding on the streets, Malone argues that the street is also a place of performance and identity formation. Jonathan Ilan, in his amazingly well-researched book *Understanding Street Culture*, goes further, suggesting that the street can be a site of cultural display, where competition and banter sometimes are merely means of providing entertainment, but often, besting your mates cracking jokes or killing it in freestyle rap ciphers affirms a (sub)cultural identity and also allows for the honing of skill sets in music, art, fashion, and so on that have significant exchange value in the (sub)cultural industries. As Ilan shows for rap (and grind in the United Kingdom), the lyrical depiction of often—but not always—exaggerated street life is commodified, which provides both a career opportunity for the participants as well as a mechanism for their further exploitation in the market.[20]

Skateboarding Scholarship

Most of the scholarship on skateboarding revolves around the idea of play as resistance. American studies scholar Michael Willard suggested nearly two decades ago that skaters have some special insight to teach us about resistance and the operation of everyday space, calling skaters "urbanologists" whose approach to space highlights how space is ordered and how aggressively its boundaries are enforced.[21] Woolley and Johns argue that skateboarders treat the city as a playground, while sociologist Francisco Vivoni also sees skating as a site of potential politics. Sociologist of sport Becky Beal has been working on the question of authenticity in skating for the past decade and insists, quite correctly, that skating can be a site for the formation of male identities.[22]

Despite the popularity of space in urban sociology, very little attention has been given to skateboarders by urban sociologists. There is only one academic book on skateboarding and only a limited number of journal articles.[23] In addition there has yet to be a single ethnographic account of the subculture. In his excellent book *Skateboarding, Space and the City*, architectural historian Iain Borden argues that recreational skaters' use of space is a direct critique of architecture as a form of social control. An additional aspect of Borden's argument, that skateboarding is an act of spatial resistance, revolves around the notion that skating is antithetical to production. Borden argues that skateboarding, besides critiquing the elements of control embedded in public space, is a threat to the modern capitalist state because skaters are seen to be simply having fun and disengaging from the system of production and are simply taking up space. He writes, "Like the homeless, skateboarders occupy urban space without engaging in economic activity."[24]

Though Borden's argument about resistance as an abstract feature of the act of skateboarding is well thought-out, this claim about skateboarding in practice could not be further from the truth. While it is certainly a plausible argument that the general public's disdain for skating might stem from this impression, the actual practice of skateboarding is not mere play but work, creative, productive work that results in a commodity—the video clip—that is shared with a global subculture, which causes other skaters to buy products associated with their favorite skater. Not only do video clips allow skaters to turn their play into work, they also become the record of subcultural knowledge, and thus making videos of oneself and one's peers, even if it does not lead to a career, is part of the process of subcultural participation. Many skaters who are not at the am or pro level also film video clips most often strictly for their own use, to learn from, to see themselves in action, or simply as a personal record of an accomplishment. However, Borden's argument that many skaters are not engaged in economic activity is a misreading at best. Borden's interpretation of skateboarding, while fascinating especially as it illuminates some heavy theory, ultimately plays only a small role in the practice of professional skateboarding.

The most fascinating scholarship on skateboarding comes from someone who, unfortunately, no longer writes about skateboarding. Ocean Howell was a legendary professional skater and is now (at the time of this writing) an Associate Professor of History and Architectural History at the University of Oregon. Howell's two articles on skateboarding provide unbelievable ground-level insight into the actual architectural obstacles skaters face. Howell understands that modern public space is a simulation, defensively designed to select for the right kinds of users while deterring those deemed unworthy.

Space/Enclave

Much of the scholarship on skateboarding utilizes the notion that skating is an act of spatial resistance. This book is the first ethnography of skateboarding and describes the processes by which professional skateboarding subculture operates. This effort to understand culture as it is lived and practiced requires what Paul Willis calls an "ethnographic imagination."[25] Here I expand on the theme of the subculture career that I began with *Graffiti Lives* to show not only that (some very talented and very lucky) skateboarders create careers out of their subcultural participation, but that in doing so, they also create subcultural enclaves, similar to an ethnic enclave in which a specific ethnic group is concentrated in a single space in the city, which upon reaching critical mass creates economic opportunity and social mobility. Subcultures draw new members to the city in the hopes of participating in the subculture industry, and out of these enclaves communities are formed.[26] However, though ethnic enclaves have a relationship to a specific place, the specifics of that particular place are in a sense random. There is nothing special about the area around Canal Street in Manhattan that is attractive to Chinese folks; it is Chinatown because that is where Chinese immigrants settled and thrived.

Professional skateboarding occurs in California not only because that is where the skaters are, but also because that it where the spots are, and because of the weather they can be skated all year round. Skateboarding subculture therefore occurs in social spaces and also physical spaces, where skaters have relationships not only with other skaters, but also with specific architectural forms. Professional skateboarders use public space to progress their discipline, and this process makes sacred the spaces that have been the sites of their history. That is to say that skateboarding is emplaced in Los Angeles and the surrounding California cities not only because that is where the majority of people in the skateboarding industry are, but also because that is where the places (spots) are.

Skateboarding is an interpretive activity; it involves seeing the world through a creative prism, in which the banal and the everyday (stairs, handrails) become sites of groundbreaking achievement. This creative prism extends beyond the trick and the space to also include a photographic/cinematographic imagination in which the performer and the documenter have a keen sense of how best to convey a particular trick and spot to make it look good on film. These activities infuse space with meaning, making it a famous spot to cherish, to talk about, to trek to, and, for some, to perform at. In this way skateboarding can be thought of as the task of making the mundane a site of subcultural appreciation; at the very least it is the activity of imagining how the everyday could potentially become something very special.

Through this process skateboarders have the potential to shape the discussion surrounding public space. Through their actions they are actively transforming space and demanding inclusion as members of a public with their own specific right to the city. Through an absolute refusal to accept the argument that skateboarding is a criminal act that destroys public space, skaters are beginning to make the case, somewhat successfully, that they have the right to public space and are actually productive users.

Overview

After providing a brief history of skateboarding and an introduction to the terminology, this book focuses on skateboarding places in an effort to show the relationships to space that skaters have maintained over an extended period of time. Professional skaters perform tricks (and document them), but their complexity is too great to understand without also understanding where they do them. I have chosen place as a starting point because it also allows the reader to experience skateboarding's progression. From place we move to tricks and careers and finally address the significance of skating for urban sociology.

On Language

As an outsider trying to learn the terminology of a specific group, one can pause conversations only so often to ask for clarity; thus terms must be learned in context, which means that most ethnographers spend much of their early time in the field in near complete ignorance. Learning the language and understanding rules of interaction is essential to any study of a group and was one of my main goals in approaching this topic. This required paying very close attention, and eventually through context and strategic inquiry, I came to understand the language and (some of) the grammar of skateboarding. The most important of these is the naming of tricks, a highly complex system that follows a strict but almost impenetrable logic. I devote an entire chapter to skaters' use of language when it comes to naming tricks, and the pitfalls I experienced in my attempts to understand it.

I wanted to mirror in print some of the process of learning vocabulary in everyday speech. The first time I use a specific skating term, I define it, but thereafter I use the terminology as if readers are fluent in the language of the subculture. I apologize to confused readers, who can find a glossary in the back of the book. It is my goal that this usage will help readers better incorporate these terms into their own speech and will be better prepared, if not necessarily to start a dialogue with a skater, should the occasion arise, to at least engage with the ideas and practices of this subculture on its own terms.

Method

This study is the result of intense engagement in the field. I have followed skateboarding subculture and specifically the professional career of my younger brother and main contact, Aaron Snyder, for over 20 years. In the summer of 2008 I began a rigorous ethnographic study and quickly discovered that I actually knew very little about skateboarding. Every summer between 2008 and 2016 I made at least one trip to Los Angeles to do research.[27] In total I have taken more than ten trips to research skating, and each time in Los Angeles I stayed with my brother Aaron, which allowed me almost complete immersion in the culture of skateboarders.

It is strange for me to call him Aaron. In our family he was given the nickname Boo by my grandfather when he was still in the womb, and it stuck. However, Aaron never let his friends call him Boo, so for the duration of this project I'll have to call him by his given name.

I also was able to develop relationships with other skaters who provided untold insight and inspiration. I was extremely lucky to have witnessed the progression of the careers of Nick Tucker and Aquil Brathwait, and this project would not have been complete without their input. Matt Gottwig was one of the earliest contributors; Robbie McKinley was also extremely helpful, and provides a slightly different take on the skate career narrative; Kelley Hart also was helpful and generous, as was Diego Najera; additional shout-outs to Paul Hart and Sebo Walker. I am so honored and humbled that these folks agreed to share their lives with me, and I'm so proud of what they have accomplished. I was also able to reconnect with Troy Turner, Aaron's childhood mentor, whose insights and openness for dialogue were essential to this project. And then there is Dr. Pete Lehman, a great skater in his own right, but who went on to pursue a doctorate in comparative literature. Pete came on board, serendipitously, out of the blue; he was a fellow groomsman at Aaron's wedding, and in my role as best man I had the opportunity to email him a lot. Once I asked him a skating question and got six pages of notes; I asked if he'd be willing to read the book in draft, and he knocked it out in two weeks, with 13 more pages of notes as well as running comments. Pete could be considered the co-editor of this book, and he helped to make it so much better.

My two main skateboard media contacts are RB Umali, *the* skateboard cinematographer in New York City, where I live, and Atiba Jefferson, an accomplished skateboard photographer in Los Angeles. I met these gentlemen in 1998 when Aaron was in New York shooting tricks for the 1998 video *Fulfill the Dream*." I maintained these relationships over the years and was able to expand on them for this project. In 2010 I also had long informal interviews with RB in New York City and with Atiba in Los Angeles. I maintained these relationships over the course of the project, and I tell their stories in this book in order to highlight the importance of the subculture media for the purpose of establishing subculture careers.

My brother provided complete access to his world, and I was able to learn in a shorter time what under normal field circumstances might have taken years. Unlike ethnographic relationships in which a good amount of time and energy must be spent toward establishing trust and developing a rapport, working with my brother allowed me to skip this phase and jump immediately into the deep end of the subculture, though it still took time for me to be able to have actual conversations about skating.[28]

My relationship with my brother however, has changed; he is still my best friend, but now we also work together. No longer am I Aaron's mentor, as I had been since he was a child; instead I am the student and he is the teacher. Aaron takes seriously his ongoing role as my teacher, and quite frankly seems to cherish this role reversal.[29] Initially when I was in his world, I was not a professor, or author, or elder, I was simply someone who didn't skate. After seven years the relationship has become a little more equal, and most of my skateboarding informants know that I am a "professor," but mostly they're just happy that an outsider has tried to understand them.

At the beginning of the project Aaron simply introduced me as his older brother who was "working on a book," and no further questions were asked. I was free to take photos, shoot videos, ask questions, and reveal my role as a researcher in my own time. In fact I didn't even need what my students and I have called a "pickup line," the prepared statement researchers use to explain themselves and their reason for intruding; I just do my best to observe and stay out of the way.[30]

When you do fieldwork in your own city, you can remove yourself from the field setting, decompress, and become yourself again; when you are living with your informants, every moment is a learning opportunity, so you have to be okay with the fact that there is no chance to just "be yourself." This has long been a challenge for anthropologists, but one fewer sociologists have had to endure.[31]

When I am with Aaron, we both become consumed with all aspects of skating, and during those times I have trouble processing all of the information and even remembering what I'm about. Most of the time I feel like I'm in a foreign country where I don't fully know the language. Even though my brother provided access, this complicated the research. I was included in conversations and skate sessions as Aaron's older brother, but from this the assumption often followed that I was a skater and understood what was being discussed. In truth, early in the process I was lost. Luckily when I got the chance I could ask for explanations, but this was usually after the fact. This meant a constant balancing of the insider/outsider dynamic. In the beginning I was assumed to be an insider, and was spoken to as such and was thus lost; however, the more I learned about the subculture, the better I was able to communicate my questions, which also led some skaters to assume that I skated, which led me again down a path of confusion. At this stage I spent considerable time convincing skaters I was an outsider, and explaining why a college professor would write about skateboarding. Often these conversations forced skaters to think beyond the confines of their subculture and were fruitful, other times not.

I also must admit to being very conscious of my body throughout this project. Skaters are young and athletic and in excellent shape, and the condition of my rounder, heavier body was a constant source of embarrassment and shame, and I found myself trying to explain my body in a way that I was not accustomed to. Often skaters would bring this up to me in coded language saying, "so . . . you *used* to skate," meaning that I obviously didn't skate anymore because of my weight.[32] (Editing this paragraph convinced me to lose weight.)

Age also played a big role in this research, as I was obviously older than most of the people I spent time with. Eventually this worked to my advantage, as skaters were intrigued by the fact that I was a college professor, and lived successfully outside of the world of skating. Some even expressed the desire to take my classes.

By the summer of 2014 Aaron's skateboarding friends got used to seeing me around, and as I became more conversant in the language of skateboarding, I was able to get into more and more real conversations, with a broad range of folks, not only skaters like Nick and Aquil as mentioned, but also magazine writers like Mackenzie Eisenhour, skate shop managers like Sean McNulty, and Red Bull brand managers like Mike Guffy. Strangely as the project progressed, skaters began to ask me whether or not I was going to include them in the book. My response was always "of course," and the skaters were genuinely pleased.

Techniques

In my research on graffiti writers in New York City (2009), I used a sketchbook to allow writers to illustrate certain words, which instigated a dialogue between myself and my contacts. This sketchbook or blackbook, which cultural criminologists call an "interactive device," allowed me to witness graffiti without encouraging illegal activity, and it inspired writers to teach me about their culture.[33] In this research on skateboarding I began by asking skaters to take me to photograph some of LA's most famous "skate spots." This method allowed the skaters to teach me about their specific uses of urban architecture without having to risk injury or arrest. By focusing on sites first, this book looks at how certain skateboarding spaces are sites not only for performance but also for the transmission of knowledge.[34] This is especially helpful if you are an outsider as skaters cannot help but give you a lesson if you ask about a particular spot. This was my original goal, and it has remained a staple of this research throughout, though more and more there was no longer a need to be at a specific spot. Through this process I began to develop a foundation of knowledge about skateboarding history, tricks, and spots. This gave me a vocabulary to talk with skaters about their subculture, which helped to develop some trust.[35] I transferred the skate spot photos to my iPhone and was able to easily show them to skaters, which then instigated discussions of their subcultural landmarks and skating in general.

These strategies borrow from Collier's technique of "photo elicitation," which is the practice of using photographs in research interviews.[36] This method allows informants the opportunity to act as teachers, describing to the researcher what the photos show. In my case it was also proof that I was diligently trying to learn about skateboarding. I also immersed myself in the architecture of both New York and LA, trying desperately to find spots on my own.

As the years went by and I learned more about the subculture and the practice of skateboarding, I was better able to see architecture from a skater's perspective. That said, in all of my searching I was able to find only one unknown skate spot that actually appealed to pro skaters. (Now two.)

These techniques complement more traditional ethnographic practices of participant observation and writing field notes. Each night I would compose a short outline and the following morning would spend roughly three hours writing up a detailed narrative of the previous day. In some cases, I would read my notes to my brother, or ask for clarification on certain things.

Good ethnography involves paying attention not only to what you see, but also to what you hear. In the case of skateboarding, this meant both understanding what people were describing and listening to the sound of skateboarding, of wheels rolling on concrete, the perfect pitch pop of an ollie as the wood makes contact with the concrete, and the music and rhythm of a well-executed grind, where the metal trucks make a ringing metallic ping as they contact a metal rail.[37]

It is important for me to say at the onset that I am not a skateboarder, and for the most part I do not participate in any of the subcultures that I study. I can "roll around" on a skateboard, and what this has taught me is how utterly difficult even the most basic skateboarding tricks are. My goal in this research was to see the world like a skater and discover skateboarding places; never did I even consider attempting to successfully land skateboard tricks, mostly because I do not want to get seriously injured. I've tried, in my 40s, over and over again to ollie on my skateboard, and each time I am forced to give up huffing and puffing after 20 minutes. Clearly skateboarding, like learning a foreign language, is something much more easily mastered by the young.

Many researchers, like Howard Becker, Martin Sanchez-Jankowski, Mitch Duneier, Loïc Wacquant, Sudhir Venkatesh, and Tanya Bunsell, gain insight into the worlds they study by being or becoming participants.[38] Clearly, one way to study groups of which you are not a member is to engage in the activity that will make you a member, all the while keeping at the forefront the notion that you will never be a true insider. Much recent subculture research has continued this tradition of basing one's ethnographic authority on the fact of one's personal experience doing, or learning how to do, a particular subcultural activity.[39] In many instances these authors were subculture participants prior to becoming scholars.

(The most frequent questions I get asked are "Do you write?" and "Do you skate?")

While there is a long tradition of ethnographic researchers who remain outsiders to the groups they study; for example, in well-known studies of the homeless and drug users, the researchers did not sleep on the street or use drugs.[40] Most people assume because I advocate for the cultures I have studied that I have participated in them, but I am neither a graffiti writer nor a skater; I am an ethnographer and a sociologist. I do not possess the skills, talent, courage, or drive to become a skater or, in my earlier work, a graffiti writer. I want to emphasize that to become a skateboarder requires an investment in time and pain that at this stage in my life I cannot afford. Actually, even if I had started young, I wouldn't have what it takes to be either a skater or a graffiti writer (which is why I'm a scholar and a teacher; as they say, "Those that can't do, teach").

This of course makes my job of explaining what skaters do more difficult, but not impossible, and there is a larger ontological point here. While it may be impossible to ever know the experience of the other if you haven't lived it, there is something to be said for empathy. In this way the point of my outsider research suggests that understanding and appreciation can help us comprehend things we may dismiss, or of which we are ignorant. It is here where my political commitments come to the fore. My task is to attempt to understand, appreciate, and describe skateboarding culture in an effort to change the minds of those who would dismiss it as stupid or misguided.

Ethnography gives us insight into worlds we would never otherwise know, and in doing so it's possible, as Patricia Hill Collins suggests, to empathize from the particular to the universal.[41] It is easy to dismiss cultural practices and people we don't understand; if, however, we assume that others' cultures are at least as nuanced and complex as we know our own to be, we may have a starting point for cross-cultural understanding.

Camera as Interactive Device

When street skaters are attempting tricks that have never been done before on a specific obstacle, there is usually a skilled photographer and videographer present. But it is common practice for those who are not skating the particular obstacle to shoot photos and video also. In these instances, I've found it useful to use a small video camera or my phone, which allows me to participate in the action while also documenting it.

While many researchers talk about the power of photography and the use of visual imagery in their scholarship, I have found that cameras and video cameras are also excellent "interactive devices."[42] The immediacy of digital technology allows me to share these images with skaters, which can instigate further social interaction. This process increases my ability to understand skateboarding itself as my contacts often describe to me in detail what I've documented.

There were also trips to skate parks and skateboard contests and endless film sessions watching videos of skateboarding. In my time in the field I was able to photograph approximately 50 of the hundreds of skate spots in the LA area and took over 500 photographs and 20 videos of skaters and skateboarding. Through these processes I was introduced to other skaters including Troy Turner, Mike Plumb, Brian Hansen, Don Ngyuen, Billy Roper, Brian Lotti, Billy Rohan, Marko Jazbinsek, Matt Gottwig, Kimathi Smith, Yuto Kojima, Sebo Walker, Aquil Brathwaite, Nick Tucker, Corey Smith, Robbie McKinley, Sean Malto, Shane O'Neill, Sewa Kroetkov, Chris Cole, Torey Pudwill, Jeron Wilson, and Boo Johnson, as well as photographers Shad Lambert and Atiba Jefferson and filmmaker RB Umali. I also continued to follow these folks through social media sites like Instagram.

Immersion

Immersion as an ethnographic term means to immerse oneself in culture, and although California is the main setting for this fieldwork, New York City also played a key role, keeping me immersed in the culture, yet in a slightly different way than it's classically understood.[43] I used what I learned in LA about the criteria for skate spots to constantly scrutinize the architecture in my own city for possible skate spots. While I did not immerse myself entirely in the subculture of New York skaters, mostly because of time constraints, I engaged in an activity that skaters the world over partake in.

The act of reading urban terrain for possible skate spots was similar to reading the walls of the city during my graffiti research. Even though good skate spots are rare, especially in New York, the act of creatively interpreting urban space is constant and an entirely new way of seeing the world. Walking and looking therefore became a critical part of my methodology, even when I wasn't in LA. Sociologist Timothy Shortell has written extensively about the necessity of walking for understanding urban space, and as a method for exploring "quotidian mobility."[44]

When I first began this research my skateboarding imagination was incredibly limited and spaces that I thought would be good for skating were entirely not. Whenever I came across a potential spot I would photograph it and text it to one of my contacts for confirmation or dismissal. In order to understand what makes a spot good for skating, you have to understand skateboard tricks, and it took me years to acquire even a fundamental understanding. But as I progressed in my knowledge, my spatial imagination improved.

Most of my "finds" were dismissed out of hand; I did however, after years of trying, find a legitimate spot near my home in Red Hook, Brooklyn. I showed it to Aaron and he encouraged me to send it to skateboard cinematographer RB Umali, who eventually filmed a pro skater doing a "gap to 50–50 grind." Even though many of my finds were false, their real significance is the way this project changed my way of seeing and looking at urban architecture. I am not a skateboarder, but I learned in some small way to view the city from a skater's perspective.

The process of going to photograph existing famous spots, along with watching videos and reading magazines, slowly started to have an impact. The more spots I was exposed to the more I began to understand the criteria and the creativity that go into interpreting a potential site in a completely different way than it was intended. So I was immersed in the culture of skating, but I was also immersed in the architecture of my own city in a new way, again. Now I too was trying to discover places of creative potential. This took a long time, or put another way, although I was quickly able to immerse myself into the culture of skaters, I had to spend years trying to understand skaters' tricks and their landmarks before I became immersed in the city the way skaters are.

PART I

Immersion

1

Skateboarding and the City

A Quick History of Skateboarding

Skateboarding began in the early 1960s when California surfers attached roller skate wheels to wooden planks to "surf" the sidewalk when there were no waves. By 1964, skateboards, as they came to be called, were being mass-produced.[1] Skateboarding remained relatively dormant until 1972, when the invention of the urethane wheels rekindled enthusiasm and kids flocked to the sport, skating down hills and in empty swimming pools all across the country. The rise of this movement is documented in Stacy Peralta's award-winning 2001 documentary *Dogtown and Z-Boys*. The Z-Boys were a crew of surfers who hung out at the Zephyr Surf Shop in Santa Monica. When the waves died down in the early afternoon, they spent their days adapting their surfing style to skateboarding. Eventually their progressive styles transformed skateboarding and established it as a professional pursuit. Tony Alva, Jay Adams, Stacy Peralta, Wentzle Ruml, Peggy Oki, and Paul Constantineau were some of the early pioneers and skating's first superstars.

These glory days were short-lived. Though skaters and skateboard companies made small sums of money, the skate park owners did not. Poor original designs made upkeep at the parks incredibly expensive, and this, combined with rocketing insurance costs, forced many owners to close the parks and cut their losses. By 1980, park skating and the movement it spawned had all but ceased.[2]

When skateboarding was no longer viable as a profit-making entity for outside investors, skateboarders themselves began to invest in their own industry. In 1981 a skater named Fausto Vitello, who also owned Independent Trucks Company, started *Thrasher* magazine, the first to be written and photographed "by skaters, for skaters."[3] Once skaters themselves began to control the content of their culture, they also began to define the standards of subcultural progression for themselves.

In the 1980s skateboarding resurfaced on "half-pipe" wooden ramps. Riders like Lance Mountain, Steve Caballero, and Tony Hawk of the Powell-Peralta Bones Brigade, all of whom skated "vert" on ramps with transitions to vertical walls, dominated the scene. There was also a secondary discipline called "freestyle" in which skaters used smaller boards, rode exclusively on flat ground, and concentrated on board manipulation. Rodney Mullen was the innovator in this discipline and won every contest he entered, but freestyle skating would be short-lived. Still Mullen invented hundreds of the tricks that would go on to form the foundation of street skateboarding, including the flat-ground ollie, the kickflip, and the 360 flip, and he eventually skated street himself.

By the late 1980s skateboarding began to change direction. Vert skating, which was the exclusive domain of those who could get access to ramps and pools, started to succumb to the democratic impulse of street skating, which could be done anywhere. This was a move skating was destined to make as kids all across the world who didn't have access to ramps or skate parks began to skate and explore their cities, searching for obstacles that could be used for performing tricks.

Natas Kaupas and Mark Gonzales are most often credited with the invention of street skating, freeing skaters from the confines of the ramp and unleashing them on the curbs, stairs, benches, and handrails of the world. Gonz rode for Vision Skateboards and pioneered numerous tricks and techniques, which expanded skaters' imaginations as to what could be skated. Natas originally rode for Santa Monica Airlines, which eventually became part of Santa Cruz Skateboards. On Santa Cruz he had two groundbreaking parts in the influential videos *Wheels on Fire* (1987) and *Streets on Fire* (1989), which showed skaters the world over what could be done with simple urban obstacles. *Streets on Fire* was also one of the first videos illustrating that street skating was becoming more popular than vert. Natas also had the first pro model signature shoe for a then fledgling company called Etnies.[4]

At this point in the process, skate company ownership began to change, and thus skaters began to take a controlling interest in their own industry. Beginning in the mid-1980s and coinciding with the emergence of subculture media, skateboarders got frustrated with the big companies (Powell-Peralta, Santa Cruz, Tracker, Independent, and

Vision) that ruled skateboarding and began to find ways to take ownership of skateboarding companies.[5]

One of the pioneering skateboard owners was former pro freestyle skater Steve Rocco, who convinced fellow pro skaters Rodney Mullen and Mike Vallely to invest their own money to help him start World Industries. Rocco began World Industries in 1987 and made an active push to chip away at the domination of the "big five" in the marketplace. He did this by enticing the best skaters to join his company, and paying them $2 per board sold, rather than the industry standard $1.[6] World Industries eventually became extremely successful, and spawned other skater-owned companies. In 1989 Rocco convinced Mark Gonzales to start Blind Skateboards, an intentional slight to his former sponsor Vision. In 1991 Blind would release its groundbreaking film *Video Days*, directed by a young Spike Jonze (who would go on to become an Oscar-winning filmmaker) and featuring Mark Gonzales, Jason Lee, Rudy Johnson, and Guy Mariano. This video, along with early H-Street videos like *Shackle Me Not*, are often cited as the most influential videos in the history of street skateboarding. Street skateboarding, in turn, would also have a huge influence on vert skaters, who then incorporated street tricks on the ramp.[7]

By the early 1990s Rocco's World Industries dominated the skateboarding industry and had numerous brands under their distribution company, including Blind, Foundation, Plan B, and 101 Skateboards. In 1992 as an exercise I asked Aaron to write me a letter explaining the state of skating. As a 15-year-old kid in Madison, Wisconsin, he was well aware of the details of the skateboard industry in California. He wrote:

Now, on to World Industries. A couple of years ago, former pro skater, Steve Rocco came out with a small little company called World Industries. People started getting into them and before you knew it Rocco expanded and started Foundation, then Blind, then Ghetto Wear clothes, then 101, and finally Plan B. Rocco would do anything for riders. He stole almost every top professional with all his money. This money started going to his head until he and his companies controlled 75% of all the skate market. With all this power he could do anything, and did. He would put extremely obscene graphics on boards (he came out with Fuct Clothing), and any company that disagreed with what he was turning skating into, he would literally destroy, and if any of his team riders left to a different company, he would devote whole page ads dedicated to making fun of them and ridiculing them beyond belief. Anyway, there really is nothing people can do, people have tried and failed miserably.[8]

I was astounded that he had that much knowledge of the skateboarding industry at such a young age. The story of Rocco would eventually be made into a documentary film, *The Man Who Souled the World*, and I already knew the roots of the story from a 15-year-old's letter written 25 years ago. (It turns out that Aaron wasn't completely unique; almost all skaters on his level know the industry inside and out.)[9]

By the early 1990s, convergent with the rise of consumer video cameras, street skating had become less about competing in contests and more about "progression" and showcasing that progress on videos and in the pages of magazines. This also resulted in new jobs in the skate industry: the photographer and the video "filmer." The filmer must be a skilled skateboarder because his job requires him to skate along with the rider while filming, and thus most photographers and filmers are very good skateboarders who had promising careers as "ams" (amateurs), they were just not good enough to go pro. These subculture documenters are highly skilled and adept at using the latest in digital technology, from cameras to flashes and drones, which give skateboarding a supremely professional look. Today skateboarding videos and magazines exhibit extremely cutting-edge camera work and design layouts, and some of the most highly skilled skate videographers go on to become successful filmmakers.

Yet despite all of these technological improvements that have advanced the documentation and marketing of skating, the skateboard has remained unchanged. A wooden deck, made from seven plies of compressed maple and covered with grip tape, rolls on urethane wheels that are attached to the board by metal trucks. There have been slight deviations in size and shape, but the basic materials have not changed. Because skateboard decks are disposable, there is no business impetus to create a more technologically sophisticated product. Riders buy a new deck every four or five months, and professionals and skaters who get their boards for free ride a new one every week, or even every day. (They usually give their gently worn boards to the younger kids at the spot, as described below.)

In 1993 Plan B riders Mike Carroll and Rick Howard, along with filmmaker Spike Jonze lured riders away from Plan B to start their own company called Girl Skateboards and then its offshoot Chocolate Skateboards, which remain two of the top companies in the industry. (The website celebritynetworth.com, though unreliable, estimates Rick Howard's net worth to be $45 million.) Other significant skater-owned companies are Baker Skateboards, started by Andrew Reynolds ($10 million) in 2000, Almost Skateboards, owned by Rodney Mullen ($30 million) and Daewon Song ($1.2 million), and DGK (dirty ghetto kids), established by Stevie Williams in 2002.

More recently this trend of skaters starting their own companies has come back into vogue. Jason Dill and Anthony Van Engelen started a company called Fuckin Awesome, which in 2015 *Transworld* magazine named company of the year. In April 2014 Paul Rodriguez started Primitive Skateboards, which by 2016 would become a powerhouse brand with pros Nick Tucker, Bastien Salabanzi, Carlos Ribeiro, Shane O'Neill, Devine Calloway, Brian Peacock, and their newest pro, Diego Najera.

Skaters also own their own shoe companies, including Lakai, DVS, DC, and Huf, which employ former skaters as shoe designers. In the last five years Nike has made a serious effort to dismantle skater-owned shoe companies. Nike currently sponsors 21 professional skateboarders, including Paul Rodriguez, Sean Malto, Shane O'Neill, Theotis Beasley, Luan Oliveira, Eric Koston, and most recently Nyjah Huston. Nike's encroachment into skateboarding has been a long and complex process. For the most part they have done a good job of making some skaters quite wealthy, without infringing upon its DIY ethos. This however is starting to change, as more and more Nike is designing shoes according to their athletic standards, rather than those of the skaters they sponsor. And they're expensive; Paul Rodriguez's Nike SB 8 sells for $130, and looks like a tennis sneaker. (One of their marketing missteps however implored skaters to look beyond the fact that their shoes are ugly, and instead focus on their technology. Needless to say this campaign didn't last.)

Street skating is by far the most popular form of skateboarding in the world; however the term does not necessarily denote a person who rides a skateboard down the street as a mode of transportation; those folks are called "long boarders." Street skating is the term for skaters who search the concrete universe for "spots," unintended architectural formations, to perform tricks on. Street skaters do tricks on "benches," "ledges," "stairs," "handrails," "gaps," "bumps," "banks," and "walls," to name a few of the urban obstacles skaters creatively reinterpret. This move from the confines of ramps and parks turned skaters into urban explorers constantly scanning the built environment for "skateable" spots. These spots must meet very specific criteria, such as the height of the obstacle, the smoothness of the ground, and the "roll away," in order to be "skateable."

The market research company Board Trac estimates that skateboarding currently generates $5 billion in revenue worldwide, and despite the mainstream appeal of made-for-television mega-ramp contests like the X Games, street skateboarding is the most popular form of skating in the world, mostly because it can be done anywhere.[10] Content analysis of the main skateboard magazines, *Transworld*, *Thrasher*, and *The Skateboard Mag*, and their accompanying websites reveals that most of the coverage is devoted to street skating, which in nearly every American city is illegal and thus requires constant hassles with cops and security.

Ollie, Nollie, Regular, Goofy: Trick Basics

The first thing to understand about skateboarding is that everyone has a natural "stance." If you first set foot on a skateboard and put your left foot on the front of the board and "push" with your right foot, it is called "regular-footed stance." If you are more comfortable putting your right foot forward and pushing with your left foot, your stance is "goofy-footed," though there is nothing goofy about it. Nor should it be construed regular skaters are righties and goofy skaters are lefties; this distinction does not apply. Aaron is goofy-footed and right-handed at everything, I am regular-footed and left-handed. It should also be noted that the breakdown of regular versus goofy skaters is roughly equal, and even though the terminology suggests otherwise, there is no hierarchy between the two stances.

Skateboarding tricks are extremely difficult to understand if you do not perform them; they are, however, slightly easier to understand if you think about them from the perspective of the board only. By imagining a skateboard without a rider you are relieved of the various complications of stance and turning direction, which predict such qualifiers as "switch," "regular," "frontside," "backside," and "fakie." Essentially the board can flip only in a finite number of ways. It can flip along the x-axis and along the y-axis and can rotate only clockwise or counterclockwise. For example, a "kickflip" requires ollieing into the air and using the toe of the front foot to flip the board counterclockwise, while to perform a "heelflip" the skater uses the heel of the front foot to flip the board in the opposite direction or clockwise. The board can also be rotated along the y-axis where the board rotates parallel to the ground. The easiest way to do this is "backside," in the direction of your heels. You can do this 180 degrees for a "shove it" or 360 degrees for a "360 shove it," that is, if your body stays in the same position.

If you combine the x and y flips and use the front and back feet to flip the board 360 degrees on both the x- and y-axes it's technically a "kickflip, backside 360 shove it," which goes by the shorter name "360 flip" (sometimes also "three flip" or "tre flip"). Then you add body movement; so if you rotate your body 180 degrees while doing a 360 shove it, you've done a "big spin." If you stay on the board and ollie into the air and spin with it 360 degrees, it's a 360 ollie. If you spin your body and board 180 degrees "front side" (toes first) while kickflipping, it's a frontside kickflip or "frontside flip." Spin your body the other way and kickflip the board (heels first) for a "backside flip." Ride backward, you're going "fakie"; ollie into the air for a "fakie ollie," kickflip the board for a "fakie flip." Ride forward and spring the board into the air off of the nose, rather than the tail, and it's a nose ollie or "nollie." Flip the board with the toe of your back foot for a nollie kickflip (nollie flip); flick it with the heel of your back foot for a nollie heelflip (nollie heel). There are also "hardflips," which are essentially frontside shove it kickflips and involve turning the board the hard way and flipping it. "Ollie impossible" is a slightly more complicated board rotation, where the rider gets the board to rotate around the back foot; these are fairly easy to recognize but difficult to explain. These tricks are the basic elements of street skateboarding and can be combined to form even more complex tricks.

Kickflips and Heelflips

The most natural way to flip a skateboard, if you are a skilled regular-footed skateboarder, is to pop the board with your back foot and when the front of the board is up in the air, you flick your toes out over the left side of the board to make the board flip one time in the air for a "kickflip." This was the first trick to be invented, but skaters are also intent upon learning everything they know the opposite way also. So the same trick can be done "fakie" or going backward, or off the nose, "nollie," or you could change your stance from "regular" to "goofy" and do the trick "switch stance," which means opposite roles for your feet. So from this one basic motion a skater can perform four different tricks, kickflip, fakie flip, nollie flip, and switch flip. By doing the basic tricks fakie, nollie, and switch, skaters increase their trick vocabulary and the difficulty.

The degree of difficulty can be understood in how skaters learn the various tricks. The kickflip, after the ollie, is the first trick most skaters learn, and from there they move on to learning it fakie, nollie, and switch, which gives a basic understanding of the relative difficulty of each technique.

These rules also apply to heelflips, which require a different foot movement but can also be done fakie, nollie, and switch. For the novice skateboard watcher, "heelflips" are slightly easier to identify than kickflips because the front-flipping foot thrusts out and the heel of the foot flicks the board the opposite way, clockwise in the case of regular-footed skaters. You can also get a sense of what trick the rider is going to do by the pre-trick foot setup; for heelflips the front foot is placed with the toes hanging off the board and the heel in the center.

There are also kickflip varials. "Varial" is the term for rotating the board 180 degrees on the horizontal axis and is synonymous with "shove it." A varial flip or varial kickflip is essentially a backside 180-degree kickflip, or one-half of a 360-degree flip, but no one calls them 180 flips. A "hard flip" is also one of the hardest tricks to understand, and it wasn't until 2015 that I actually understood. A "hard flip" is a frontside varial kickflip, rotating the board the opposite, and much more difficult, way from the varial kickflip. There are also backside varial heels and frontside varial heels.

Rotations of the board and the body, either separately or in conjunction, add another layer of complexity (but skaters don't refer to it as a rotation). Rotating the board parallel to the ground is called a varial. The easiest varial trick is a "shove it," where you flick the board 180 degrees, and the easiest and most natural way to flick it is backside, thrusting your back foot toward your back, away from you in a sweeping motion to get the board to rotate 180 degrees. Most of the time you never hear anyone say "backside shove it," but if you rotate the board the opposite way, which is much harder because you are essentially using your back foot to push the board away from you, it's a frontside shove it (sometimes written as "FS shuv"). If you ollie into the air and flick the board 180 degrees it's called a "pop shove it." Rotating 180 degrees while doing a kickflip is a frontside or backside kickflip, shortened to frontside flip or backside flip, depending on the direction you're turning. These tricks are then learned fakie, nollie, and switch to create even more difficult tricks. Riders become known for perfecting certain tricks, the most notable of these is the "frontside flip," which is said to be "owned" by Andrew Reynolds. Josh Kalis was known for his 360 flips.

These combinations take incredible amounts of time to learn on flat ground, and once the foundation is established a skater takes these tricks to architectural formations in the street, which then increases the complexity and danger of their performance.

There is another category of tricks that can't be done on flat ground, called grinds and slides, which are performed on handrails and ledges. Sliding on the tail of the board is a "tailslide," on the nose a "nose slide," and on the middle of the board a "board slide" or "lip slide," depending on the approach. Grind a rail on the axles of both trucks for a "50–50 grind," back truck only for a "5-0 grind." "Blunt slide" is when a rider slides on the back portion of the truck, rather than the axle. Even though in theory I know what a "front blunt" or a "nose blunt" is, I often misidentify them.

"Feeble grinds" and "smith grinds" look the same when the rider is on the rail and are differentiated only by how the skater approaches the rail. For a frontside feeble grind you approach the rail, ollie your front trucks over the rail, lock your back trucks in, and grind with the nose of the skateboard angled below the rail. For a smith grind, the grind is essentially the same but you approach the rail from the opposite direction, ollie up to the rail, and turn and lock in your back trucks. A "crooked grind" is where you ollie up onto a rail, place the front truck on the rail, and angle the board, ideally 45 degrees to the rail; angling the board the opposite way you approached is called an "overcrooked grind" and is a Sean Malto specialty.

The real element street obstacles add, however, is danger. For pros, falling on flat ground while attempting a trick is pretty harmless, but falling badly while trying to 50–50 grind on a rail could result in broken bones, concussions, or worse. All of these tricks are incredibly scary and require an amazing amount of courage.

Overcoming the mental challenge that fear presents is one of the most critical aspects of being a skateboarder. For skaters who are invested in progression and pushing themselves, this requires not only immense courage and physical toughness, but also extreme mental strength. Skaters have to focus completely on the trick they are attempting and somehow block out any thoughts about how badly they could get injured. For some skaters this evolves into what they generally refer to as "the madness," and for Andrew Reynolds, Paul Rodriguez, and others this results in a series of OCD-like behaviors and ticks that they believe help them to clear their minds and focus on the trick. Andrew performs a series of ticks based upon the number three. He taps his board three times, taps the wall three times, asks the filmer if he is ready three times, and finally goes. Before every attempt Paul removes his hat, puts it over his face, and says a prayer.[11]

As skateboarding has evolved and progressed, the amount of risk that skaters take on has become difficult to comprehend, especially since most skate videos are a showcase of successful makes; for the most part they do not show the painful process. As riders attempt more and more difficult tricks on bigger obstacles, the amount of falling and pain and dedication involved is staggering, and truthfully it's difficult to watch on video, let alone witness firsthand. House of Hammers is a website run by Baker Skateboards, and one of their segments is titled "What's a Guy Gotta Do?" It shows the process that skaters go through to perform their tricks. For example, Andrew Reynolds recently did a varial heelflip down the Hollywood 16, which took 75 tries. That means he fell on the concrete from approximately eight feet in the air 74 times in a row; in the end he was bruised and bloodied, but the final result is amazing.

However, just watching the video and counting the attempts made me cringe.[12]

Not all skaters are "gnarly." While it may be an oversimplification, it is practical to understand skaters on a technical/risk continuum. Some skaters are extremely "tech" and have amazing control of their skateboards. They do super-complicated, precise tricks, which are often slightly less dangerous than those of the "gnarly" skaters, who do less technically sophisticated tricks but take enormous risk. Today's best skaters accomplish both, called "tech-gnar." One thing that is easy to forget as you marvel at all of these flips and flicks of the board is that skaters are manipulating the skateboard with their feet.

Ledge Trick

A description of a single ledge trick reveals the complexity of skateboarding culture both spatially and linguistically. The "Wilshire Gap to Ledge" is a famous spot of major accomplishment on Wilshire Boulevard in Los Angeles. There are two ledges, about waist high, with an approximate six-foot gap between them, so you have to ride atop one of the ledges, ollie your board into the air, and land on the second ledge to do the trick and then "pop" off the ledge and land on the ground. When skaters say "gap" they mean a space that has to be ollied over. When they say "gap to . . ." it means that first you have to ollie over the space and then do the trick. So "Wilshire Gap to Ledge" therefore means you need to ollie over a space and onto the ledge and lastly, once you're done sliding on the ledge, you have to "pop" or ollie off of it, and sometimes another trick will be added "out."

Guy Mariano's "switch, back tailslide, to shove it, out" in 1996 is one of the most incredible tricks to be done at this spot and codified its fame.[13] When you look at the spot on video, it seems relatively unassuming; it doesn't appear as intimidating or scary as the huge handrails or gaps that the super gnarly dudes do. But when you go there and stand on it and visualize what actually needs to be done, it becomes clear how incredibly difficult and dangerous this obstacle is. First off, unlike with stairs, for example, there is no logical way to exit the trick midflight, and run down the stairs. Performing a trick requires 100 percent commitment from the very first try. No working your way up to it.

Wilshire Gap to Ledge, Los Angeles. Photo: Gregory Snyder.

Skateboarding is a subculture of spatial manipulation and visual documentation, but it is also linguistically precise, like musical notation. The description of the trick and the spot reveals exactly what was performed. All you have to do is tell skaters that "Guy Mariano did a switch, back tail, to shove it out, at the Wilshire Gap to Ledge," and they will visualize exactly what happened, because this is an amazingly precise and efficient description of exactly what happened and where.

The first part of the description, "switch," means that Guy, who normally rides with his right foot on the front of the board and pushes with his left, is doing the opposite, meaning that he's trained himself to ride a skateboard "left-footed," even though he's naturally "right-footed."[14] The second part of the description refers to the trick actually done on the ledge, a "backside tailslide," shortened to "back tail." This means he rides atop the ledge and pops the tail to fly over the gap, turns his board 90 degrees in the air, rotating counterclockwise or in this case "back side," to land the tail of the board on the ledge. He must maintain his balance and slide the wooden tail of the board over the waxed concrete ledge approximately three feet, and then "pop" the board again to get off the ledge and rotate it, "to shove it," a 180-degree rotation clockwise, which goes against the circular momentum he gained from turning "backside," and land on it while descending and falling back toward the ground. Also amazing is the fact that it took me 200 words to describe what skaters describe in 13: "switch, back tail, to shove it out, at the Wilshire Gap to Ledge."

Public Plazas: Filling the Voids

In the 1960s and 1970s planning commissions in cities across America allowed developers to increase the square footage and thus the height of their buildings if they agreed to create public plazas. However, many of these so-called "bonus plazas," which in theory sought to create urban safe havens by isolating the space from the street, actually failed to attract everyday citizens. There was little available seating, as planters were too high to sit comfortably and ledges were canted to prevent seating, and thus citizens rejected these spaces. These empty public spaces created a void, which was then filled by drug dealers, drug users, and the homeless, so regular citizens felt that the spaces were unsafe.

Sociologists Benjamin Shepard and Gregory Smithsimon argue in their book *The Beach Beneath the Street* that it wasn't a failure of architectural design that made the plazas unsuccessful, but an intentional effort by developers to use design to discourage loitering.[15] Because the plazas were to be open to the "public," there was an attempt to use defensive design strategies to filter the public.[16]

Concerned about the dearth of citizen activity in urban plazas, the city of New York hired urbanist William H. Whyte to study public plazas. In the influential film *The Social Life of Small Urban Spaces* (1980), which showcased his findings, Whyte made the obvious but forgotten observation that successful plazas were those that attracted citizens.[17] He stated that the number-one public activity in city spaces is "people watching other people." Therefore, he recommended to New York's planning commission in the 1980s that plazas should have adequate seating space, access to food, and ample trash bins, and most importantly they should not be cut off from the main event, what he called "the action of the street." He argued that spaces that fit these criteria successfully drew people together—a concept he called triangulation—while those that did not became sites of illicit activity.

This lack of civilian use of public plazas, however, contributed to the history of skateboarding. These plazas that many had thought of as failures of urban design, like Justin Herman Plaza on the Embarcadero in San Francisco, the Courthouse in West Los Angeles, Love Park in Philadelphia, and Pulaski Park in Washington, DC, were actually skateboarding paradises. Here the lack of everyday citizens worked in the favor of skaters, who, undeterred by the bums, utilized these spaces to spend hours learning and perfecting their tricks.[18] The most famous of these spaces became sites for the progression of skateboarding and the formation of tight-knit subculture communities. The skateable architectural forms that existed in these sites, as well as the lack of policing, created opportunities for the skaters who had access to them. These plazas therefore spawned the most progressive skaters of the generation, and most of the top pros of the 1990s and early 2000s began their careers performing tricks in these spots. It would be difficult to understate the importance of Embarcadero, Love Park, and the Courthouse to the history of skateboarding and the formation of professional careers.

The tricks performed at these plazas were showcased in 1990s skateboard videos, which gave the spots worldwide fame and attracted more and more skaters. As the plazas became populated with skaters from all over the country and the world, agents of social control began to view skateboarders as problematic. Soon those plazas, which had fostered skateboarding and launched professional careers, were shut down.[19] Cities passed ordinances making skateboarding illegal and cops started kicking skaters out and ticketing them for skateboarding in public plazas.

Ocean Howell argues in his 2001 article "The Poetics of Security: Skateboarding, Urban Design, and the New Public Space" that when the skateboarders were removed these public spaces, the illicit activity returned. He writes, following the great urbanist Jane Jacobs, that "ironically, defensive design [to keep skaters out] also destroys the self-regulating potential of the space by reducing the number of eyes in the space, and thereby creates a vacuum that can be populated by indigents."[20] Criminalizing skateboarding and removing skaters from public plazas essentially gave them back to the indigent folks, in whose hands they remain to this day.

The story of Hubba Hideout illustrates this phenomenon. Hubba Hideout is a small skyway in San Francisco just around the corner from the Embarcadero, and was originally known as a place where folks could smoke "hubba," or crack cocaine, without being seen.[21] Skaters discovered it had a unique architectural element with steps and a ledge going down the stairs, which opened up new possibilities for tricks, as well as presenting a risky challenge. And as Howell writes, "when skaters took the place over, they actually made it safer."[22] The space was constantly populated with skaters, which thus made it a difficult place to smoke crack in seclusion. Hubba Hideout attracted skaters from all over the world, and despite the years of being a well-known spot for illicit activity, it was skateboarding that attracted the police. In the late 1990s the police kicked the skaters out and the city installed skateboard-prevention devices. In the mid-2000s city workers removed the brick pavement, leaving only dirt.[23]

Hubba Hideout, 2009. Photo: Gregory Snyder.

Author buying Hubba Hideout Tech Deck. Photo: Aaron Snyder.

In 2009 I visited Hubba Hideout and learned that it is once again a homeless crack hangout (although when I told its current resident that this spot is legendary, he was quite proud). Today Hubba Hideout is completely unskateable, but in any city if you ask skaters where there is a good "hubba," they won't take you to a crack spot, but to a ledge going down stairs. Hubba Hideout has its own Wikipedia page; in addition, the toy company Tech Deck, which makes tiny finger skateboards, has also produced a toy replica of Hubba Hideout that is available at your local Target. (Actually they are no longer available, which means that the one I own is a collector's item.)

The "LA School" of Urban Sociology

Urban sociology has its roots in the Chicago School that arose at the University of Chicago's Department of Sociology in the 1920s. The department was chaired by Robert Park, who encouraged the use of ethnographic techniques to explore the city and quipped that "civilized man is at least as interesting as primitive."[24] Park used this as a rationale to suggest that his students could learn about society and human behavior by studying the modern city. Park and his students utilized the city as a "laboratory for learning," and they produced numerous classic ethnographies, including *The Gang* (Thrasher), *The Hobo* (Anderson), and *The Taxi-Dance Hall* (Cressey).[25]

One of their most important theoretical legacies is the Concentric Zone Model. With this model Ernest Burgess sought to explain the growth of a city by showing how social mobility is reflected spatially. For example, as industrial workers increased their assets they were likely to move further out from the industrial center of the city to enjoy more space, less pollution, and the increased life chances that a better neighborhood provides. Burgess argued that the catalyst for this movement was the "invasion" of newly arriving European immigrant groups seeking to realize their American dreams in Chicago factories. The new arrivals would engage in "competition" with the more established ethnic groups, and the result would be what he called "succession," where, for example, a once Irish neighborhood transitioned into an Italian enclave, as the more successful Irish, threatened by the lower-class status of the newly arriving Italians, moved out in search of better spaces.[26]

The Concentric Zone Model therefore does a good job of explaining neighborhood turnover, though it is strictly limited to the social mobility of European non-Jews. Burgess may have recognized that black folks and Jews did not have the same opportunities and were forcibly retained in a single area of the city, but he never mentioned it. He in fact designates the "black belt" by constructing a large pie-shaped swath in the middle of his radiating circles, but never analyzes it apart from one line, "Wedging out from here is the Black Belt, with its free and disorderly life."[27] However, W. E. B. Du Bois had shown 25 years earlier in his now classic ethnography *The Philadelphia Negro* that spatial mobility according to class, just like that described by Burgess in the Concentric Zone

Model, existed in the 7th Ward in Philadelphia, even as racial segregation persisted.[28]

The racial blind spots notwithstanding, the Chicago School model of a city that had its financial and industrial hub centrally located held sway for nearly the rest of the century, in part due to its "beguiling simplicity," as urban geographer Michael Dear has described it.[29] This model even works to explain postindustrial cities. When the factories leave, unemployment escalates and government policies and white flight create segregation, extreme poverty, high crime, and military-style policing of black and brown neighborhoods, which is to say that when the center implodes, "inner cities"—as they've come to be known—are what is left, creating a situation that has been referred to as "hypersegregation."[30]

In the mid-80s postmodern geographers like Michael Dear, Steven Flusty, Mike Davis, and others began to conceptualize Los Angeles as a new urban model that provided an alternative to the Chicago School. Los Angeles does not rely wholly upon mass transit, and never had a financial and industrial core from which to radiate out concentric zones. From an urban perspective, what makes Los Angeles special is the fact that it has no center. For some this makes it a postmodern city, but it is necessary to think of an LA School of urbanism because of all the ways that it fails to conform to the time-honored traditions of the Chicago School, thereby teaching new lessons about how we conceptualize cities and the movement of their populations.

The idea of a center-less city can be understood simply as the outgrowth of cars replacing mass transit systems, which bring folks from the periphery to the interior; but this is not to say that LA is a city without industry; in fact it is home to the oil, agriculture, film, and aerospace industries. In his tour of the "60 mile radius" surrounding LA, Edward Soja refers to LA as the Keynesian ideal, where the city is home to one of the most sophisticated government-sponsored private industries, the military-industrial complex, along with the massive entertainment machine.[31]

So the Los Angeles of the LA School is, according to Soja, a "polycentric, polyglot, polycultural pastiche"; there is no center in both reality and metaphor. The Chicago School's concentric rings create a simple cognitive map that can be applied metaphorically as a model to explain urban growth and the movement of populations. Burgess's human ecology model suggested that population movement was a "natural" process that followed a pattern of "invasion, competition and success" (even though it's problematic to suggest this process is "natural" rather than human-made). The LA School does not describe the movement of people because there is no movement, no social and spatial mobility.

As Mike Davis shows in *City of Quartz*, LA is a fortress, an extremely segregated place with very little internal population shift, and until recently gentrification and displacement were not a concern.[32] That is to say there was no need for invasion and competition because there was space for everyone, and people stayed in their place. And for a very long time that's what they did. (Robert Weide's recent research shows an active process of ethnic cleansing of indigenous people's neighborhoods, to make way for the "hipster colonials.")[33]

This suggests that the spatial logic of Los Angeles does not follow the classic model, where upward social mobility radiates out from a center. With the Chicago School model, the more wealth you amassed, the farther you moved from the center of the city and the more life chances you accrued. Certainly successful Angelenos live in bigger, nicer homes in better neighborhoods than those home to less successful folks, but the spatial logic does not follow a simple cognitive map, which radiates out from a center. Beverly Hills, Malibu, Brentwood, and the Hollywood Hills are disconnected pockets of wealth that do not follow a simple spatial logic (except for Malibu, which is on the Pacific).

The history of LA is one not of "invading immigrants" but of white colonizers displacing an indigenous population. California became a state in 1850 and was still part of Mexico in 1848, but it's also strange to consider that California statehood predates that of Minnesota and a whole host of other states including Utah, New Mexico, Nevada, and Wyoming, which actually gives pause to the Manifest Destiny notion of pushing west to the Pacific. America in fact colonized California and filled in the flyover states later.

In Los Angeles spatial distribution does not follow a consistent outside-in pattern. Wealth, power, and fame are not concentrated in one area. In general, the north is wealthier than the south, the west more so than the east.

For urban sociology skateboarding presents an opportunity to think differently about the cartography of the city. Skateboarders map their city according to spots, the unforeseen elements of the built environment that are the result of creative acts of interpretation and physical prowess. Because of the serendipitous nature of architectural by-products, the map of the city for skaters does not follow a coherent logic. For skaters there is no movement from the periphery to the center as a signifier of success; the signifiers of success happen at famous spots, and are shared throughout the subculture.

Skateboarding places are an interpretive by-product of the built environment and therefore do not conform to a spatial logic. Yes, there are some spots Downtown, which tends to have newer architecture, but there are spots everywhere, at schools and parks and other random places. For skaters this means that their city map is a vast array of unintentional acts of beauty that exist across an entire region, none of which would have existed without the skaters' imagination.[34] When seen from the perspective of a skater, the spatial logic of the city becomes one where there is no center, only points of extreme interest, or a "polyglot, polycultural pastiche," in the words of the LA School geographers.

Skaters skate at spots with small groups of friends and teammates, along with the documentarians, and yet when they are at a place they know who's been there before because there is a historical record of the deeds of others. They skate inside a virtual community of their imaginations and seek to progress the discipline by sharing what they've done with others. The community of skaters largely does not exist in physical space; their community is facilitated by skateboarding media and now more immediately by social media.

The cognitive map of Los Angeles covers an immense geographic expanse, but rather than "staying local" in one's specific area like many Angelenos do, skaters go to spots that suit their needs, no matter where they exist. So skateboarding defies the logic of spatial mobility of the modern city by eschewing the Chicago School idea of a center and the logic of segregation that accompanies a vast region like Southern California. In LA, you are not meant to go to, explore, or have contact with those unlike yourself. The postmodern militarism of fortress LA, as described by Mike Davis, is designed to keep people in their respective spaces to alleviate white middle-class fears of a black, brown, and poor planet. And in LA, for the most part (though foodies are changing this) there is no reason to go to an unfamiliar area, unless that space has a special quality of architectural happenstance that appeals to you.

Skaters today, like graffiti writers in New York City generations ago, actively cross urban boundaries in search of spots and in doing so understand their city in an entirely different way from the maps constructed by urban sociologists in the 1920s. In this sense skaters are postmodern explorers of the contemporary city unbound by country or continent or hemisphere. Skaters are citizens of city earth, constantly exploring, searching for new undiscovered places to expand their discipline's notions of what's possible, all the while developing an ever more intimate relationship with the urban geography of the world's built environment. And yet, those serendipitous public spaces that are cherished by skateboarders, like Embarcadero, Love Park, and the West LA Courthouse, became physical focal points not only where skaters had access to architecture that suited their needs, but also where they had each other, to hang out, to talk, and most importantly to learn and progress.

Skateboarding Subculture

Subculture should be understood simply as a smaller cultural group that exists within the culture of a larger society. This inclusive definition of subculture, which does not assume members to be working-class or deviant follows the one offered by sociologist Claude Fischer in 1975, but the idea of understanding subcultures as groups with shared interests has since been mostly forgotten.[35] There are ethnic, occupational, leisure, sport, and music subcultures, and many, many more. Subcultures are not by definition resistant or subversive, though that is the definition most commonly accepted by many scholars and journalists, but stamp collectors and Wall Street traders constitute a subculture just as much as outlaw bikers, gangsters, and graffiti writers. In fact more and more the "mainstream" increasingly includes a diversity of subcultures, some of which are valued, others not. As Fischer writes, "Cities provide the critical mass necessary for a viable subculture and the clashes that accentuate that culture. With size comes 'community'—even if it is a community of thieves, counterculture experimenters, avant-garde intellectuals, or other unconventional persons."[36]

Skateboarding is a subculture because its members define it as such. Like all subcultures it has its own distinct language, skill set, worldview, and set of values. While it is important to note that subculture beliefs, practices, and values are not static, it is also the case that often what these groups share is a recognition that they are self-consciously part of a subculture, and identify as such.[37] Skaters, graffiti writers, goths, and others self-identify as members of a subculture and define membership simply as those who are committed to the practice.[38]

Who Skates?

Skateboarding has attracted a diversity of practitioners since its inception. Skateboarders are united by the process and practice of skating and form their skater identities first and their ethnic or racial identities second. When it comes to race many people incorrectly assume that graffiti writers are black and skaters are white; my experience is mostly the opposite. Most of the graffiti writers I met were white, whereas a majority of my contacts in skateboarding were people of color. During my time researching skating there were no pro skaters who were openly gay. Until. . . .

September 27, 2016, I arrive for my last research trip to LA. Aaron and I are catching up, and while scrolling through my feeds I notice that folks are posting stuff about legendary skater Brian Anderson. "BA" as he is also known has played many groundbreaking roles and won skater of the year from *Thrasher* magazine in 1999. In recent years, he has been less of an active pro and has done sneaker designs for Nike (the BA Project) and owned a short-lived board company.

We figure out all the attention has something to do with Vice Sports, and a quick search reveals the title "Brian Anderson on Being a Gay Professional Skateboarder." We are stunned and thrilled. The fact that Brian Anderson is so many people's favorite skater means that even the most homophobic skaters will have to reassess their notions. But it's not even an issue; the culture has rejoiced, calling it a "big day in skateboarding history." There has been nothing but positivity and support for Brian Anderson and Giovanni Reda, who conducted the interview and filmed most of it. The next day *Rolling Stone* picks up the story, followed a day later by the *New York Times*.[39]

I will say, however, that all of my skating contacts are male, though I did encounter some female skaters at Stoner Plaza. There are professional female skateboarders who have made impressive contributions to the culture. The first great female pro street skater was Elissa Steamer, who inspired the current generation of female pros, which includes Lacey Baker, Alexis Sablone, and Leticia Bufoni.[40] However, despite repeated attempts, I was unable to develop anything more than a cursory relationship with female skaters.[41] This is in part because I did not want to simply reach out to female skaters solely because of their gender, and this is likely the same reason that female skaters tend to be suspicious of male researchers.[42] Although she did not participate directly in this project, former pro skater Jaime Reyes is a close friend whose career I followed closely when she rode for Rookie Skateboards—an all-female team—during the late 1990s and early 2000s, and her response to being a "female skater" was that she's just a skater. There are certainly fewer financial opportunities for female skaters, and those who do receive opportunities tend to also be judged by their appearance. But this is changing; there are two female-owned skate companies and a foundation, and for the past two years women have competed in the Street League Super Crown Finals.

Skateboards are not very expensive (especially compared to snowboards, BMX bikes, and motorcycles), which means that skaters come from a range of class backgrounds, from the suburban upper-middle class to the working class and urban poor. While class is not a determining factor in nourishing skateboarding talent, it does require parents who are either extremely supportive or, in many cases, absent. However, it is true that the kids who can get access to technology (video recorders, computers, etc.) or can afford to go to skate camps like Camp Woodward have a better chance of making a career within the skateboarding industry.[43]

This group of people self-consciously constitutes skateboarding subculture. They are involved and have contributed, on whatever scale, to the production and progression of skateboarding. They are distinct from those kids who simply own skateboards and have chosen "skater" as their identity by dressing in skater fashions available at the local mall. Skating is something that cannot be faked; therefore a skater is not just someone who rides a skateboard, but one who has made a physical and mental commitment to learn skateboarding tricks and has knowledge of the culture.[44] Street skateboarding as I'm using it here is a diverse subculture that is based upon one thing only—the ability to perform tricks on a skateboard.

Subculture media and the Internet have made finding folks who share your practices, kinks, interests, obsessions, and style incredibly easy.[45] What scholars have been slow to recognize however is that in the 21st century subculture participation has become, for many people, more than a way to find people with whom to develop lasting relationships and ease the tensions of big city life, as Fischer described; as a subculture reaches "critical mass," it presents potential career opportunities, sometimes where none previously existed.[46]

For subcultures like skating, the reality is that, contrary to conventional wisdom, they have had a positive economic impact on the lives of many participants by providing them with career opportunities. As discussed earlier this is an idea that scholars have resisted for some time, in part because of the Birmingham School's insistence that subcultures are symbolic manifestations of radical politics.[47] Recently, Australian scholar Kara-Jane Lombard has been one of the few to understand the futility of the Birmingham School for understanding how contemporary skateboarders see their subculture. She writes, "Skateboarding has a complex relationship with commercial culture . . . at the same time there has been resistance to some instances of commercial incorporation. . . . Thus purely oppositional or resistive readings of skateboarding are problematic."[48]

The fact that people make careers out of their subcultural participation means that the radical promise that many had invested in stylistically resistant, working-class subcultures has been dashed. And while some have decried subculturalists for selling out, research shows that many people become involved in subcultures with the hope that they may be able to have a career doing what they love.[49]

Although skateboarding subculture exhibits very little stratification along the classic lines of race, ethnicity, class, or even age, this is not to say that skating has been completely exempt from the racism and classism that exists in the larger society. Jeremy Nemeth argues that at Philadelphia's iconic Love Park in the 1990s there was some tension between white and black skaters.[50] Nemeth suggests that Stevie Williams, who is black, indicated that there was a bit of segregation when the black skaters in Stevie's crew began to establish their talents in the park. In a video on Love Park, Stevie says, "It seems like Love Park was segregated. It was like they had their clique, and we had our clique. And there was always like tension and beef, and we should have just all got along."[51] Even though Nemeth believes that the segregation and tension that Stevie describes are racially motivated, that doesn't mean that Stevie's crew was entirely black (see Josh Kalis), nor does it mean that this tension wasn't also motivated by generational conflict. In the end Love Park lived up to its name, and today all the original Love Park skaters have love for each other. Unfortunately, they no longer live in the same city. Shutting down Love Park for skaters produced a mass exodus of one of the strongholds of Philadelphia's creative class.[52]

While it should be noted that the wealthiest, most mainstream skateboarders, like Tony Hawk, Rob Dyrdek, and Rick Howard, are all white, it is also the case that current superstars like Nyjah Huston and Paul Rodriguez are people of color. While it may be the case that white skaters with movie star looks, like Ryan Sheckler, are more palatable to mainstream corporations, it is important to remember that the first pro street skater to successfully secure mainstream sponsors while retaining respect from his peers was Paul Rodriguez Jr. Paul is Mexican American and white, and is the son of successful 1980s comic Paul Rodriguez Sr. Though this may have made Paul's class experience different from those of other Mexicans his age, it does not discount the fact that Paul is a brown-skinned Latin male and is the face of skateboarding for Nike, Target, and Mountain Dew (although Paul recently left Mountain Dew to start Villager Water).

The Skater Code

Skateboarding is stratified by skill level, style, and personality, where skaters who have a "sick style" and are thought to be "cool" are praised. Those who have bad style and are deemed "uncool" or "kooks" by the skateboarding tastemakers are chastised and ridiculed.

One aspect of skating's diversity that is rarely mentioned is the fact that it brings together groups of young people from vastly different age groups. This is a phenomenon unique to skateboarding where older skaters tend to look out for the "groms," little kids aged 8 to 11 or so. While skaters are engaged in edge work, and risky behavior, which can often include drug and alcohol use, they tend to try to keep the kids sheltered as long as they can. But since younger skaters tend to have a larger proportion of older friends than others in their age group, this may put them at risk to begin drinking or smoking weed at an earlier age, but again I have seen that the older skaters try to regulate this.

Case in point: In 1990 I was living in Washington, DC, and Aaron and my mom came to visit. Aaron came because he wanted to skate at Pulaski Park, an extremely famous spot at the time. My mom let Aaron, who was 13, head off to the spot by himself in a city where he had never been, fully confident that he would be okay. She knew that the skaters there, whom Aaron had heard of but never met, would take care of him. Little kids are tolerated if they are talented skaters and if they are, for lack of a better word, cool. This means they must be deferential and respectful.

When young skaters are too cocky, or if they show up other skaters in a disrespectful fashion, like attempting the same trick someone else is trying and landing it on the first try, they get shunned by the skating establishment.[53] In skate terms, they get "hated on," and while skaters don't exhibit the classic modes of stratification (race, class, gender), they love to "hate on" other skaters whom they feel are not doing it right. The "right way" is a fluid concept as what's cool in skating is constantly being debated and argued. Most of these debates focus on style, trick selection, or clothing choices, but it should also clearly be understood that the "hate" is motivated by jealousy. Many of the people who complain the loudest about other skaters could never accomplish the feats they're critiquing, which means that sometimes there is no reason at all for the scathing critiques that some skaters receive.

The practice of "hating," which also can be considered a form of peer review, sometimes involves a real and nuanced critique of skaters' abilities or choices, such as that they skate too slow, land difficult tricks but with little grace or style, are boring and lack charisma, or over sell and show off too much. There is a long list of skating dos and don'ts, but most of them are unwritten. One of the biggest taboos, however, is cheering for yourself when landing a trick. Skateboarders tend to appreciate humility, and skaters who do so much as fist pump when landing a trick are severely criticized. And while the above are in many ways legitimate arguments, many skaters get "hated on" simply because people don't like them personally. These guys are considered "kooks," and even though they may be talented skaters, their inability to get along with other skaters, essentially to conform to subculture norms, eventually leads to their being ostracized and sometimes even excommunicated.

It is a tall order to expect skaters to be cool and mature at such a young age, especially for those who are receiving so much attention, fame, and even money from older people. Nevertheless there is a strict code of conduct, and those who don't follow it will be shunned and may even lose their sponsorship. A lack of charisma or a bad personality however can be overcome with pure talent.

Parents can sometimes also play a role in this process. If skaters' parents behave like parents involved in so many other sports, demanding that their children receive the respect the parents believe is due, the skate gatekeepers will not respond. It's difficult to understand what this code is; at the same time, skaters spend a lot of time with each other, so the level of scrutiny extends far beyond simply how one skates. When skaters go on tour together they are with each other day and night, and tiny transgressions become annoying and exasperating to those making the rules.

Skating has a very strict set of rules of interaction that are always changing according to who the rule makers are. The rule makers' power comes not from a privileged racial, class, or ethnic position, but from their skateboarding prowess and position within the industry, combined with their likability. And knowing the rules is part of being a member of the subculture. For some this comes easy; despite their youth they understand and respect older skaters, have a strong sense of self, and can withstand the criticism; for others this can be quite daunting, further complicating a difficult adolescence. For some, success at a young age, combined with money and easy access to drugs and alcohol, sadly often results in substance abuse. (The good news is that in the past 20 years there have been some very high-profile pros who have saved lives, and skate careers, by publicly getting sober.)[54]

The truth is, if you are good at skating but nobody likes you, it will be difficult to succeed at skateboarding unless you are extremely talented; on the other hand, if everybody likes you, you may be able to have a successful career if you have a good style, even if you're not the most talented skater in the world. For example, Skater X is universally loved; I've met him personally and he is a super sweet guy, always smiling, very positive, and extremely consistent on his skateboard. He has all of the big-name sponsors and is quite likely a millionaire. He is also tall and gangly or short and hunched over, and to my eyes appears to have a poor style compared to other skaters. But I have never heard even the most cynical skaters say a bad word about him. No one "hates on" this guy because it is simply not fashionable to do so, and because the guy is just such a wonderful, positive person, people are interested in his skating.

Kids grow up and change their ways, and free themselves from the aegis of a domineering parent, and when the skating community comes around, their talent is finally rewarded. There are others, however, who never quite get it, and despite overwhelming talent, in the words of photographer Shad Lambert, "they get kooked out of the game," and left with no way to make a career in skating.[55]

2

Skate Spots

Scanning the Terrain

I am sitting in the passenger seat as Aaron drives through the streets in his West Los Angeles neighborhood. As he drives, his head swivels back and forth scanning the terrain. This is my first trip to LA and I see apartment buildings, sidewalks, lush greenery, and parking lots, but for him every glance is a calculated gaze as to whether or not something is "skateable," and if so, in what way. He is looking for ledges, and rails and possibility. As we drive, he rattles off crazy talk like "you might be able to switch flip, 5–0 that; or, that could be a possible board slide spot, if. . . ." It almost seems like a mental exercise, keeping the mind and the eyes sharp just in case there might be some "new spot" that he hasn't yet noticed. Because spots are rare and liable to get skateproofed as soon as skaters discover them, and the fact that skaters often get ticketed or kicked out by police and security, skaters are also, always, looking for new spots. They are continuously honing their architectural imaginations by constantly scrutinizing urban spaces in the hope that there might be an undiscovered skate spot.

***

Skateboarding at the highest level requires spots to skate. Over the years the places where tricks have been filmed have made famous not only skateboarders, but also the spots. Spots evolve and develop their own history according to the feats performed; therefore to learn about famous skateboarding spots is also to learn about the history of street skate-boarding.[1] Good skate spots become stages for performing tricks and inspire skaters to invent new and more difficult tricks to perform, thus adding their names to the history and legend of a particular spot. Skate spots become invested with deep meaning for members of the subcul-ture, depending upon the feats that have taken place and as a result are treated with great reverence. So much so that when spots are destroyed or made "unskateable" by police and security guards, skaters will write

R.I.P. after a spot in magazine articles; consider "Carlsbad Gap, R.I.P." or more recently and for skaters more heart-wrenching, "Love Park, R.I.P." As former skater turned scholar of comparative literature, Peter Lehman puts it, "what is mourned is not the object itself, but the death of the ongoing skate history attached to it."[2]

For skateboarders, a skate spot is any place or obstacle that is "skateable"—meaning it fulfills the basic requirements for doing skateboard tricks. While on the surface it would appear that professional skateboarders would have a nearly infinite amount of urban public space upon which to perform, in fact these accidents of urban design where skaters film tricks are quite rare.

Although in theory street skating has the possibility of repurposing any element of the built environment, finding obstacles that meet a pro skater's criteria and are thus "skateable" is actually quite difficult. Skaters tend to focus on specific sets of obstacles, which include flat ground, ledges, bumps, banks, stairs, gaps, manual pads, flat bars, and handrails. Within these categories there are also terms that indicate even greater specificity, like "hubbas," "pier 7s," "euro gaps," "grass gaps," "double and triple sets," and "kinked rails." These terms can also be combined to describe more specific obstacles (e.g., "bump to ledge" or "gap to rail").

For a spot to be skateable, the ground (concrete, blacktop, brick, marble, granite) must be sufficiently smooth so that the relatively small and hard skateboard wheels will roll properly. Ledges and rails must be smooth enough to grind the metal trucks or slide the wooden nose or tail. Skaters may engage in guerilla architecture and employ a number of techniques to alter the quality of a spot, thus making it easier to skate. Skaters will repair cracks in the concrete, cut "skate stoppers" off of rails, remove pieces of chain-link fence, or simply apply wax to a ledge, all in an effort to make a spot skateable. Pro skaters are looking for obstacles that best showcase their specific skill sets; the "gnarliest" skaters who do the most dangerous tricks, like Nyjah Huston, Aaron Homoki, and Andrew Reynolds, skate extremely big gaps and huge handrails, but generally stay away from ledges, while others like Guy Mariano prefer to perform their technical wizardry on medium-sized rails, while still others, like Mike Mo Capaldi and Shane O'Neill, are masters on ledges. Therefore obstacles that are perfect for some skaters don't work at all for others.

In addition, skaters like Brandon Westgate, Raven Tershay, and Jordan Sanchez become known for creatively skating difficult obstacles that most other skaters would avoid.[3]

Skateboarders skate at "spots" that involve unintended uses of architectural spaces, but do not always significantly alter or vandalize the space. In many instances skaters have created functionality of a space in ways that were unimagined by the original designers. This reappropriation is only temporary, and without a properly trained eye the general public has little knowledge that the bench or set of stairs that they are sitting on might be famous to a particular group.

Not all skaters skate the same spots, and one can get a very clear understanding of a skater's skill, creativity, and style just by looking at photographs of the obstacles a skater has chosen to skate. A quick primer is that technical or "tech" skaters who do more intricate and complicated flips of the board tend to perform their tricks most often on ledges, flat bars, smaller rails, and "manual pads" (raised surfaces that are good for doing front or back wheelie tricks). The "gnarly" big-risk, big-reward skaters perform on bigger, more dangerous obstacles like huge sets of stairs, big gaps, and massive handrails. Of course the best skaters in the world can skate everything.

Ledges

A "ledge" or bench is a piece of urban furniture normally used for sitting. Marble and other hard surfaces make ideal ledges for skaters and are usually about 18 to 24 inches high and of sufficient length to slide on the trucks or on the wooden deck. Ledges are the sites for some of the most technical skating because skaters can essentially do three tricks in one: the trick into the slide, the slide, and the trick out of the slide. The names of tricks that are done on ledges often reveal their complexity— "fakie ollie, to 5–0 grind, to fakie 360 out"—and great ledges have become famous subcultural landmarks. When I show skaters my photo of the famous DWP Ledges in Los Angeles, they immediately rattle off a series of historic tricks that have been done there, a fact of which I'm sure few employees of the LA Department of Water and Power have any knowledge.

Gaps, Handrails, and Banks

A "gap" describes any space that a skater has to ollie over. There can be flat-ground gaps like the sand gaps at Santa Monica beach or down-hill "grass gaps" like the Carlsbad Gap. Stairs can also be skated as gaps (skaters simply fly over the stairs) and do the same set of tricks, but stairs are also more specific because of the number of stairs and their height. Famous spots include the Santa Monica Triple Set, the Holly-wood 16, Wallenberg, and the El Toro 20.

Handrails refer to the rails that accompany the stairs upon which skaters perform tricks. In general, a 5-stair rail is easier to skate than a 12 or a 16. Smaller rails tend to accommodate harder tricks while more basic tricks are done on the bigger rails. No matter the size, it takes an enormous amount of courage to skate a handrail.

Handrails must be sturdy enough to support the weight of the rider and usually 3 to 8 stairs minimum to 16 to 25 on the upper limit. The more stairs the longer the grind distance, which increases the speed

Santa Monica Triple Set. Photo: Drew Vaz.

Hollywood 16. Photo: Aaron Snyder.

and the danger because you have farther to fall. But sometimes skaters require smaller rails for doing technical tricks, like the most recent six-stair rail on which Guy Mariano did the first ever switch 360 flip, nosegrind.

A bank is an angled obstacle to which skaters go up, do a trick on the top of the bank, and come back down. The most famous banks in the world are the Brooklyn Banks in NYC and the Car Wash Banks and Radisson Banks in LA.

New spots are places of enormous creative possibility because no one has yet to do any tricks on them. Finding them is tricky not only because

Wallenberg, San Francisco.

of skaters' specific architectural requirements, but also because of cops, skate stoppers, sidewalk cracks, and pedestrians. Spots are also time-sensitive, as most are in use by civilians during the week and especially at daytime, so finding a "weekday spot" is even better.

Skaters have also been known to engage in DIY architecture to make spots skateable, often repairing sidewalk cracks with a substance used for auto body repair, Bondo. They also will bring generators and cinematic floodlights to skate a spot at night if there is no way to skate it during the day.

***

I am once again driving down Wilshire Blvd. with Aaron and as we pass a drugstore he lets out an "ohhhhhh" and we take a quick, slightly precarious left, across oncoming traffic, to go see the possible spot. This happens often as I drive with Aaron and most of the time, as he says, "it turns out to be a bust," but these sidetracks are a common part of urban travel for the skateboarder.

I wait while Aaron goes to check the spot. Sure enough when he returns he says that the "bump to wall" that he thought he saw from the street was no good. We get in the car and drive down the alley a bit further and as we pass the entrance to an underground parking garage, he spots a metal rail attached to a wall that was put there to prevent cars from damaging the wall as they enter. It is yellow and rusted. Aaron stops the car abruptly, gets out, and goes crazy. "Holy crap. This is sick." Excitedly he grabs my camera to photograph it, then he grabs his board from the car to test the spot, using his hands to slide the board. "It'll need more wax, but you could 'back tail' or 'crooks,'" he said referring to two tricks, in which you slide or grind on the rail. He said this spot is now on the top of his list, meaning he wants to do a trick on it and share the documented video of it with other skaters. Aaron tells me I've just witnessed a "sighting in the wild," a rare moment when a spot is actually "discovered."

Some skaters require different types of spaces dependent upon not only their style of skating, but also their stance. Since the rail

Walgreens Rail. Photo: Gregory Snyder.

can be approached from only one side, "goofy-footed" riders can do tricks only with their back facing the obstacle, called "backside," while "regular-footed" or left-foot-forward riders can do only "frontside" tricks. Of course riders could also do a trick "switch," meaning changing their stance, but that increases the level of difficulty. This suggests that the spot itself plays a role in determining the range of creative possibility.

The beauty of finding a new spot, aside from the simple joy of discovery, is that no tricks have been done on it yet. Every possibility is available to the rider who makes the discovery. But this act of architectural appreciation also goes on in the abstract. Skaters often imagine skating spots that they'd never be able to skate, such as museums, federal buildings, and the like.

The LA County Superior Courthouse on Wilshire Boulevard is a beautiful building with curved architectural flourishes that look interesting and are attractive to skaters.

***

As we approach, Aaron knows the drill and leaves his skateboard on the sidewalk. I take a photo and immediately a guard comes out to tell us that I'm not allowed to photograph the building (because of terrorism). We're just looking at the building, and enjoying it from a different perspective. Aaron walks around the area describing to me all the different ways you could skate this spot, if you could actually skate this spot. Essentially we are appreciating the architecture, however, not as it is, but as it could be, by imagining different ways it could be used.

In April 2015, Trevor Colden filmed a Nike ad in which he performs a trick on this obstacle; it is unclear whether or not Nike facilitated permission.

The Ethos of Progression

Pro skaters skate obstacles that help them contribute to the "progression of skateboarding." Progression is achieved essentially by increasing the degree of difficulty at existing spots or by finding new spots that meet specific criteria for a specific trick. This means that skateboarders

LA Superior Courthouse. Photo: Gregory Snyder.

are constantly scrutinizing public space and imagining how it could be skated. It should also be noted that the so-called "big pants, small wheels" era of the early 1990s, which boasted progression merely for the sake of progression, is an era that is not remembered fondly among skaters because of the complete lack of style with which tricks were done at the time.[4]

The ethos of progression is persistent throughout the culture and is just as strong with filmers and photographers as with skaters; not only do they want to shoot the most progressive tricks, they also are committed to progression as it relates to improving how skating is documented and presented. As RB Umali says, "progression in filming is about trying to improve the quality of the image and the way you do that is by learning about all of the available products and programs that could potentially facilitate that." From being among the first to fit VHS cameras with fisheye lenses to going digital almost a decade before the rest of society, as well as leading the way in the transition to HD filmmaking, skateboard documenters have been and continue to be on the leading edge of the video revolution. In their role as filmers, skateboard cinematographers are not only camera operators, location scouts, and encouraging supporters of skaters engaged in dangerous activity, but also independent filmmakers responsible for editing the content (utilizing professional software like Final Cut Pro and Premiere), scoring the film, and using various other postproduction techniques to produce cinematic representations of skateboarding. Filmers may be skaters first, but they are also in many ways the arbiters and curators of what gets seen by the larger subculture, and their aesthetic shapes how skating is viewed. The best filmers do not take this role lightly and are committed to sharing the knowledge they've amassed with other skaters and filmers, thereby contributing both the finished product (videos of progressive skating) and their technical innovations to the rest of the culture, who adopt these new practices to varying degrees.

The skateboarding industry has many different roles including but not limited to pro skaters, filmers, photographers, designers, team managers, marketing folks, web engineers, and social media experts, all of whom also skateboard. For skateboarding culture therefore, progression is not simply limited to tricks and spots but is an ethos that values the idea that the goal should be to contribute to the betterment of the culture on any level. While this isn't always the case, it is nonetheless an ideal that is upheld and consistently preached in magazine editorials, in videos, and on social media. Progression isn't just for the most advanced skaters and the best filmers; any skater can contribute to progression. It is an inclusionary ethos; progression happens when a groundbreaking new trick is accomplished, but it also happens when a group of skaters get together and force their local communities to build them a proper skate park, or when skaters seek new spots to skate in new cities in China or Dubai, or when Oliver Percovich organically developed the Skateistan

Project (now an award-winning NGO that uses "skateboarding as a tool for empowerment" for boys and girls in Afghanistan, Cambodia, and South Africa) on a trip to Afghanistan.[5] Progression also happens when cinematographers like Ty Evans and the Brain Farm production team push the limits of action documentary filmmaking by using remote-controlled drones, Red cameras, handheld MōVI stabilizers, and a device called the "Spot Over" to advance "gyro-stabilized" cinematography, to create the feature film *We Are Blood*.[6] Not only did they use the most advanced equipment, they got to use it for free. As Ty says in a recent interview about the folks who sponsored the gear:

> We've been fortunate enough that a lot of these companies have been partners of [our] film and they want us to use this equipment and show the rest of the world what's possible with it. Companies like Shooter, Freely Systems, Radiant Images rental house, Intuitive Arial with their helicopters, Digital Sputnik with their lights, Maxx Digital with their hard drives, and then at the very end Dolby came in and let us do an Atmos mix, which no one has ever done in action sports, let alone skateboarding. It was just crazy to have the relationship with all these people and have them support the film and let us show the world what's possible with their equipment.[7]

Progression at its best then comes in many forms, and it inspires the entire culture to continue to learn. In fact, for many finding how they can contribute to this thing they love is an essential part of finding their place in skating, and in life. However, while the ethos of progression is open to all, the rewards are not shared evenly. There is a crude amount of financial inequality that exists within skateboarding, with those at the top—skaters, filmers, and company owners—reaping most of the rewards, while many others struggle financially. While skaters are a collective, they do not use their financial power collectively. Money is something that skaters rarely talk openly about; while they are unified by the act of skating and a commitment to progression, they are divided when it comes to the distribution of rewards. There is no union, no group of skaters advocating for fair contracts, no fund that skaters contribute to in order to help out aging skaters. In this realm all skaters are out for themselves.

There are many different disciplines in skateboarding culture, and while the documenters (filmers and photographers) disseminate skating achievements, many others become experts in marketing, digital editing, graphic design, shoe design, social media networking, and skate park design, to name a few. Here, if we expand on Sarah Thornton's idea of subcultural capital, if subculture knowledge adds value to one's status and is a form of capital, we should also understand that knowledge gets passed around and becomes part of the currency of exchange.[8]

As former skater turned college professor Pete Lehman describes:

> In terms of this knowledge, the practical education [of skateboarding] cannot be separated from the creative or inventive practice—that is, the activity of skating teaches much more than tricks, skaters also share environments and their relation to those spaces is itself a learning experience, with numerous applications. My inclination, would be to stress the multifaceted cultural aspects of this knowledge. Thinking about some of the videographers, graphic designers, ramp builders, etc. that I've known or met, I wonder whether their desire to learn those skills can be separated from the fact that they are contributing to framing, constructing, and developing that activity they love—that is, the subcultural practice of skateboarding, to participate in the transformative landscape of skateboarding. Not just reproducing something fixed, but contributing to its progression.[9]

Progression therefore is dependent upon the communication of ideas that everyone can build upon, which helps to encourage skateboarding's culture of innovation. In a recent *Wired* magazine article titled "Silicon Valley Has Lost Its Way. Can Skateboarding Legend Rodney Mullen Help It?" Brendan Koerner highlights Mullen's sudden new career as a sought-after speaker on the tech circuit.[10] During his nearly three-year recovery from injury—when he had to painfully jab, poke, and hammer at his hip and thigh to release the scar tissue that had nearly fused his femur into his hip—Mullen mastered Linux, an open-source computer operating system favored by the world's best hackers.

With his mastery of Linux suddenly came new opportunities. Rodney Mullen's TEDxUSC Talk, "Pop an Ollie and Innovate," which he gave reluctantly, has generated over 2.4 million views and thrust him into the new role of tech star. Mullen's talks are designed to inspire Silicon Valley's innovators and as his speaking career has flourished he has also landed an array of consulting gigs, advising the head of virtual reality at a USC research lab and collaborating with the Smithsonian to launch a project about skateboarding history and innovation.[11] Koerner writes that both "hacker and skate culture are proudly open source, filled with innovations that improve upon the nonproprietary works of generations past,"[12] or as Mullen put it in his 2012 talk, "Take what other people do, make it better, give it back, so we all rise further."[13]

This irony is not lost on most skaters, whose world revolves around a very simple device: a wooden deck with aluminum trucks, urethane wheels, sealed ball bearings, and a sheet of grip tape unifies a global culture. Over the years there has been almost zero innovation in the skateboard itself. The major technological change occurred in the 1970s when urethane wheels replaced metal ones. Since then, except for some experimentation with shapes, there has been no effort whatsoever to "improve" the skateboard. This is not to say however that skaters are a low-tech culture; in fact the opposite is true. Skateboarding is a visual culture, and one of the ways that skaters learn and progress the culture is by studying videos, often in slow motion, of other skaters. Skateboarding therefore has always been at the leading edge of video technology because the documentation and showcasing of the culture necessitate the latest technology. While the skateboard needs no technological improvements, the culture relies heavily on technology to communicate feats, and thus skateboarders are at the leading edge of digital video technology.

This advancement has been led by the photographers, cinematographers, and editors who contribute to the progression of skating by improving the aesthetics and efficiency of documenting and disseminating skating. And their technological proficiency has then filtered into the rest of the community who are keen to adopt new innovations. So while the device that fuels skaters is extremely simple, they are a culture that embraces new innovations in technology, and are quick to master complex devices, computer editing software, and of course social media; they are what the tech industry would call "early adopters." As RB Umali says, "sometimes people exaggerate and say skaters set all the trends, but we definitely are up on what's out there, as far as video technology is concerned."

Excavating the City: Historic Skate Spots

On the first day I begin research for this book, Aaron brings me to the place where skating began in the early 1970s. Jeff Ho's Zephyr Surfboards, located on the corner of Bay and Main in Santa Monica, just up the hill from the beach. This surf shop, with its pioneering board shapes and rebellious attitude, served as a hangout for young surfers. When the surf day ended around 10 A.M. they would pick up skateboards and attempt to "surf" the hill down Bicknell Avenue.[14]

The last 100 yards of Bicknell are a steep hill leading down into a beach parking lot. In this area of 300 or so square feet, Aaron points out spots that tell the story of over 30 years of skating history.

Aaron takes me to the bottom of the hill and points to a strip of sidewalk raised curb-height off the ground that separates the road on the left from the parking lot. He calls this the first "manual (or manny) pad." A manual is a sustained wheelie where a rider balances on the back wheels

Bicknell Avenue Hill. Photo: Gregory Snyder.

or, in the case of a nose manual, the front wheels. A rider approaches the concrete sidewalk from the asphalt parking lot and ollies to get the board off the ground, then lands only on the back (manual) or front wheels (nose manual) and sustains momentum across the four-foot concrete sidewalk or manual pad and then ollies off the sidewalk from the wheelie position.

There are hundreds of variations that can be created on this simple theme, and for a time this was one of the most famous spots in the world. Aaron then scrutinizes the obstacle like an old tracker and tells the story of what went on in this space merely by reading the terrain. Although never having skated here himself, as a master of manual skating, Aaron reads the land:

> If you're looking at where people are gonna skate it from, most likely it's going to be right here in this little path, you can see there are cracks leading up right here. And on the other side the smoothest landing area is right here. If you turn this way there's a big blind crack right here, and a nice smooth section right to the side of it. So you can bet that about 90% of the people that ever skated this spot skated it right here.[15]

He spreads his arms about three feet wide to indicate the path taken by very famous skaters decades ago.

Our next stop is approximately 20 yards away—the rounded curbs that line the bike path along the beach. There is sun and sand and surf and palm trees, and none of this natural beauty inspires Aaron's creativity; he is excited by man-made architecture, in this case the curbs. He rarely goes swimming and does not surf; in fact, the thing that the Z-Boys did to pass the time when they weren't surfing is now the main passion for Aaron, so that the curb is more significant than the ocean. As bikinied women cruise by on rented bikes or roller blades, Aaron explains that the rounded tops of the curbs were critical to the early part of street skating because they were easier to manipulate than regular curbs and skaters could progress and explore the limits of their imaginations.

Ten yards away are ledges approximately 18 inches high, and Aaron says that when the top skaters were skating the 6-inch curbs they couldn't

Santa Monica beach curb. Photo: Gregory Snyder.

even imagine skating the ledges because it would be impossible to ollie up that high. It wasn't until the 1990s that skating had progressed to that level.

So this space of 30 or so square yards represents almost 30 years of street skating progression and magazines showcasing tricks from these spots, which are physically close to each other yet separated from each other temporally in terms of skating progression. It took 30 years to cover a distance I can walk in 30 seconds.

Next, Aaron takes me to another famous spot he calls the "sand gaps," and when we arrive he shows me two empty four-square-foot spots in the concrete, where palm trees had died or been removed. "Are you kidding?" I think, as this looks like nothing special. But from a skater's perspective the squares are nearly perfect. Aaron informs me that the closeness of the two gaps requires riders to be very technical and very fast doing back-to-back tricks. And the ledges in the background make this spot especially good for skating lines, or continuous tricks in a row.

Skating is about progression, increasing the degree of difficulty and creativity. Tricks are done first on smaller obstacles like curbs

Sand gaps, with ledges in the background. Photo: Gregory Snyder.

and when mastered are brought to bigger, more difficult obstacles like ledges, and finally to more dangerous obstacles like stairs and handrails. This progression takes years and is inspired by skaters' architectural imaginations.

Aaron then takes me to the Radisson Banks behind the Radisson Hotel in Culver City. This spot has been skated since the late 1980s, and Aaron recently fixed it up so it could be skated successfully again. He used Bondo to make the spot "grind better," and he says that he also made it easier for someone to "blunt slide" it. At this point these words mean nothing to me. However, I do understand that skaters are not simply content to reinterpret available architecture; they also physically change spaces—often forgotten, unexplored, ugly spaces—in ways that make them usable to a skateboarder.

What is beauty to a skateboarder? A skater sees urban architecture in aesthetic terms, which are completely different from those of the general public. The skater sees the world as a simple bipolarity, skateable or unskateable, so that skaters who use their creativity, wit, and daring to turn something unskateable into a skateable spot have essentially transformed something mundane into something beautiful. Skaters in many ways are artists, or guerilla architects, transforming unwanted space into usable public art.

Backtail, Death Ledge, July 23, 2008

On this particular day we are at one of Aaron's secret illegal skate spots to photograph a "backside tailslide." The spot is a concrete aqueduct in Culver City located behind a grocery store, just under the 405 freeway. Despite the whizzing cars above, the place is quite serene. Someone has stenciled "you are beautiful" on the wall, but Aaron, who reconstructed this spot, calls it the Death Ledge.

This spot had never been skated before and work needed to be done to make it skateable. Two weeks prior Aaron used a leaf blower to clear all the debris. On the second day he taped off a spot on the ledge, and painted it with clear lacquer spray paint. On day 3 he sanded it smooth and then waxed it, thereby making the spot skateable. Aaron was keen not to use colored paint because he didn't want to identify the spot to other less skilled skaters because he says he would have been bummed if someone had gotten severely injured.

The purpose of all this effort is to shoot a photograph of a trick to be included in *The Skateboard Mag*. This will be used to advertise Aaron's "Mag Minute," curated by photographer Shad Lambert, a one-minute collection of tricks that will be shown on the magazine's website. This also is the last time that Aaron will participate in the skateboarding industry as a skater; that day, Aaron viewed this simply as another effort to contribute to progressive skateboarding, and an opportunity to increase his reputation. Looking back, it was a last-ditch effort to try to hang onto something he loved but was slipping away.

Shad has a massive camera bag that he tells me holds approximately $25,000 in camera equipment, which he has accumulated over time. His main camera is a Canon 5D HD-SLR; his bag also houses three lenses, multiple lights with radio-controlled setups, tripods to hold the lights, filters, and other gadgets.[16]

Shad decides that the best place to shoot Aaron's trick is from up on the hill looking down on him so the viewer can get a real sense of the space. The problem with this spot is that there is a fence in the way. Aaron gets bolt cutters from his car and snips a tidy one-foot-square opening in the fence. Neither of them have any problem with this minor act of vandalism because now Shad can poke his head and camera through to get the shot. Sometimes spaces must be altered not only to make them skateable but also for the aesthetics of proper documentation.

Shad then goes about rigging his lights. It is a bright sunny day, but he needs a flash to stop the action. He rigs a light on a tripod and instructs Aaron where to put it. He also gives fellow skateboarder Billy Roper a light to hold. Both lights are connected to the photographer's camera via remote control and are set to go off when he presses the shutter.

Aaron then proceeds to ollie up to the 18-inch ledge and turn his body and the skateboard backside (back facing the obstacle) in such a way as to slide the wooden tail of his skateboard approximately two and a half feet, and then "pop" (ollieing once again) off the ledge. In the event that Aaron missed badly he could fall 15 feet down, so he had to push this critical fact out of his mind.

Hopping fences. Photo: Gregory Snyder.

Shad Lambert photographing through the fence. Photo: Gregory Snyder.

According to Aaron, this is not an extremely difficult trick, but to an outsider it appears highly complex, and a bit impossible. Just the simple ollie, the foundation of street skateboarding, employs Newton's third law of motion, and is completely counterintuitive. The skater stands on the board moving forward with the back foot on the tail and the front foot over the bolts. He jumps up into the air while using his back foot to thrust the tail of the board down onto a hard surface like the street. The skater hovers over it in the air, for an instant, essentially waiting for the "equal and opposite inverse reaction" to occur, as the board "pops" up, the skater slides his front foot forward, creating friction with the grip tape, which levels the board out. The amount of downward force applied to the tail is the exact amount of height or "pop" the board will get off of the ground. (Most folks say that it takes between six months and a year to learn how to ollie properly.)

In pro skating the goal is not simply to land the trick but to do it well; you must also have style. The trick has to look good, and by the fourth or fifth unsuccessful attempt, the pressure on Aaron to land the trick perfectly begins to mount. As he becomes fatigued, the possibility of real injury increases, making it difficult for me to watch. In this way the pro skateboarder is more like a stunt person in a movie shoot than an athlete. The skater must perform the trick, perfectly, with camera and crew waiting around, all wanting to see the trick completed before they get kicked out of the spot, the cops come, or they lose the light.

Finally, Aaron lands the trick to his satisfaction, and Shad shows him the digital image on the back of the camera to confirm.

Next, Shad needs to go to another spot to photograph someone else, so we quickly pack up and drive to the Texas Gap, at a church on Texas Avenue in West LA. When we arrive at the "session," Alex Gourdouros, a 17-year-old skinny kid with long stringy hair and an "am" or sponsored amateur for Foundation Skateboards, is hurling himself over the "gap," and each "fakie 360" attempt ends in a bone crunching fall on the concrete.

There are approximately 50 tricks that make up the foundation of skateboarding. Each varies in difficulty, and most can be combined with other tricks to create new ones. A "fakie 360 ollie," for example, is actually a "fakie ollie" and a "360 ollie" combined. Essentially a "fakie 360 ollie" is a 360-degree twist while riding fakie, or backward, so you're ollieing with your dominant foot, off the front of the board, and spinning your body with it 360 degrees. (Steve Caballero was the first to master this, and thus it is called a "caballerial" or "cab" for short.)

Each time Alex approaches the obstacle I am filled with anxiety. I don't want to witness a gruesome injury, but I also don't want to miss it if he is successful. After at least 30 attempts, Alex sits down on his board and stops trying. He is bruised, battered, and deflated. This is the second time that the obstacle has beaten him, and it's clear that the knowledge that he'll have to heal up and come back another day weighs on him heavily. Three months later I'm flipping through the pages of *The Skateboard Mag* (October 2008) and come across Shad's photo of Aaron that

Texas Gap, West LA. Photo: Gregory Snyder.

I witnessed. Nearly a year later, in the June 2009 issue of the same magazine, I see a beautiful photo of Alex's finally completed "caballerial" over
the Texas Gap, along with an interview written by Shad.

Field Notes: Spot Hunters

DOWNTOWN LA

> In Downtown LA skateability is less a function of architecture and more a
> question of security guards, surveillance cameras, and police. Most of the
> spots we go to haven't been skated in a while as the enforcement of "no
> skateboarding" has become more and more strict.
>
> The first stop is at the famous DWP Ledges at the California Department
> of Water and Power. These ledges have been skated for years but have only
> been minimally damaged because the marble is of extreme high quality. The
> benches are approximately 18 inches high, and there are two of them spaced
> a perfect distance apart so that two consecutive tricks can be performed.
> Aaron had tricks in the video Fulfill the Dream filmed here. Jason Dill

Alex G. skating Texas Gap. Photo: Gregory Snyder.

killed the spot in the Alien Workshop video; Mike Carroll, Eric Koston, and others have done incredible, mind-bending, and difficult tricks here. Aaron treats these benches with near sacred reverence, and he is not the only one; they are simply the most famous and most esteemed benches in the world.

How did someone figure out that the DWP had good benches? Well, for one, skaters always look at federal and municipal buildings because they use taxpayer funds and usually use better materials.

***

Next Aaron takes me to the newly built Santa Monica City College. He checks out all buildings during their construction phase for possible skate spots. This space had purposefully rough ground and used a slate material that was undesirable for skaters, and they had also skateproofed spots before skating had ever even happened. Skate prevention obviously played a role in the design of this new space; however it is clear from their prevention plan that they don't know where the skating would take place.[17] They've put skate stoppers on things that would never be skated, and thus added costly and unsightly defensive design elements that do not stop skating. This is akin to putting a "Keep Out" sign on a place that no one would want to enter. Skaters notice these tactics, which confirm that their "enemy" is ignorant of their actual processes.

Skate and Appreciate

Brian Lotti began his professional skateboarding career in 1991 when he first appeared in the H-Street video *Now-n-Later*. He was extremely influential and was generally considered to have one of the best styles in skating. Today Lotti, who went to college in Hawaii and studied art and film at the University of San Francisco, makes films that use skateboarding to engage a dialogue about the use of public space. His film *1st and Hope* is an intimate look at the relationship that skateboarding has to Downtown LA and shows the other side of skating. Rather than the old slogan "skate and destroy," Lotti and his crew of stylish, athletic skaters adhere to the mantra of skate and appreciate. They carve down hills and cruise through various parts of Downtown Los Angeles, from Little Tokyo to the China-town rails, the DWP, and finally Staples Center. As they glide through the city they do tricks, spontaneously reinterpreting the city as they go. They never linger long enough in one particular area to get kicked out. Most skate videos show only money shots, but *1st and Hope* provides a little context and most of all some romance in its love affair with the city.

I met Lotti at a BBQ in the summer of 2008 at Griffith Park. I told him I was researching skateboarding and asked if I could call him. Aaron and the other skaters were starstruck around him, but I actually felt comfortable because he is closer to my age and has experienced more outside of the subculture than most skaters.

Lotti begins by telling me he likes to cruise through Downtown LA and tells me about his film *1st and Hope*, which I purchase later in the day. Lotti says in the film "we're playing the city as if it were an instrument, as strings to be plucked on a guitar."

We begin to discuss the attitude that American politicians and security guards have toward skaters and Lotti bemoans skaters' inability to realize some "political power as a collective group." I tell him that it's surprising that pro skaters do not take a more activist position and use their significant financial power and in some cases celebrity status to try to bring about some dialogue with city officials. He says that he hopes that this will change soon.

Lotti tells me he has just finished his second film, *Free Pegasus*, about a day of skateboarding in Barcelona, Spain, a place, according to Lotti, that is much more "liberal and democratic" in their attitude about space and who gets to use it. He says that in Barcelona when they skate, citizens watch and applaud and treat them like "performance artists," while back home they get the same treatment as "terrorists and homeless dudes." Lotti insists that public space should be "dynamic space, used for multiple purposes, some of which no one has ever thought of before, by a diversity of people." He goes on to explain that skating has the possibility of being a type of "street theater: in which skaters are not only having a dialogue with the built environment and other skaters, but also with fellow citizens." In this way skating has the power to transform public space with its subtle segregations and barriers into a place where citizens might, as members of a collective, witness acts of creative, dangerous, architectural interpretation, and might come to view the open spaces of a city as sites for the creation of urban community that cuts across lines of race, class, gender, and ethnicity. Lotti talks about how when he skates in Barcelona, and rarely at home, there is a sense of "oneness" between himself and others around, with whom he shares nothing more than a feeling of collective humanity.[18]

This is the same type of argument that urban planners and advocates for green space make for the necessity of parks, where everyone can come together and do their own thing. Skating takes the built environment and turns it into a spontaneous park. Because skaters are seeking the best skate spots, they are not concerned about ethnic or racial demarcation in a neighborhood. Therefore, a skate session is also an incidence where white, black, and brown skaters find themselves in a neighborhood communing with the locals, a momentary antidote to segregation.

Brian talks a lot about segregation and makes me think that in many ways skaters are agents of desegregation. They are a multicultural, diverse group of mostly men who visit all areas of a city, regardless of the racial, class, or ethnic makeup of the neighborhood, for the purpose of skating a particular spot, and when they go to these areas they are forced to engage with people unlike themselves, often also spending their money. The people in the neighborhoods witness folks whose love for skating cuts across lines of race, class, and ethnicity. For the skaters themselves their desire for skateable architecture has turned them into world travelers and individuals who have a diversity of cultural experiences within both their own cities and cities all over the world. It is possible that someday skating could be a focal point for collective activity.

3

Skateboarding Basics

The Grammar of Skateboarding Tricks

Name That Trick: Stoner Plaza

Five years into my study of skateboarding, Aaron decides that it's time to test what I've learned. While skating flat ground he devises a game for me. He'll do five tricks and I'll try to name them. Now this would require no effort at all for any single one of the approximately 50 kids there, but for me it requires total concentration. I have to pay attention to his stance, whether he pops the board off the nose or the tail, whether he spins his body and in which direction, whether he's frontside or backside, and finally what the board is doing and how he manipulated it. Did he use the toe of his front foot or the heel of his back foot or vice versa?

He says that he's starting me off easy, but it doesn't feel like it to me. I study him; he rides backward, pops the front of the board, and does a kickflip. I meekly say, "fakie kickflip?" Yes. I got it right. Whew. For the second trick he's riding forward and again pops the front of the board, which in this case makes it a nollie, or nose ollie, then he flips the board with the heel of his back foot. I know this one. "Nollie heel!" I exclaim. Hooray, two for two. The third trick is one that he knows I know. He rotates the board 360 degrees while turning his body in the same direction 180 degrees. This is the only trick that looks like this, and I confidently tell him it's a "big spin—named for its inventor Brian Lotti" (the California Lottery at the time was called the Big Spin). Now I'm three for three and Aaron doesn't want me to get too cocky. Now he's riding backward and spinning and flipping, and I have no idea. I guess "Nollie frontside flip?" "Nope, half-cab kickflip." This means he's riding backward, popping off the tail of the board, which appears to be the front, rotating his board and his body 180 degrees (half-cab means half of a caballerial), and also flipping the board with his front foot, which appears to be his back foot because he's riding backward. This trick could also be called a fakie frontside flip, but no one calls it that. Now my head hurts, but I focus for the last trick. He's riding forward and popping with the front foot, spinning his body and the board 180 degrees clockwise, or in this case backside, and flipping the board. I can only guess. "Nollie, backside flip?"

Aaron says "Yup" and I can't believe it. I got four out of five correct and it's taken me only five years to learn. But next Aaron gets a little cruel and does some crazy trick. I have no idea what it is, even though he shows me three times. "You'll never get this, skaters even have a tough time with this one, it's called a nollie undervarial flip." I don't even try to understand.

Grammar Counts

When I return home I decide to test my progress in trick description. I give myself the challenge of deciphering every trick in Aaron's most famous video part in *Fulfill the Dream* (1998), when he was an amateur for Shorty's Skateboards. I was inspired to do this by a skater whom I met at Stoner Park who told me he had just rewatched Aaron's part the night before.

For skaters, naming tricks is instantaneous; for me it is an arduous process that requires constantly pressing pause and rewind and pushing the limits of what I've learned in the past five years. The video is 3:07 long and contains 37 tricks (38 actually, I missed one). It takes me over an hour to compose my list, and when I'm finished I am exhausted. I contemplated rewatching the video to proofread my trick list, but I don't have the energy.

The only thing I can compare this to is foreign language study. Once you have passed the beginning phase and have gained some conversational prowess, you then have to deal with the rules of grammar. In 1991 I was staying in Germany with my foreign exchange brother Claude. I studied German in high school, and while in Germany I studied the language's grammar every day. This was extremely difficult, and every night I would wait for Claude to come home and correct my mistakes, of which there were many. I left Germany after three months and lost interest in my study of German, mostly because it was hard. Studying skateboarding tricks is much harder. Understanding the basic trick vocabulary is somewhat easy, but to comprehend the grammatical rules in which these variables are combined is daunting, especially from someone who has never actually skateboarded.

There is a precise grammar in the naming of tricks that follows logical rules that are easy to forget. For example, a nollie, or nose ollie, is an ollie off the nose of the board, which is easy to recognize, but not every ollie off the front of the board is what it appears to be. If a rider is going backward, or fakie, and ollies with the lead or front foot, it looks as if he is riding switch stance and doing a nose ollie or nollie, but looks can be deceiving. There is no such thing as a switch nollie; it is a fakie ollie.

Finally, I make it to Aaron's last trick. First I determine the stance—it appears to be switch because his left foot is forward. I pause the video. Then is the ollie off the nose of the board or the tail? Pause. The nose. What happens to the board in the air? Does it flip? Does it rotate? Pause. What part of the board is landing on the obstacle? The tail, the nose? Pause, rewind; pause, rewind. The front truck or the rear truck? Is the board straight or angled? Okay. Now what happens after he's finished grinding the ledge? It's a 360 flip (tre flip, three flip). Now I watch the trick again all the way through, and look at my notes. I determine that the trick is a switch nollie, onto a bench, switch 5–0 grind (on the front truck) on top of the bench, switch 360 flip out. I believe that I have rightly identified this trick and I am proud of myself, and very impressed with Aaron because after 16 years I now understand that this was a pretty amazing trick.

I text Aaron, "I've just finished transcribing your entire Fulfill the Dream part. Is it possible that your last trick is a switch nollie, switch 5–0, to switch 3, out?" His response comes in seconds. "Fakie 5–0, Fakie tre flip, out-NBD." I'm crestfallen, having made a classic error and one that is an inside joke to skaters, as everyone knows there's no such thing as a switch nollie. A nollie is riding forward and popping off of the nose of the board; a fakie ollie is riding backward and popping off the tail, which because he is riding backward appears to be the nose, hence my error. However, if I had paid attention to the grammar of my own description, I would have understood the error of my ways. Switch means opposite, and nollie means a nose ollie while going forward; therefore my description translates to "opposite forward," which any 10-year-old will tell you is ridiculous. You don't say opposite forward, you say backward, or fakie in the language of skateboarding.

This isn't simply a problem of syntax. First, while rolling backward on a skateboard is difficult, it's not as difficult as riding switch stance. Second, when you describe a trick as switch you're indicating that you're doing the hard work of the trick with your nondominant foot. However, since Aaron has changed only the direction he's going, he is still popping the board with his dominant foot, so even though he appears to be riding switch and ollieing off the nose for a switch ollie, since he is popping the front of the board with his usual dominant left foot, it's not a switch-stance trick but a backward trick. As a result, there is no such thing as a switch nollie, and anyone who makes that mistake is a dummy who doesn't understand the logic of skateboarding. Now, this is not an uncommon mistake, but a critical one nevertheless, and I am upset with myself for making it. (And sadly this won't be the last time I make this mistake.)

I type up my full list and email it to Aaron. I have described 37 tricks, and my hope is to be better than 50% (still a failing grade mind you). In fact, I'm secretly confident that I've done much better than that and that Aaron, my younger brother and my teacher, will be impressed with all that I've learned.

It is 9 A.M. Pacific. Aaron is just starting his workday and replies that he'll get to my list when he can. Within the hour however he has returned my test. I got 17 of 37 correct, for a score of 46%. Damn.

However, the stunning fact for me is that Aaron graded my exam based upon memory. He did these tricks 16 years ago and has a photographic memory when it comes to his video part, and it's not just his own. He also has all of the major parts of his generation memorized, and the more I'm around skaters, the more I come to realize that *all of them* have this ability to not only decipher in an instant a rider's stance and then all of the variables that go into naming a single skateboarding trick, but also to remember entire clusters of tricks in a single viewing.

Now to my credit Aaron's style of skating is purposely hard, and technical. The fakie 5–0, fakie tre out had never been done (NBD) before. Aaron skates this way in part because precise control of his board and making new combinations out of a finite set of variables excites him, but it is also a lot safer. Aaron's technical skating excuses him from having to jump down huge obstacles, but it's also a lot harder to understand.

Looking back on this video part brings up a lot of memories for Aaron, some good, some bad. Shorty's was the biggest team in skating at the time, and *Fulfill the Dream* won video of the year. Aaron's part was well received and it seemed to him and to his friends and family that he was on a path toward becoming a professional, but the skateboard industry is more complex than that. He would not become pro for another four years, and with a different company.

Learning to Skateboard: Aaron Snyder

When I began this project there were still many things about Aaron's skating development and career that I didn't have details about. When he was younger it was often hard to get details about his skating because we did not share a common language, and because some of the things I was asking him to explain (essentially why he got fired) were understandably difficult for a young person to articulate, especially when doing so required some honest reflection. Inspired by Mitch Duneier's *Sidewalk* in which Hakim Hassan, the key informant, writes the afterword, I wanted to have Aaron write directly about his experiences, in order to diversify the voices in this book. Having him write also served a methodological purpose of getting him to understand the project from my perspective. And he's a good writer, and I wanted to challenge him to tell his story in his own words.

> I grew up skating in Wisconsin in the mid-1980s through the 1990s. In the beginning, when I lived in Green Bay, I had one mentor, Troy Turner. He was older than me, and he was a truly incredible skateboarder. From my perspective, what he was doing seemed like magic.
>
> He would create dozens of tricks that no one had ever seen. During the winter he would come over to my house because my parents let us skate in a 15- by 40-foot room in the basement that had smooth cement floors. "I thought of a new trick" would usually be one of the first things to come out of his mouth. "What if you ollied and started to turn like you were going to do a 180, but then at 90 degrees you counter your motion back against the direction you've already spun? I call it the 'ollie north.'"
>
> He would then proceed to work out the mechanics of the trick he had created in his mind, and by the end of the day he'd already mastered it and was working on different variations as well as the task of "practical application," that is, now that I've learned a new trick, how can I apply it to the

world around me? Can I do this trick off of steps? Can I do this up something? Can I do this into a slide or grind on a curb or rail?

There was no way to know it at the time, but what Troy was doing was breaking new ground and helping to lay the foundation for everything that has come since.

Keep in mind that at this time there was no Internet or home video cameras. Everything we knew about skating came from reading the articles in skateboard magazines and looking at the still photos. Troy read an article about how freestyle legend Rodney Mullen had invented an ollie where the board flips under his feet and then he lands back on it. Not knowing exactly how Rodney managed to get the board to flip Troy set out to figure it out. The only thing he knew for sure was that it was based on the ollie, which meant that at the very least he knew that it would require him to jump and pop the board off the ground with his left foot and then figure out how to make the board flip with his right (lead) foot.

What Troy discovered is that there are actually two different approaches to this concept. With one you slide the heel of your lead foot over to the edge of the board, leaving just your toes on the board to balance—then you pop and "kick" your lead foot out off the end of the board, causing the board to flip clockwise. The other was to do the exact opposite and slide your front foot the other way, hanging your toes off the edge and leaving only your heel on the board. Then as the board pops you "kick" with your heel out in front of you, causing the board to flip counterclockwise.

I'm not sure how long it took him to learn, I don't think I ever asked him. What I do remember is that he called them "toeflips" and "heelflips," and he made them almost every single try. Keep in mind that this was in an era when street skating was in its infancy. The "ollie" was just about the most progressive move out there. The majority of street skating was going off plywood "jump ramps" while bending down and holding onto the board. It was utterly mind-blowing to see somebody not only not holding onto their board to get into the air, but to have the board flip freely in the space below him while he guides it back onto his feet and then land back on the board. I can't believe how lucky I was to witness that firsthand. Troy basically taught himself the kickflip and the heelflip, cornerstones of all modern-day street skating based on an article he read. Actually to be fair, Rodney Mullen clearly invented the kickflip—but at the time he was the only person to do it and he was a freestyle skater, which meant he rode a board that was much smaller and easier to manipulate.

Over the years I lived in Green Bay and skated with Troy I saw him invent tricks that would become staples in today's world of skateboarding. Back then these tricks were being brought into the world by a 13-year-old kid living in the Midwest.

Troy even would come up with creative names for the tricks he was inventing that would eventually make their way into the skate lexicon but used for completely different tricks: Troy's version of the "ollie north" was what would eventually become known as the "shifty ollie," currently the term "ollie north" is the name of a trick where you ollie and kick your front foot off the board aka "ollie one foot." . . . Great minds think alike.

The genius didn't stop at just inventing tricks; he saw things years and decades in advance. I remember a specific conversation I had with him sometime in the 1980s where we were discussing the future of skateboarding. At the time the coolest trick around was called a "hippie twist"—it involved going off of a jump ramp holding onto your board (also called "early grabbing") and spinning 360 degrees before landing. I theorized that in the future people would be going off jump ramps and doing 720s. In my mind it was the natural progression; if people were currently able to spin around one time, then eventually they'd be doing two spins. Troy gave it barely a second thought before responding with "no they won't, they'll be doing hippie twists the other stance." (Meaning that he anticipated that skaters would learn tricks the opposite stance, what we today call switch-stance skateboarding.)

Now skating never evolved to the switch hippie twist because over the next few years skaters learned how to ollie higher and flip their board without the assistance of their hands, which led to the demise of the "jump ramp era." Skaters no longer needed a ramp to get up off of the ground. But the fact that Troy predicted people learning how to skate both stances in the middle of the 1980s still blows my mind. Today nearly every pro skater can skate both stances. If Troy had grown up in California, he likely would have been a skateboarding legend.

Saying that the first year of skating was incredibly difficult would be a massive understatement—especially at a time when street skating was still in the early stages. It took me a full year to learn how to ollie, and that was with putting in at least four hours a day skating. When I finally had gotten to the point where I could comfortably ollie up a curb, it felt like a massive accomplishment.

Soon after that came the first skate contest that I ever entered, put on by a local hardware store. I had been skating for about a year and a half, and this was the day that changed everything for me, because I saw Troy Turner do things on a skateboard that seemed utterly impossible. Troy was older than me and had also been skating for longer, but I knew I was looking at something special.

Even though I wasn't nearly on the level that Troy was, I was still probably the second best skater in town. And above all else skaters gravitate toward talent, because the only way to improve your own skating is to surround yourself with people who can push you. So Troy and I became fast friends, skating every day together and thus getting better at an accelerated rate because we could feed off of each other's ability. Over the next few years

Aaron Snyder in *Green Bay Press Gazette*. Photo: John E. Roemer.

skating completely took over my life, and more and more I found myself not quite being able to relate to the other kids my age. I was the only skateboarder in my entire school, and it consumed every moment of my free time other than playing Little League baseball, and I was pretty damn good. But even a natural talent for baseball couldn't put a dent in my desire to skate all the time. So it wasn't long before baseball was out too (much to my father's dismay).

When I was 12 we moved to Madison, Wisconsin. At first I was crushed to have to move away from my friends, especially Troy. But as I quickly found out, Madison is a bigger city with better spots and more skaters. It's pretty unbelievable to think that within a week of moving to Madison I had met and become friends with Dave Mayhew, Tyrone Olson, and Pete Lehman— all of whom would eventually move to California in pursuit of a dream to skateboard all year around, and three of the four would become pro. (Pete Lehman recently got his PhD and is working as a professor.) Tyrone Olson is still living in San Diego and skating professionally, and Dave Mayhew found incredible success by having the highest selling signature skateboard shoe of all time: the Osiris D3. When his skating career was nearing its end, he decided to move back to Madison and opened up a skate shop called Alumni. He has also worked with the local government to secure land and financing for a large skateboard plaza right in the heart of town.

By the time I was in high school I had absolutely zero interest in academics. None. I couldn't even pay attention. I'd sit in class all day fantasizing about tricks I wanted to try, spots I wanted to skate, and the possibility of one day having a board with my name on it. My grades were terrible, barely passing. Didn't care. My parents were distraught and incredibly concerned for my future. Didn't care. My teachers and guidance counselors would tell me how smart I was and that I just needed to apply myself.

Didn't fucking care.

If it wasn't about skateboarding, there was no use for it taking up space in my brain. And trust me, this isn't an unfamiliar story for skateboarders. There's a popular saying among skaters that "skateboarding is a drug." And it's very much true. It gets under your skin and starts to dictate everything that you do, say, or think. It will make you completely ignorant to everything outside of your little bubble. It is all-consuming.

I'm not really sure when the plan for our "skate crew" to migrate to Southern California after high school came about. Maybe it never did. But

I always felt like it was inevitable. Looking back, I don't know why I thought it was a very good plan. In the early to mid-1990s it was unheard of to move somewhere with the sole intention of skateboarding full-time. The only professional street skaters were from California, where skateboarding was born. But a change was coming and everyone in our crew could feel it.

Dave was the first to move to San Diego. He was the oldest and (arguably) the most talented guy in our crew, which made him a pretty good litmus test for the rest of us. It wasn't long after Dave's move that he became friends with Marc Johnson, a skater who was quickly becoming one of the emerging greats from a new generation of skaters.

In the beginning of 1995 I got a phone call from Dave. I was a senior in high school counting down the months and days until I could free myself from my cold Wisconsin prison and get to the promised land of California. "Aaron, here's the deal. . . . Marc Johnson is going to switch over and ride for Maple Skateboards and he wants me to join him. I told him that I didn't want to leave you behind, and that you should also come over and ride for Maple . . . sound good?" Hell fucking yes it sounded good. Getting sponsored by a company that was making real headway in the industry was the goal from the beginning. To have this happen before even moving to California was a dream come true. So in the early summer of 1995 I packed up my 1986 Honda Civic hatchback and headed west.

I had been living in California for only about three weeks when I got a call from Brian Emmers. Brian was 16 years old at the time and living in Green Bay, and had become Troy's protégé after I had moved to Madison. He was also way more talented than me and my entire crew.

Brian told me that he was wasting away in Green Bay and that he wanted to come out to California and stay with us. He figured that if we were out there pursuing our dreams, he could too. A week later, a 16-year-old Brian Emmers had taken up residence on our couch, and we were on our way to an entirely new life.[1] I don't think in our wildest dreams any one of us could have predicted what the next few years would bring.

Moving to San Diego with a board sponsor (Maple) already in hand was a huge advantage; I didn't have to worry about where my next board was coming from or who I had to politic with in order to get a sponsor. I just had to skate.

The first few months of California were truly dream-like. I had spent my whole life as a skater living vicariously through magazines and videos coming from Southern California and now I was here. I could go to the very same spot that my favorite skater had done a trick on and admire how amazing it was. I could film myself skating spots that my heroes had skated. I could feel the presence of skateboarding history, and I wanted desperately to contribute to its lineage. And, for an all too brief period, I did.

Right before my 1986 Honda Civic hatchback was all packed up and ready for the cross-country drive from Wisconsin to California, I sprained my ankle badly. This meant that I couldn't skate for the first few weeks in California. It was torture; my friends and I would go to the famous spots we had grown up watching on video, and the level of energy and excitement of possibly contributing new tricks on them was huge, but I couldn't skate. Accomplishing tricks at these spots was also our first experience that our crew may have been as good as we always thought we were. Watching my friends take their shots at NBD (never been done) tricks on famous spots fueled me like nothing else, and when my ankle finally healed enough for me to skate again, I came out on fire.

Over the next month or so I was putting down NBDs left and right. Then one day at PB Middle School, I bit off a little more than I could chew. PB Middle had a set of very small four-stair handrails that went down at an angle, causing the railing to be longer than a normal four-stair would be, thus inviting all sorts of original tricks to be done on them. I went there to do a nollie, frontside noseslide down it. I had never seen one done on a handrail before so I wanted to be the first. Surprisingly I landed the trick fairly easily. Next, I wanted to do a nollie to backside lipslide, another trick I don't remember having seen done down a rail on video yet (but I'm not going to claim first on that one). That one also came fairly easy. Up next was a switch, smith grind. This was something I definitely knew had not been done before on a rail. The trick was actually very new even for pros to do on ledges, so it was certainly a "hot" trick at the time. I think I made it in fewer than 15 tries. In hindsight, this should have been the point where I stopped and cut my losses. Instead, I tried to quadruple up on my daily NBD count and try a switch frontside nosegrind. The bitch of it is—I had it. I knew on the very first attempt that I could do this trick, that I could also do a 180 out of it, and that my stock was going to be rising quickly . . . and then I came off of the rail with my left (lead) foot about one inch too far forward, folded it over the front of the board, and felt it crunch against the ground as the momentum from my board rolled right over it. In that single moment I felt my skating life was over. I had waited and dreamed of finally getting here. I had battled injury for the first few months, and on this day had finally gotten back to the point I was at when the injury had first occurred in Madison over a year ago. One fucking inch.

In a sense, I was right. That ankle injury kept me off the board for five months. Maple Skateboards put out a video called *Seven Steps to Heaven*, and even though my part had a few good flashes, which showed what might have been, overall it was a big disappointment not to be able to make a bigger impact with my first part out in California.

A few months after the video came out, I was let go from Maple Skateboards.

***

It was not until I got Aaron to write this that I actually understood the whole story; although I remember the injury, it never occurred to me that getting injured at the wrong time might have an adverse impact on one's career. I naïvely figured that injuries are part of the game, and the company would wait for you. Nope. However, at the time, I remember that Aaron's biggest complaint about his Maple part was that he did not have complete control in the editing process, which can have a big impact on how the skating is presented. But the truth is that despite Aaron's early progression he wasn't able to get enough of it on film to have an impact.

Troy's Story

Troy Turner was Aaron's childhood mentor, and hence he was also a family friend. Troy was at our house seemingly every day, and I had a sense that he was way better than Aaron, but I never really understood that he was genius better. As I've come to understand with this project, there are so many elements to making a skate career besides talent. Timing, geography, and luck also play huge roles, so I began to theorize that there are "Troys" all over the world—folks who were light years ahead of their peers, but also ahead of their time. The industry hadn't yet become professionalized enough to recruit talent from outside of California, and without the resources to get yourself there, or an amazing bit of luck, you remained unknown. In the book *The Impossible*, Cole Louison recounts the story of Rodney Mullen, who was living in Florida, literally bumping into Stacy Peralta at the skate park, and Stacy, who owned Powell-Peralta skateboards, recognized Rodney's genius immediately and invited him to California to compete in freestyle contests.

Most skateboarders learn to skate from skating with other, usually older, skateboarders. In Aaron's case this person was Troy Turner. I was just heading off to college when Aaron and Troy started skating together, but I could tell that Troy was a special little kid, and I proceeded to share with them both all of the things that I was being exposed to in college, especially music and film.

In his youth Troy was a brilliant skateboarder, but he was a little too old and a little too far removed geographically from the skateboard industry to make a career of it. Troy wound up bouncing around from Arizona to Green Bay and eventually settled in Chicago, where he went to UIC (University of Illinois–Chicago) and studied film. Big-city life eventually wore Troy down, however, and in 2003 he had a crisis and moved back to Green Bay to be nearer to his family. Nowadays Troy drives a delivery truck and makes art.

Troy was in many respects a childhood genius. He began skating in 1986 when he was 12 years old and by the end of the year he was one of the best. He saw skateboarding as an art form and just by looking at magazines was able to understand, execute, and even innovate tricks that were being done by only a small number of people. For a time in the late 1980s and early 1990s he was probably one of the best in the world, but because Troy was in Green Bay, nobody, except Aaron, knew it. I'm sure that there are many "Troys" out there, amazingly talented kids who never received proper recognition, but subcultures should also be understood as learning networks, and some folks are simply best suited to be teachers.

By 1991 Troy had made some headway in the industry and had picked up some big-name sponsors in Planet Earth skateboards, and Airwalk shoes. One of the highlights of his life was that Tony Hawk at one time called his house. Troy was traveling to California to "basically audition for Chris Miller, and Brian Lotti." However, during the layover in St. Louis, Troy was skating outside the airport and sprained his ankle and couldn't skate up to his potential in California. When he returned from California he received a letter stating that "due to the economic downturn we are cutting you from the team."[2] From there Aaron put Troy in touch with

Troy Turner skating S-rail. Photo: Grant Brittain.

Ken Park, whom Aaron had met at skate camp. Ken was starting a new company out of Colorado, called One More Skateboard Company. During a trip to Colorado Troy got a trick on the famous S-rail, which even wound up on the contents page of *Transworld* magazine with the caption "Troy Turner came all the way from Green Bay, Wisconsin to Boulder, Colorado to try his luck on the S-rail."

But One More quickly became one less skateboard company, and Troy had no other contacts in the industry. In 1992 Troy graduated from high school and decided to move out to Arizona with a crew of BMX riders, because in Troy's mind Arizona was closer to California than was Wisconsin.

While the start-up costs to becoming a skateboarder are significantly less than those in many other subcultures, it does take money and resources, which Troy didn't have, to get noticed. Living in Arizona with a bunch of 18-year-old BMXers was ultimately a bit too crazy for Troy, and within a year he returned to Green Bay and stopped skating. "I just wanted to be normal," he said. He moved in with his girlfriend and tried to get a job. Around 1992, more and more cities were making skateboarding illegal, and Troy was becoming less and less interested in being part of an outlaw subculture.

In 1992 Troy entered the regional NSA (National Skateboarding Association) skateboarding competition at Turf Skatepark in Milwaukee, and he didn't even make the finals. Dave Mayhew and Aaron both qualified for the finals that were to be held in California. At that point Troy realized that Aaron and Dave were much more advanced than he was, but Troy was cool with it. Troy said, "I had pushed my protégés as far as they needed, and I felt like I was ready to retire."[3]

Troy and Aaron had not seen each other in over 20 years, and I thought it might be nice to have a reunion, and essentially thank Troy for all that he had taught Aaron. I flew Troy out to LA to hang with us and to attend the Street League Contest. My assumption was that Troy would be somehow bitter that he never was able to make a career in skateboarding, but I was wrong. I also learned that I had a much bigger impact on Troy than I knew, and surprisingly Troy thanked me for all the music and films I had exposed him to in his early years. After all of these years Troy is still an amazing person, and I'm happy to say he's once again part of our family.

The timing of Troy's trip could not have been better. We saw the opening of the Courthouse, where Troy spent a good portion of the time staring at Eric Koston, his childhood idol, and we watched the best skaters in the world at Street League. When we dropped Troy off at the airport and said our good-byes, he texted, "Thanks. I had the time of my life thanks to u guys."

Old Man Skateboarding

August 2014. It's taken me six years, but inspired by my recent trip to California, I'm trying to skateboard. Not really skateboarding as much as what skaters call "rolling around," which means riding a skateboard the way most of the population would understand it. But I also am trying to understand what it entails to ollie a skateboard, so I'm gingerly giving it a go.

It started innocently enough. My wife and daughter wished me to accompany them on their late summer walks to the pier, and I decided to ride my skateboard. Luna says, "Daddy you're skateboarding?" Well not exactly, but yes Luna I'm on my skateboard. I practice wheelies, what skaters call manuals, and it takes an amazing amount of core strength to hold the front of the board up, and I can do it for a few seconds, but it feels a little bit like skating. But then there's the ollie. First, to prepare I looked at some "how-to" videos on YouTube and got some good advice. It's easier if you think about it in three separate motions, although it has to be done all in one. Pop (the tail), slide (your front foot up the grip tape), and jump. I'm beginning to learn that the sliding of your foot up the grip tape is the key to the whole mess, but it's such an uncomfortable movement and requires a weird amount of groin strength, for lack of a better word. The other piece of advice was to practice in the grass so the board will be stable and it won't hurt as much when you fall. However, finding grass for a 46-year-old man to practice skateboarding without drawing too much attention to how foolish he looks is tough. Luckily we live in Red Hook, an out-of-the-way Brooklyn neighborhood, close to the waterfront with an adequate amount of grass for me to give it a try.

Over the three nights I tried I made small improvements, which boosted my confidence slightly, that is until I decided that I would give myself the test of trying 10 ollie attempts in a row. Mind you that even one attempt requires an unbelievable amount of muscle strength and coordination, and leaves me huffing and grunting like the old fool that I am for attempting this. So, boom, attempt number 1 goes okay, attempt number 2 is a little better. Wow, maybe I can actually do this I think, as I launch into my third attempt, and I hear a little "pop" in my right oblique muscle. Holy fuck that hurts. I stop immediately and do not skate again until a month later. However, this time knowing just what types of injuries were in store for me, my confidence and my approach had changed. Others advised that I should practice while rolling on the street, which I attempted a few times, but after a small fall I quickly became too scared to try with the dedication this act deserved.

Now the weather is changing and classes are back in session so I haven't been trying to skateboard. What I've learned is what I already knew—even the simplest acts of skateboarding are incredibly hard—but what I've experienced in this brief moment is the crushing realization of how much dedication it takes to become a skateboarder, and consequently how much failure is involved. Progress is so slow and excruciating that I couldn't imagine spending a year (which is the consensus of how long it takes) learning how to ollie, mostly because it takes that long to train the specific muscle groups that have no real-life application. And that's the thing: I'm just not willing to put in the work. All I have to do is commit to practicing, but I don't. And I hate myself a little bit for it.

What I think is even harder to comprehend is that the people who are dedicating themselves to this pursuit are children, 10- and 11-year-olds, making progress in tiny increments, day after day after day after day, until one day, they get it, and they can ollie. Malcolm Gladwell suggests that it requires approximately 10,000 hours of practice to become a master at something; for skating this means that it takes about five and a half years to master skateboarding.[4] Most of the kids who go on to become pros first start to get noticed when they are 14 and 15, which is about right, but they do not truly master skating until they mature physically, around 17 to 19, coming out to roughly 13,500 hours (5 hours a day, 365 days a year).

As Aaron describes above, his first ollie was a moment of extreme jubilation, which is understandable, seeing how he'd been failing for so long. This dedication in the face of overwhelming odds is impressive, and shows just how committed skaters are to the process of learning.

As for me, I'll never get it. This is painful to admit, but interesting in light of my previous work on graffiti. Certainly talent plays a role, but really it's the dedication and the commitment to be good or even great at something that requires an incredible amount of risk and hard work that separates the good from the great. That is the most impressive fact about these subcultures, and also one of the things that explains the tendency toward career making.

Both skaters and graffiti writers have told me that once they were successful in their respective disciplines, they felt like they could be successful at anything because nothing else was as hard. To this end, many skaters and writers put just as much time, energy, and courage into their careers as they originally put into learning how to skate or to write. This is one of the reasons that skaters have been so successful as entrepreneurs, producing a self-sustaining subculture that provides opportunities for skaters to make lives for themselves. But skaters have also been extremely successful outside of their subculture. The documenters, the photographers, filmmakers, and editors, all say that nothing is as hard to capture on film and then convey as skating, which makes all other pursuits, according to them, almost easy.

PART II

The Professional World

4

Professional Street Skateboarding

The Skate Plaza at Stoner Park

In 2010 the skateboard plaza at Stoner Park opened, and immediately was recognized as one of the best-designed skate plazas in LA. The plaza was built by the West Los Angeles municipal government, along with significant input from the West LA community of skaters, including Alec Beck and Aaron Snyder.

The community that was fostered between Alec and City Council Chair Jay Handal during the construction of this project would provide a foundation for the skaters of West LA and municipal leaders to enact historic change. This relationship led to the most significant act in Los Angeles skateboarding history, and public space in general; the decriminalization of skateboarding at the Courthouse, one of LA's most cherished and historically relevant skateboarding places. There will be extensive details provided later in the book, but both of these places should be considered skateboarding "success stories." Now, however, the focus is on Stoner.

The skate plaza looks less like a typical "skate park" with gray concrete and an imposing fence, but more like a Zen garden, which combines elements of subcultural beauty with more traditional notions of beauty.[1] The park has black and red swirls built into the ground and planters with actual trees and plants in them. Not only is the design perfect for contemporary skating, in part because the obstacles were modeled on actual street spots, but the aesthetics of the park signal to skaters that they are worthy citizens, rather than a nuisance that should be fenced off from the public.

Alec Beck, a self-proclaimed skate activist, is the skater most responsible for getting Stoner Plaza built to the specifications that skaters wanted. (He even brought beer and donuts to the workers during construction.) The idea for Stoner Plaza came about because of local politicians' frustration that skaters kept skating the West LA Courthouse Plaza, despite

Stoner Skate Plaza. Photo: Gregory Snyder.

Stoner Skate Plaza. Photo: Gregory Snyder.

the fact that it had been skateproofed and criminalized. One day Alec met West LA Neighborhood Council Chairman Jay Handal, who told him he was befuddled by the fact that two skaters who were ticketed and told to leave one day were back skating the very next day. The councilman was astounded that they would return having been previously ticketed and realized it was going to take more than simple policing. He asked Alec what it would take to keep them from skating the Courthouse, and Alec replied that they needed an adequate skate plaza. Thus began the series of meetings that included local skaters and local politicians that would eventually result in a skate plaza being built in Stoner Park. It was also the case that a portion of Stoner Park at the time had fallen into the hands of one of the local gangs, and thus the plaza fixed two problems—it provided a place for skaters to learn and to congregate and reclaimed a place that had developed a gang presence.

It is a beautiful sunny Sunday afternoon and we arrive at Stoner Park around 1 P.M. Stoner Park has six nice tennis courts, two of which are not being used, two basketball courts, where three white kids are lazily shooting baskets, a large pool that is pleasantly uncrowded, and a skate plaza that is teeming with kids representing a range of age groups, ethnicities, and genders.

There are a crew of 10 women, seemingly in their late teens and early 20s. One of the riders is 19-year-old Samarria Brevard, whom I recognize from watching her on TV in the X Games Street Finals the day before. A young African American female skater is taking a rest next to me, and we engage in conversation. She tells me that I just missed seeing Leticia Bufoni, the gold medalist, and Lacey Baker, the silver medalist, who were flying around the park. She heads off to skate with the rest of the women, who all skate together and move in unison from obstacle to obstacle. They represent a wide range of skills, but Samarria clearly stands out.

They move to the center stage platform—which was made to resemble the Courthouse in West LA—and there they start to do tricks that get the respect of the men. The men I'm sitting with give respect by saying "yeahhhhh" each time one of them lands a trick. (They do this for men also, and it shouldn't be seen as condescending.) At one point Samarria lands a 360 kickflip off the stage as well as a "big spin"; impressive.

The girls keep to themselves, and have very little interaction with the boys. This is not uncommon. I'm told that when a group of skaters come to the park together they usually skate together; however this many women skating the park together doesn't happen very often. In fact, there are only a handful of women who are regulars at the park, but today they are making their presence felt.

Aaron is one of the oldest skaters, if not the oldest skater, at the park and he's also the only male who was a former pro. There are no other pros or sponsored skaters there that day because for ams and pros Sunday is a work day; they're somewhere trying to get tricks on street obstacles.

There are a few things that I've come to understand about skating from watching Aaron. First off he's my younger brother and I love to watch him skate, especially because I can also ask him about it immediately and learn something. And second, Aaron has perfected interesting, creative tricks that for him are not very dangerous. Aaron does not like to get hurt, even more so now that he's older, so he tends to do more technical tricks on the smaller obstacles. He skates within himself, but even to an outsider like myself it's clear that today he is head and shoulders above the younger kids who are still learning how to master skateboarding. (On weekdays the park is filled with big-name pros and up and coming amateurs practicing for the main stages of the street; then Aaron's skating looks more plebian in comparison.)

At one point some kids are skating the five-stair handrail and their friends are filming with their iPhones, which they have specifically rigged for shooting skateboarding.[2] These teenagers are busting their asses trying over and over again to "smith grind" the rail. Aaron stands holding his board staring at the rail, waiting his turn. He then skates toward it, ollies in the air, and cleanly "front board slides" it first try. I asked him what the stare-down was all about, and he said that it required total focus and commitment for him to execute this relatively simple trick. Even when he makes it look easy, it most definitely is not, and the possibility of real injury is always looming in the background. (The rail is based on an actual street spot—the rail at UC Irvine where tons of progression took place, including the first ever "switch frontside bluntslide" by Eric Koston in 2000.)

The third thing I've learned from watching Aaron skate is that for many skaters body type is an indication of style. By watching Aaron so closely I have come to learn about style and realized that for his body type Aaron has good style. Aaron is one of only a small number of pro skaters who are over 6 feet tall and he's lanky, with incredibly long arms, and most big dudes in skating don't look that great (except for Andrew Reynolds, Brian Anderson, and Dylan Rieder). Most tall riders are known for their power and risk taking and less for their style. Size is somewhat of a disadvantage in skateboarding, as being lower to the ground and closer to the board is an advantage, and thus the majority of pro skaters are by most measures short. Also, bigger kids (Americans mostly) are more likely to get wooed by coaches in team sports, though this is changing.

Career Stoners

In 2004 Aaron moved from Huntington Beach, California, to Los Angeles. He had just lost his Darkstar Board sponsorship, but he was making some money acting in commercials (Old Spice) and decided to move to LA to explore the entertainment industry and to be near the famed West LA Courthouse. Soon thereafter Brian Emmers, a childhood friend of Aaron's who was also a protégé of Troy Turner but never fulfilled his promise, started to come up from San Diego to skate with Aaron on the weekends.

One day Emmers asked Aaron if he could bring along his "little homey," a 13-year-old kid whom he'd met at Pacific Drive, a skate shop in San Diego. Nick Tucker did one trick and got Brian's attention. Nick was with his mom, a Japanese African American woman, and Emmers asked her if it would be okay to take Nick, whose technique had impressed Brian, to LA to skate. Nick's mom agreed.

Nick Tucker then started to accompany Emmers on his trips to skate with Aaron. Brian and Aaron took an active role mentoring Nick, teaching him about tricks, trick selection, and how to present his skating, but most of all Brian and Aaron, both of whom suffered crushing defeats at the hands of the skate industry, were determined to use their experience to teach Nick how to make the most of his talents and specifically what *not* to do.

As Nick grew he started to become more physically powerful, and his skating got very good. He got on "flow" (free product, no dough) from the most well-known company in San Diego, but Aaron and probably Nick knew that it wasn't a great fit, evidenced by the fact that he was never actually put on the team. By this point however, Nick's talent and style were undeniable, and still he was being slighted by his board company and had no prospects for making any money. In 2012 Nick decided to quit and move to LA, in the hopes of getting a new sponsor.

The repercussions from this seemingly benign move were far-reaching. Many in the San Diego crew felt that Nick had betrayed them and assumed that he was difficult to work with. As a result, despite Nick's talent and style he has had a difficult time securing a board sponsor and is still not even officially an am, though he is on flow with Expedition skateboards (academics: flow = adjunct professor, am = tenure-track).

July 2012

Saturday is a workday for sponsored skaters, and Aaron and his crew are texting back and forth trying to figure out where they're going to skate. Of course everyone knows that the "meet-up spot" is Stoner Plaza, located on Stoner Avenue in West Los Angeles. The park was completed in 2010 and since then has become one of the most popular legal skate spots in all of LA. It is in essence a training and learning facility where kids young and old can practice their skating and hone their careers.

When we arrive around 1 P.M., the plaza is teeming with a diversity of kids of various skill levels. Aaron points out a few pros warming up, and I sit down to watch the skating. While Aaron is stretching out his aging body, he points to a blond, shirtless kid in his early 20s who is flying around the park, hitting every obstacle with speed and grace. His name is Sebo Walker and he is Stoner Park's first success story. Shortly after Stoner opened, Sebo drove his van from his home in Oregon and parked it on the street next to the park. His van became his new home, and his plan was to skate the park every day, and improve his skating. Within months Sebo got sponsored by Lakai Footwear, one of the most prestigious sneaker companies in the skateboard industry, and Aaron proudly says that Sebo is the first skater whose career was nurtured by Stoner Plaza. (Two years later, Sebo was featured in *The Skateboard Mag*'s "new jack" section with a lengthy interview in which he describes the joys of van living, art making, and skating. He also discusses getting sponsored by Krooked Skateboards, a company owned by legendary skater Mark Gonzales. In 2016 Sebo became a professional skateboarder.)

Then Aaron directs my attention toward Nick Tucker, whom I had yet to meet. Nick is 22 years old and identifies as "black, white and Japanese" (his dad is white, his mom is African American and Japanese). He has a lazy Afro and an effortless, yet technical skating style, which he makes look easy. He is extremely talented, and everyone knows it, and yet he currently does not have even a board sponsor.

Everyone is properly warmed up and Aaron announces that it is time to "take it to the streets." We pile in cars and head to Aaron's crib for a medical break and a final discussion of where to skate. We are joined by Aquil Brathwaite, a 25-year-old pro for a small company called Selfish Skateboards. Aquil grew up in Newport, Rhode Island. His parents are African American, his father a retired Navy SEAL. Paul Hart is also part of the session; he is 20 years old and also sponsored, and the only white dude in our crew, besides Aaron and myself. (A year from now Aquil will leave Selfish Skateboards to ride for the more well-established Powell Skateboards, and Paul will be riding for Cliché Skateboards and Globe sneakers. His April 2015 part in the Cliché video *Gypsy Life* generates amazing reviews. *Thrasher* magazine writes, "There are special times when somebody becomes a household name overnight. This is one of those moments.")

Nick is working on a video part for his clothing sponsor Primitive Apparel, and the purpose of this street mission is for Nick to get a "clip," meaning documented video evidence of a progressive trick. Aaron, Nick, and Aquil discuss different spots and what tricks they would do. Nick tells the story of getting a really difficult trick at the Courthouse a few weeks ago, but that he wasn't happy with it and would "be down to go and redo it." Aaron agrees with this immediately because he knows that if Nick successfully lands the trick it will put him in conversation with some of the best skaters of the previous generation, and it is essentially a good career move.

It's not clear that Nick knows all of the history of the Courthouse, as does Aaron, but he does realize this is a landmark space. The Courthouse, however, is locked; there are skate-stopping devices on all of the ledges. The only obstacle that can really be skated is the stage at the small amphitheater, which is 25.5 inches high and the ultimate test for skaters who have the "pop" to get up to it and the technical proficiency

Nick Tuck after completing his trick. Photo: Gregory Snyder.

to land in a manual. The difficulty of skating this obstacle and the complications that illegality presents have severely limited its use over the past ten years. But Nick has a big trick in mind, so the potential of getting hassled by the police is worth it.

In the mid-1990s the entire plaza at the Courthouse was a skateboarding proving grounds, and was the site of some amazing tricks, many of which were showcased in the Girl Skateboards video *Goldfish* (1993). Prominent pros like Stevie Williams and Eric Koston have also done groundbreaking moves here.

The authorities have put barriers in place all over the ledges to prevent skating; however, it is still possible for precise skaters to skate the stage. Aaron believes that Nick has all of the tools to be a top pro. Therefore, Nick needs to do a trick that's never been done, an NBD at the Courthouse that showcases his talents. Nick is attempting to do a "switch heelflip—switch manual—switch heelflip," which means he will approach the obstacle riding switch, ollie the board with his nondominant left foot, and soar up into the air and over the 25.5-inch ledge, while flicking the heel of his right foot to rotate the board one revolution on the longitudinal axis, land on top of the stage in a switch manual, which means only on the back wheels, balance on them across the entire length of the stage (approximately 10 yards), and then do another switch heelflip off the stage, landing safely on the ground.

Nick's talent and style are palpable even to an outsider like me. Within three tries he's landed the trick, but when he views the playback on the video camera he's not completely happy with it, so he gets back to work. Within 20 minutes he's landed the trick perfectly, and all of the other skaters and myself cheer his accomplishment. We are gone before anyone comes to kick us out or issue tickets.

Later Aaron puts this trick in historical context. Eric Koston, a legendary skater who was the undisputed best in the world for the past two decades, did a switch ollie up to the stage, landing in a switch manual, and then performing a switch heelflip off of it in 2001. Then in 2003 in *The DC Video* Stevie Williams, a well-respected pro and also the first African American to have a signature skate shoe, did a switch heelflip up to the stage and then a switch manual off of it. What Nick has done is essentially combine both of these legendary skaters' tricks, doing a switch heelflip up to the stage, which was Stevie's trick, landing in a manual, which both Eric and Stevie did, and then a switch heel off of the stage, which is what Koston did in 2001. (Nick knew only of Stevie's trick; he didn't know what Koston had done until I told him on July 24, 2014.) To grasp the significance and the difficulty of this, one only has to reflect on how easy it is to imagine a skater doing a switch heel up and out because Koston and Williams had essentially each completed half of the trick already, and yet it took 9 years for someone to actually do it. While Nick's trick is interesting on its own, when put in historical context it becomes even more exciting. Aaron, and lots of other skaters, have imagined for years that someone, someday might be able to combine both tricks, which is exactly what we witnessed. Aaron's level of appreciation is increased by his knowledge of subcultural progression. Skating is unique in this way, where often things are imagined years in advance of their actual accomplishment.

Now some would say that Koston's trick, switch ollie switch manual, switch heel, was slightly easier than Stevie's because Koston's only had to switch ollie up onto the stage; there was no heelflip involved, which is what Stevie added to the equation. He switch heelflipped up onto the stage, which is significantly more difficult than switch heelflipping off the stage.

In March 2013 Nick's switch heelflip, switch manual, switch heelflip at the Courthouse became public in his part for the Primitive Apparel video *Pain Is Beauty*.[3] This trick will put him one step closer to his goal of getting a legitimate board sponsor.

When I return the following summer Nick's sponsor list has grown to include SUPRA Footwear, Primitive Apparel, Mountain Dew, Grizzly Grip, Venture Trucks, Diamond Hardware, Andale Bearings, 9Five Sunglasses, Bones Wheels, and Dakine bags, but he still has no board sponsor, which is key for building a pro career. This is starting to become an issue. The longer this persists the more the industry will assume that the unfounded rumors about Nick are true, which will compound his difficulties. Nick however is tireless at using social media, especially Instagram, to build a following. How he does it I'm not sure, but he currently has 500,000 followers (@nicktucker).

***

On April 10, 2014, I arrive in Los Angeles to continue my research. This same day Paul Rodriguez, one of the most recognizable names in skateboarding, launches his new board company called Primitive Skateboards and announces Nick Tucker and Carlos Ribeiro as the new amateur team members, bestowing upon them instant credibility. In the video introducing the team, Nick does a nollie heelflip, backside nosegrind, nollie heelflip out on a picnic table (NBD) and solidifies in the skate community's mind his inclusion on the team.

Aaron is giddy with excitement that his friend, whom he loves like a little brother, has finally gotten his due, yet he cannot yet congratulate Nick in person, as he is in China filming for the big-budget skate movie *We Are Blood* with legendary skateboard filmmaker Ty Evans.

On April 16, my last day in LA, Nick comes over with Aquil, and Aaron gives Nick a massive hug. Nick explains to us that he's known about this now for four months and can finally talk about it freely. The plan he has worked out with Paul Rodriguez is that Nick will work all summer on his part for the Berrics website (www.theberrics.com), which will come out in October. This video will cement in people's minds that Nick is ready to become a pro skater, and if all goes according to plan, they will turn Nick pro in January 2015. As we are chatting Nick mentions a spot that I know and gives me an enormous compliment for recognizing it. "You're sure you don't skate?" he asks. However, seconds later I piss it all away. Nick decides to give me a friendly test and shows me a video of a trick on his phone and asks me to name it. Yikes, now the pressure is on. I know what Nick's stance is and he appears to be riding switch and popping off the front of the board, and I meekly say, "Um switch nollie?" Before I can even finish my sentence Aaron, Aquil, and Nick are laughing wildly and making fun of me. I immediately recognize my mistake. "No fakie flip," I say, but the damage has already been done. "Damn," I say to Aaron. "I can't believe I made the same mistake again." As the laughter dies down I remind myself, there is NO SUCH THING as a switch nollie; if it looks like a switch nollie, say fakie. Luckily I've gotten to know Nick and Aquil, so they don't judge me too harshly and I'm included back into the conversation. But damn if ethnography don't make a 45-year-old man feel like a naïve 12-year-old.

Nick Tucker: Pr@ Skater

Thursday October 30, 2014, 9:30 A.M. Pacific, Paul Rodriquez posts to his 709,000 Instagram followers, "Help us celebrate our newest pro at Sheldon Plaza on Sunday, November 2 at 1 P.M. Skate jam, autograph signing, giveaways and more!"

Within an hour 23,000 people have "liked" it, and over 200 people comment, all speculating who the new pro will be. Some say Chris Cole, some say Keelan Dadd, some say Bastien Salabanzi. I text Aaron, who is vacationing in Mexico, and within minutes he confirms that this weekend Nick Tucker will become a professional skateboarder. Nick is surprisingly absent from Instagram, and I know from conversations with him that he doesn't want to jinx it, but I send him a message of congratulations anyways. (Originally Nick was slated to go pro in January 2015, but with the opening of the Courthouse in 2014 providing so many possibilities for Nick to skate, he is going pro two months ahead of schedule, and considering how much he makes a month, it would not be farfetched to say that the unlocking of the Courthouse has been lucrative for Nick.)

On the day that Nick goes pro he is going to be making a yearly income that is twice what I make as an associate professor and that in the coming years he will be making sums that I will likely never make in my lifetime. But skaters don't like to talk about money.

Nick's Golden Hour

On Thursday March 19, Nick announces via Instagram that the video part he's been working on since getting on Primitive Skateboards will premiere Friday morning on the Berrics website, the most viewed, most prestigious site in skating. The Berrics also has recently purchased *The Skateboard Mag.*[4]

So on the same Thursday that he announces the premier of his part, the Berrics puts up an "Anthology of Nick Tucker" showing all of his exclusive Berrics footage to get viewers ready for the full part the next day. That same Thursday, *The Skateboard Mag* arrives in my mailbox with Nick's first "Pro Profile," which includes a short interview, but mostly just amazing photos of Nick's tricks. The full interview is on *The Skateboard Mag*'s website, and in it Nick has high praise for the work Brian Emmers put in mentoring him.

> Oh, my god. Brian Emmers made me a VHS tape. He had foreseen this whole thing all along. At the time, I didn't get it. I was like, "Okay. Cool video. Thanks [laughing]." But in a way he implanted these skateboarders in my mind: Mark Appleyard, Paul Rodriguez, Mikey Taylor, and Guy Mariano, and just showed me the way, through this video. I didn't really appreciate it at the time. But now I understand. And in many other ways, he mentored me and basically kept my head on straight. I thank God for him. Brian Emmers is the man.[5]

On Friday morning I watch the video. Amazing graphics light up the screen: *Primitive Presents Nick Tucker's Golden Hour.* (This is a cinematographic reference to the hour shortly before sunset when the light is best, a suggestion that this is finally Nick's time, and an allusion to Primitive's practice of giving each new pro a golden foil board.)

My first impression of Nick's part is simply joy. I've known him for a few years now, and it feels great to see such a nice, humble dude showcasing his brilliance to the skateboarding world. Nick is a very special skateboarder. Everything just looks so easy—the way his body flows, the effortless flicks of his feet, the clean and quick rotations of his board, the massive "pop," and my overall inability to actually decipher what is happening. Meaning, I can tell that his tricks are very complicated, and that it's unique to have that much technical skill and that much style and power, but as to actually comprehending what is being done, I am utterly inept. I watch it four more times throughout the day, and start to get a little better understanding of Nick's tricks, and a few texts back and forth to Aaron help. I think I know what Nick's last trick is, but am hesitant to risk it, so I simply text Aaron for confirmation. It's a trick that Nick is known for, a switch inward heelflip, but to do it up the 25.5-inch stage at the Courthouse, into a manual is unbelievable.

The Switch Inward Heel to Manual

Nick is a master of the "switch inward heelflip," and during the entire process of filming for this video part, his goal was to have the switch inward heel to manual at the stage be his "ender," which is usually the trick the rider deems his best and also the most challenging. This trick took him months to accomplish. He went to the Courthouse five separate times. This means that on four occasions, after trying for four or five hours, he had to admit defeat, drag himself back to his car, drive home, and lie in his bed, sore and tired, wondering if he would ever be able to land it. Nick tells me that this process was mental torture.

There is no way to describe a switch inward heelflip in anything other than skateboard terms. An inward heel is essentially a backside shuvit, heelflip; a switch inward heel is a backside shuvit heelflip with your opposite stance. Nick uses the ball of his back, left, foot to snap the board into the air and flick it to get the board to rotate 180 degrees on the x-axis. *At the same time* Nick will kick out his front foot, in this case his right foot, and use his heel to get the board to flip one full rotation on the y-axis. This trick is quite rare, and not that many people do it well regular-footed, but to do it switch and make it look good is even harder. To do an inward heel your feet are in a sense working against each other, while obscuring your view of the skateboard during the trick. But it's not the difficulty of the trick that makes it special; it's the style with which Nick does it. Nick has trained himself to be ambidextrous, and his "switch inward heels" look like pure athletic magic.[6]

Nick approaches the stage and pops the board into the air, right leg goes one way, left leg the other, and it all comes perfectly back around. Nick lands on the back wheels only, and completes the manual, across the entire length of the stage, and ollies off. But there's more context here. In some skate videos a rider will present the full part and then fade to black, and there will be an encore, a few more tricks, "after black."[7] These tricks are usually the most dangerous, and the fact that Nick can generate this amount of buzz with manual tricks is further testament to his ability. As the screen comes back Nick knocks out four tricks, all on the Courthouse stage, each one more difficult than the previous. Nick starts off with a nollie heelflip, nose manual, nollie front foot flip (NBD), then a backside 180 kickflip, fakie manual (NBD), followed by a switch frontside 180 kickflip, manual, backside 180 kickflip (NBD), and ending with his switch inward heel (NBD). With these tricks Nick has now firmly chiseled his name into the history of the Courthouse.

The following day the Berrics releases a "Process" video of Nick's "ender" for the *Golden Hour* video. On the first day Nick gets in 11 tries before it starts to rain. On day 2 Nick tries and fails over and over again. Aquil holds up his phone with the timer going and announces, "5 hours and 24 minutes, soccer games don't even take that long." A few moments later Aquil offers some sage advice.

"Your board is done. You're fuckin' killing yourself and you have to go on a trip tomorrow. You still have four days to come back after that trip to get this trick."

Nick responds, "So I should try one more?"

Aquil, "Try one more solid one and then call it." Nick tries again and fails and decides to come back another day.

Nick arrives at the Courthouse on Thursday, March 19. He says to the camera, "the part drops at 11:59 P.M. tonight. It's crunch time." The trailer for the part is already up on the Berrics website, and Nick does not yet have the final trick. He says, "this'll close it out, so it all depends on this trick pretty much." The video shows three tries and finally he is successful.

June 9, 2015

We arrive at Nick and Aquil's apartment in Sherman Oaks, California, around 7 P.M. on a Tuesday. Strangely it is raining. Aaron and I are greeted warmly by Nick and Aquil and hugs and slap-bump skater handshakes are exchanged all around. This is the first time that I've seen Nick since he has become a professional skateboarder and I offer my congratulations. Nick directs my attention to the kitchen counter where his signature board is sitting as a gift to me. I had secretly prepared for this, and I whip out a Sharpie for him to sign it. Nick writes, "Thanks for being awesome, Nick Tucker." I'm so touched that this 24-year-old kid, who is essentially a young star, would not only remember me and agree to my incessant questioning but also thank me for it.

Nick gives us a tour of their apartment. Three bedrooms, three baths, in a brand-new building. Nick shows us his room, and I notice the Diamond sneakers on the floor. Aaron asks Nick about his new shoe deal with Diamond and Nick says, "[Aquil and I] met with them and they're gonna let us help plan the direction of the skate shoe brand." Diamond is a huge company, they make hardware and just about everything else you could imagine, from T-shirts to bed sheets and lifestyle sneakers. Nick is the first skater signed to Diamond Footwear.

Aaron leaves the room and I have Nick alone. "On the day you turned pro I estimated that you'd be making about X. Am I close?"[8]

"Yeah that's about right." This means that in less than a year Nick has gone from making just about nothing to making more than double my salary. He tells me that he's trying to "be smart and save money, and not go too crazy." But he is after all a kid making man money. When I asked him what's changed now that he's a pro skater he says, "Now I'm able to take care of my family and friends."

Aquil has also become Nick's business manager, among other jobs, and he is perfectly suited for it, being fiercely intelligent, very charismatic, and ambitious. He is also at a point where he is getting older and his own pro career has stalled. When I ask him about the Diamond negotiations, he says, "We got a three-year deal, and we're super psyched about it." Corey White, who runs the YouTube channel for the Berrics and holds a degree in new media, is also part of Nick's team. For the time being, Nick is going to be the sole "ambassador," but within a year they will add Torey Pudwill, Brandon Bielbel, Boo Johnson, and Jamie Foy.

Nick reveals being pro is great because he is finally respected, but there's also more expected of him and more demands on his time, so there is less time to produce. He has to work harder to keep up the level of progression that got him there.

The big question I had was what changed. Nick had gone through years of frustration over not being able to find the right sponsor, not being recognized for his talents, being labeled difficult to work with. Nick said that with all the frustrations with various companies and sponsors that he got to a place where he stopped trying to be part of something, meaning a team. This is interesting because it is also the case that being on a team is also about being included into a specific peer group, and getting to the point where you are invited to be on a team requires not only good skateboarding but a fair amount of glad-handing. Nick said he got to the point where he had a close group of friends from whom he drew support, so he no longer felt the need to ingratiate himself into skating's most popular cliques. This freed him up to concentrate solely on his skating, which of course led to him being part of one of the best teams in all of skating. Currently the Primitive Skate team includes Paul Rodriguez, Nick Tucker, Bastien Salabanzi, Carlos Ribeiro, Shane fuckin' O'Neill, Devine Calloway, and ams Brian Peacock and Diego Najera. Things done worked out for Nick.

Shorty's and Darkstar: Aaron Snyder

It's 1996, I'm 19 years old living in San Diego, California, and I've just been kicked off of Maple Skateboards. I don't remember being given a specific reason for being let go, but based on how my first year in California went I wasn't surprised. I had spent over half my time battling injuries and hadn't fully come back physically or mentally. The only saving grace for me was that at the time I got the boot I was almost completely healed and skating really well. So instead of feeling like I had just blown my big chance, I felt like it was they who had missed an opportunity, and I was determined to show them how wrong they were.

The first time I met Chad Muska was in Carson, California, at a pro skate contest. He was sitting with his good friend Tom Penny looking through the new *Thrasher* magazine on which Chad had his very first cover photo. These two dudes were the "it" guys of the moment, who had meteoric rises to the top of the industry. They had gone from being nobodies to living legends in less than two years. And I met them both on the same day; I was stoked.

Chad and I became friends pretty quickly even though our skating styles were polar opposites. At the time, he was riding for the company Toy Machine, but soon after a now legendary blowup at the premiere for their video, he was left board sponsor-less and in the position of being one of the most highly sought-after "free agents" in the history of skateboarding.

Instead of riding for one of the already existing "A-list" skate companies, Chad decided to partner up with the skate hardware giant Shorty's and turn it into a board brand. The announcement for this partnership immediately became the biggest news in skateboarding, and put Shorty's right at the top of the industry.

Because Chad was the centerpiece for this new brand, he was pretty much given free-reign to build the team around him. This was a tricky time for me because I knew all of this and desperately wanted to be given the opportunity to ride for Shorty's, but I was also friends with Chad and didn't want to put him in a difficult position of having to turn me down. So I never asked, I just kept on skating.

About a month later I was sitting on Chad's couch "decompressing" after a skate session when he casually says to me, "So I talked to Tony (the owner) about putting you on the team and he's down."

Gulp. "What?"

"Yeah man, if you're down to ride for Shorty's you're on."

Gulp. Over the course of two sips of beer I had gone from no board sponsor to being on the fastest growing company in the industry.

The years I spent riding for Shorty's were surreal to say the least. We were, without a doubt, the biggest thing that skateboarding had seen in over a decade. Street skateboarding had evolved from grinding curbs and figuring out clever ways to manipulate your board on flat ground to a full-blown onslaught of seemingly death-defying maneuvers. Skateboarding exploded as a result, and Shorty's was right at the crest of this wave, riding mostly (if not completely) on the immense popularity of Chad Muska.

In the years leading up to the rise of Shorty's, the vast majority of professional skateboarders were just kids doing difficult tricks. You almost never saw a picture of them not skating, and they very rarely had anything interesting to say outside of skating. In other words, they were sort of bland, but Muska on the other hand was larger than life.

Even though Chad was known for taking extreme risks and doing massive tricks, he was never reckless in his approach. I witnessed most of Chad's biggest tricks during the filming for *Fulfill the Dream*, and he would often roll up at least a hundred times, for upward of an hour, before even making the first attempt. Keep in mind that prior to every single instance of stopping short of the obstacle, he would say, "this is the one." Which is to say that even though he didn't make a physical commitment until he was totally ready, the mental commitment had to be there every time. Each time he approached the obstacle as if he was going to make an attempt, only to stop short because something, his foot placement, an errant noise, a rock, wasn't right. This activity requires so much precision and is so dangerous that attempting the trick with even the slightest mental or emotional distraction could result in dire, career-ending injury, so yes Muska is one of the gnarliest skaters of all time, but he is also very careful.

***

When Muska teamed up with Shorty's it was the perfect combination of big personality meets genius marketing. At the time skateboarding desperately needed something to come in and shake things up, and what we were ultimately left with was the new model for the pro skater: the superstar.

Shorty's, to their credit, was completely in tune with this new shift. There is no better example of this than the Vancouver contest in 1997, where Shorty's created the single most incredible piece of "skater branding" that I've ever seen. For each of the three pros at the time—Chad Muska, Steve Olson, and Peter Smolik—they created personalized "foam hands" just like the ones you see at most sporting events, but with the names of the skaters on them and a direct statement about who these people are and why you should relate to them: Muska, "the rebel," had the middle finger. Olson, "the hippie," had the peace symbol. And Smolik, the "hip-hop California native," was given the hand gesture for "west side."

Did I think at the time that I was good enough to go pro for them? Probably, but what I was still completely naïve about was that what you do on your skateboard is only a piece of the puzzle; a big piece, no doubt, but still only a piece. What you did and who you were off of your skateboard was becoming one of the things that could make or break a career. The board companies needed something kids could latch onto beyond the skateboarding. And I was so inside of my own bubble these things never even crossed my mind. In other words, I was a total skate nerd. I had no real substance to my personality outside of my skating. So Shorty's tried to create one. A perfect example of this was the invention of "Snyderman," an attempt to create some sort of Spider-Man-esque fictional character. I still cringe when I think about seeing my first Shorty's ad where I'm skating a handrail and they put graphics of webs shooting out of my hands. To me, at the time, this was the opposite of the skateboarding I had grown up on. I had given them a photo of a trick that I was very proud of—a trick that took two separate trips at two in the morning to complete (it was in front of a McDonald's, so I had to wait until they closed) and that I had hit my head on the ground while attempting the first time (the only time I've ever hit my head skating), and they manipulated the photo to take all emphasis off of the actual trick that I was doing.

Now, even with all that being said, Shorty's did not keep me from reaching my full potential and turning pro for them; fear did. Skateboarding on any level is scary. Skateboarding at the highest level is downright terrifying. Most of the time it's not skaters' talent that allows them to accomplish a good trick down something that could very well send them to the hospital, it's their ability to block out the fear and just go for it. I could never "just go for it," and it gave me mental hang-ups that became insurmountable. When faced with something that I knew I could do if only I could get myself to try, I would back down. I was a total fucking wuss.

Shortly after the now legendary video *Fulfill the Dream* was released in 1998, I was let go from Shorty's. They gave me some spiel about how they had taken so long to establish their first three pros that they weren't going to turn anybody pro for at least another two years (a statement that they did actually stick to). But I knew the truth. I just flat-out wasn't good enough to be a pro skater at the top of the industry. I was B-list at best.

∗∗∗

Getting dropped from the Shorty's roster was nothing short of devastating for me. I had worked my entire life to make a name and a career for myself. Years and years of dedication, obsession, blood, sweat, and pain, lots of pain. I had finally made it to the top of the industry, right on the cusp of a professional career with the most popular skate brand on the planet. Only to have it pulled away at the last second.

Picking up my next board sponsor was not easy. For one, I had been dropped from my last two sponsors, which doesn't exactly make for a glowing résumé. Second, I didn't have very many contacts within the industry outside of the companies I had already ridden for. So I didn't have the connections to pick up new sponsors quickly.

Third, I had been labeled (perhaps deservedly) "difficult to work with," which can be a death sentence for an aspiring skater. That and "bad style" are probably on the lowest two rungs of what you don't want to hear about yourself. Unless your skating is so good that your status as one of the elite is undeniable, nobody is going to tolerate smugness in a skateboarder. And my skating was definitely not good enough to overcome that particular personality flaw. But at least they didn't say I had bad style.

I sent out videos and letters to companies trying to get new sponsors, but nobody showed any real interest. I had to forge new personal connections if I ever wanted to achieve my goal of being a professional skateboarder. It started slowly, but eventually I picked up my first new sponsor, a popular wheel brand called Darkstar. I had heard rumors that Darkstar was considering expanding to a board company, and I set out to put myself at the top of the list of riders who would bring it to life. In 2000 I moved from San Diego to Huntington Beach, where Darkstar was located, I skated and formed friendships with the other team riders, and eventually was given the green light to be put on the team. Then, after a few more months of hard work in the streets, my day finally came. I was taken out to breakfast and told that I would be turning professional. Holy fucking shit, this was it. The moment I had been dreaming of since I was nine years old had finally become a reality. I had done it.

I can remember no prouder moment in my life than the day I was able to show my family my first pro board. And I can remember no sadder moment than the day it was taken away.

I'll say it again. Maintaining a successful career as a pro skateboarder is mind-numbingly difficult. You have to avoid injury while constantly pushing the limits of what you can do. Every trip into the streets brings potentially career-changing results; sometimes for the good, sometimes for the bad. If you do manage to remain more or less injury-free, you still have to (or are expected to) continue to improve. During the early 2000s skateboarding was made illegal in the city of Huntington Beach, California, so it was extremely difficult to actually skateboard.

Nowadays there are skate plazas and private training facilities for pros and ams to train at and learn a multitude of new tricks. I was having to learn my tricks on the fly, in real street spots, and we would usually get kicked out after only a half hour. I have no doubt that if I had access to the type of training facilities available today I would have at least had the possibility to maintain a longer pro career. My brand of skating is technical. It takes tons of practice and repetition. If there is nowhere you can go to put in the time, your ability to contribute to the evolution of skating becomes a real uphill battle.

Skating therefore became less fun and more and more stressful. Even though I was pro for Darkstar, I still had a hard time picking up other good sponsors. I wasn't producing enough because I couldn't skate enough. It's hard to imagine nowadays that there was a time when pro skaters didn't have access to something as simple as a bench to skate, but that's how it was. Skating was still very much an outsider activity, with the majority of people looking at it as vandalism and a haven for wayward youth. The only legal place to skate was the Huntington Beach skate park, which was about the size of a four-stall garage. The local officials just flat-out didn't like us and weren't afraid to let us know. We would get kicked out of every single spot we tried to skate. They even had the police helicopter fly over a local school yard to stop us from skating an empty basketball court.

***

We were filming for the Darkstar video and I was not skating well. The lack of a practice grounds had made it extremely hard for me to get into any kind of rhythm in the streets. I had a few tricks on film I was excited about but not enough for a full part. Once again, I wasn't skating up to my potential.

These were also tough economic times, and the skate industry went through a bit of a rough patch as many companies downsized. Dwindle Distribution, which housed Darkstar, made significant cuts to three of their major brands (Darkstar, Blind, and Almost), and once again I was let go.

This time, deep down, I knew it was the end for me. I had given everything I had, and it wasn't enough. I was in my late twenties, had no college education, and had dedicated my entire life to an activity that apparently didn't want me.

The only recent success I'd found was being cast in a national commercial and picking up an agent. So I moved to Los Angeles and started going on commercial auditions. Lots of auditions—soul-swallowing auditions. But what did I care, I had no better options, I was flailing for a direction of any kind.

That direction eventually came in the form of television editing. Yes, I was technically uneducated, but I slowly came to realize that I had acquired a vast amount of tangible skills during my time in skateboarding. I had learned about photography, videography, marketing, design, sales, social media, and most importantly, editing. Because I had the desire to edit my own skateboarding video parts, I learned the programs required to do so. I started using Final Cut Pro when it was in one of its earliest versions. This same program is now used to edit many television shows and films.

✳✳✳

Over the next few years I skated less and less and worked more and more. But as I became more successful as an editor, I started to really miss skateboarding. Not just riding the board, but everything else that goes with it— the community, the freedom, the thrill, and the camaraderie that come from sharing a passion for this thing that only we seem to understand.

When I tried to reintegrate myself into the skate community I felt completely lost. The place where I had skated the most (West LA Courthouse) had been completely shut down. Every planter ledge had been knobbed, and a security guard would patrol the grounds and kick out anybody on a skateboard. All the while ignoring the homeless people and drug addicts who would use the space, which was closed off from view from the street, as a haven to go about their vagrancy undisturbed.[9]

The only silver lining was that there was a brand new "skate plaza" being built right down the street from my house, but construction was going painfully slow. I would find myself driving by the half-built park on my way to work dreaming of the possibilities of what this could do for skateboarding. Stoner Plaza was not going to be just another skate park. It was, in fact, a completely new mold for what a skate park should be. Previously parks had been poured entirely in the same drab concrete gray with obstacles that seemed to have been designed by someone who had never even stepped on a board. Stoner Plaza was designed by the skaters in the community, along with a very talented designer, Colby Carter, who was a former pro himself. The completed plaza looks more like a concrete Zen garden than a skate park. Flowing designs of red and yellow swirl through the space. Trees are planted in large granite planter boxes, the same type of granite that was so famously used to construct Philadelphia's Love Park, a place that was widely considered to have the best ledges for skating in the world. In short, it has the look and feel more reminiscent of a city plaza than a skate park.

When Stoner Plaza finally opened it was an immediate success and practically a worldwide phenomenon, thanks to social media. Within days the entire skateboarding world had seen numerous photos and videos of the plaza, and you could feel a collective shift in the atmosphere. Skaters could not believe what they were seeing, and it gave them hope that maybe change on a larger scale was coming.

***

Another by-product of no longer being a professional skater was that skateboarding became fun again. Super fun. I was learning again, doing tricks I hadn't been able to accomplish as a pro. There was no pressure, and I was doing it because I wanted to, not because I had to maintain a career. I had finally reconnected with the love that drew me to it in the first place.

It wasn't long after I'd found skating again that a friend of mine called to ask me if I was going to the Transworld Skateboarding Awards that night. I told him that I didn't even know it was happening that night and that I had no way in.

"I've got a ticket for you, you're going," Marty said.

In the past this was an event that I would never miss, it's like the Academy Awards of skateboarding. In the past few years, however, I had not gone because it was a painful reminder of what I had lost. Seeing all of my peers who were still maintaining successful careers was a tough pill to swallow. I felt like skateboarding had chewed me up and spit me out, and I hadn't left nearly the mark that I had hoped I would. I always felt like I was just outside the inner circle of top skaters who dominate the skateboard industry. I had tried for years, practically decades, to find a way to break into that circle, but I never could. I wanted, like most skaters, to be able to talk to the skaters who had been my heroes and to be accepted by the people whom I had so much respect for. I could never be as great of a skater as they were, but maybe if I could convey how much I love it, how much thought I've put into in, and how much it means to me, I could be on their level in some small way.

Thirty minutes into the awards ceremony I started feeling twinges of nostalgia mixed with regret, so I got up from my seat and headed to the bar.

I ordered a Stella, and before the bartender gave me my drink I heard my name called out from halfway down the bar. I see my old friend Brian Atlas, who was a big part of the community of skaters that dominated the last era of the West LA Courthouse days, and I moved down the bar to say hello.

"Snyder! I'm so glad I've run into you; I have been meaning to get a hold of you but I no longer have your number. . . . Have you heard about Street League?" he said.

I had. Street League was the brainchild of Rob Dyrdek, a pro skater, reality TV star, and the most successful entrepreneur in all of skateboarding. Street League was created to be the biggest, most exclusive contest series in the world. He signed the top 25 skaters to exclusive contracts, essentially making every other contest out there (X Games, Dew Tour, etc.) strictly for the "B-League" pros.

"Of course I've heard of it," I said.

"Well I actually helped Rob create it, I'm the general manager. . . . How would you feel about being a judge?" he said.

There have been a few moments in my life where I have felt like fate has stepped in at the exact moment that I've needed it to, and this was one of those moments.

"It would be an absolute honor, just tell me what I've got to do."

Numbers were quickly exchanged and I walked, no, floated back through the crowd in a complete daze. I took my seat next to my friend Marty who had gotten me the ticket and sat there in silence for a few seconds, still processing what had happened. Marty shot me an odd look, and said, "You okay?"

"Yeah . . . I think you may have just contributed to one of the most life-changing moments of my life."

He had. Becoming a Street League judge was the validation that I had wanted my entire life as a skater and never felt like I had fully gotten. To be recognized as someone deemed worthy of passing judgment on the greatest skateboarders in the entire world gave me a sense of pride that I hadn't felt since I first held my own pro board. It also gave me the "credentials" to no longer be so shy and timid around the iconic pro skaters I had grown up idolizing. And so, somehow, years removed from an actual pro career, I finally gained acceptance.

Behind the Scenes at Street League Skateboarding

Since its inception in 2010, Street League Skateboarding has become what few thought possible—a prestigious contest that because of its unique format showcases the closest thing to actual street skating. It also places a once deviant subculture firmly into the mainstream. Skaters are not uncritical about this transition, yet the voices of dissent have been somewhat muted because the level of skating has been so impressive.

For nearly two decades prior to Street League, most of the top pros did not compete in contests; they made their reputations by putting out "video parts" in which they performed creative and original feats on skate spots throughout the world. Skaters who excelled at park contests were ridiculed as mere "contest skaters" because their expertise was largely on park-produced obstacles, rather than an expression of what was happening in the streets. Street League changed all that. Originally conceived by pro skater, reality TV star, and entrepreneur Rob Dyrdek, Street League signed exclusive deals with the best 25 skateboarders in the world, and hired renowned skate park builder Joe C. of California Skateparks to build street courses in arenas that were modeled on real street obstacles.

For the first three years of its existence, Street League Skateboarding was sponsored by DC Shoes, and it held four stops in the United States. As its popularity began to increase, and skaters around the world flocked to TV screens and to the arenas, bigger sponsors began to take notice.

In 2013 Nike SB became the "presenting partner," and Street League teamed up with the X Games to host Street League events in Brazil, Barcelona, Munich, and LA, along with Kansas City and Portland. (This year the X Games sold naming rights to the skateboard mega ramp competition calling it "America's Navy Skateboard Big Air.")

The final event of the Street League season culminates with the Super Crown World Championship, which takes the top eight skaters from the entire season, and presents the winner with a check for $200,000.

This will be my fifth street league event, and the more I learn about skating, the more exciting they become. This contest is held at the Prudential Center in Newark, New Jersey, but the skaters are all housed at a boutique hotel in New York's Lower East Side. New Jersey may be where the contest happens, but New York City is where the parties are.

The skaters who have earned the right to participate in this year's contest are a diverse bunch: Nyjah Huston is African American and white; Chris Cole, from Lancaster, Pennsylvania, is white; Torey Pudwill and Mikey Taylor are white; Paul Rodriguez is Mexican American; Luan Oliveira is Brazilian; Shane O'Neill is Australian; and Sean Malto is from Kansas City and is half Filipino and half white. Nyjah, Torey, Paul, and Mikey all grew up in California. Paul, Sean, Shane, and Luan are all sponsored by Nike. (In three years they will add Nyjah.)

Aaron and I arrive at the Prudential Center, and he picks up his credentials as well as an "industry" and "hospitality" bracelet for me, which gets me a seat in the arena and free food and drinks. We step into the arena to watch the riders practice. The course has been up since Thursday, and the riders have spent that time getting used to the course, developing a plan, and then honing those tricks so they can perform them when the contest starts.

Street League is unique in both its scoring system and its setup. Riders are scored immediately after they've completed a trick, so they know their scores and what they have to risk in order to improve. Prior to the advent of the ISX Instant Scoring System, the judges just huddled in a corner and then decided upon a winner, with the winner oftentimes chosen in a popularity contest rather than a test of skateboarding.

In terms of its setup, the Street League course is divided into three sections, which are now called the Flow Section, the Control Section, and the Impact Section. These are also the marketing slogans for Nike's new line of skateboarding shoes. In the Flow Section the riders come up with a "run," meaning they have 45 seconds to string together a series of tricks, all of which they have spent the past three days creating and then practicing. Each rider gets two chances to get one score. This means that if they fall they get a second chance. But as riders have become more strategically sophisticated in their approaches, they usually start with a relatively risk-free (for them) first run and then try to improve their score on the second run. This usually means keeping the same basic flow of the run through the various obstacles and increasing the difficulty on one or more of the tricks. The number of tricks per run varies from rider to rider, but most average between 6 and 10. But skaters are judged on the quality of their tricks not the quantity. The best run comes from Paul Rodriquez, who scores a 9.0. He does exactly as he practiced.

1. switch kickflip over the bump to bump
2. nollie crooked grind on the flat bar
3. backside tailslide
4. switch kickflip backside tailslide
5. 360 flip up the bank
6. switch frontside blunt slide down the hubba

Riders also need to figure out a "best trick" for the Control Section, where they get four chances to post one score. They also have a pre-determined plan for this. They've decided which obstacle they're going to perform on and what trick. Because they get four chances to post one score, they choose really difficult tricks. Some skaters choose an incredibly hard trick and figure they can make it at least once in four tries, while others put up a score and try to improve upon it with each try.

One of the things that Street League has done is to objectify the subjective. Street skating is about spots and style and what even might be called artistic expression. To achieve their desired (trick) goals, riders will attempt extremely difficult tricks, on very dangerous obstacles, that may take them anywhere from 10 to 100 attempts to land. (That of course means falling, a lot.) Street League is about not falling and landing extremely difficult tricks on command, a feat that really only the top eight skaters in the world can consistently accomplish. This fact requires extremely knowledgeable judges who not only can recognize immediately what tricks the best skaters in the world are performing, but also instantly give them a score.

Skateboarding tricks are essentially a combination of elements to make a compound. Street League judges give each of these basic elements a rough numerical value. Out of the periodic table of 52 basic skating elements, there are 21 tricks that garner 1 to 3 points, 21 tricks that garner 2 to 4 points, and 9 tricks that garner 3 to 5 points.[10] The riders then turn these basic elements into infinite and ingenious combinations to form more complex tricks that score higher points. A front bluntslide, for example, might get 4 points, but a switch kickflip, frontside blunt—like the one Paul Rodriguez did in his Flow Section—might receive 9 points. Riders are of course also judged stylistically on how well they've accomplished a particular trick, which accounts for the variance between tricks among the riders.

There are five judges—Scott Pfaff, Jimmy Gorecki, Aaron Snyder, Matt Rodriguez, and Robbie McKinley—all of whom have had a long time in the skateboard industry with varying levels of success. And most importantly they are familiar to the skaters and respected for their knowledge.

There is little separation between the judges and the skaters, and the consensus is that the judges have a difficult job because all of the tricks are so good and they've pretty much gotten it right. How they do this is difficult to ascertain.

As soon as we arrive at the site, Aaron and I sit in the stands and watch the riders practice. It's good for the judges to get a sense of the course, and Aaron and Scott usually also skate the course themselves before a contest. It's also good for them to get a sense of what the skaters are working on, and just as the skaters are practicing what they're going to perform, the judges are taking mental notes for the scores they will give, if, for example, rider X perfectly executes the switch frontside bluntslide he is practicing.

The contest's top seed and winner of 11 of the 16 Street League contests so far is 18-year-old phenom Nyjah Huston, who has been one of the top skaters in the world since he was 13. Nyjah has recently come into his own, reclaiming his life from those who had mismanaged his career. This break was further reinforced when Nyjah cut his 17-year-old dreadlocks. Three years ago as a skinny 15-year-old, he was among the slowest riders on the course; now he is one of the fastest and he speeds around the course like a silent assassin, landing impossible trick after impossible trick, listening to music and barely saying a word to anyone.

But this is not the case with every rider. Sometimes it is necessary to communicate with the judges to get a sense of how they're judging this particular course. Almost as soon as we arrive Sean Malto comes up to Aaron—as he does at every contest—and asks a hypothetical question. What score would you give a blah blah blah on the rail. Aaron responds, "high 8, possibly 9, if it was done really well." Malto says, "Scott [another judge] said the same thing." Satisfied, Malto heads off to perfect his idea.

Next we go floor level and immediately get a visceral sense of the speed and power of these skaters. On TV, and even from the stands, they appear to be going much slower, in part because you can't hear the speed of their wheels on the ground. This is especially true of Shane O'Neill. He is from Australia and has exploded onto the scene in the past four years. He is the most technically proficient skater in Street League and does some of the hardest tricks in the world. He has won Street League once before, but usually he has a hard time figuring out exactly what to do, in part because his options are so limitless. Skaters all have what they call their "bag of tricks," and Shane has by far the biggest bag.

Shane is another one of the skaters who Aaron says always comes and asks about tricks and looks for feedback on his plans. Shane is working on a trick for the best trick or Control Section, and he asks Aaron about what he thinks of a particular hypothetical situation. Aaron replies that the trick Shane was considering would garner only a 7. Shane goes quiet and someone says, "clearly not the answer he was hoping for." Shane skates off to come up with a different plan.

When he's gone I ask Aaron what it's like when one of the most talented skateboarders in the world asks you about a trick that you could never do in three lifetimes, and you say, "Ahh, not so great only about a 7." Aaron chuckles at this irony, but there is no question that his expertise is respected by the skaters. However, to an outsider, it's sort of like a guy who drives a Honda telling a millionaire that he was silly to buy the Jaguar XJ and instead should have purchased an Aston Martin. (Incidentally that is exactly what is happening: Aaron does drive a Honda, while Shane is a millionaire who drives a Jaguar XJ.)

We watch as Shane tries a few more ridiculously impossible tricks and then rides over to present his new idea. "How about a switch heel, feeble grind on the flat bar?" Now Aaron gets excited. "If you could do that, that's the trick to do." Shane goes and tries it and by the fourth attempt he makes one. Holy crap. Robbie says "NBD" as in it's never been done before—not NBD in a contest, but never been done before, ever. Felix Arguelles, a 41-year-old pro and on-air analyst for the event, corrects him. "Jereme Rodgers did one, but I won't tell Shane."

Shane comes back to check in with Aaron as to what type of score this trick might generate. Aaron tells him he has to grind on the rail a little longer, then it would be at least a 9. Again this is astounding. As a fan I have just witnessed only the second iteration of this trick in the history of skateboarding, and my brother is telling him, honestly, that he needs to do it a little bit better. And Shane agrees.

What is incredible about this is the camaraderie among the skaters and also the lack of ego. Shane doesn't become upset in the slightest degree, nor does he say "Fuck you, you try it." Aaron admits later that if he'd tried that trick 15 years ago in his prime, every single day until today, he still wouldn't have made it. This part of skateboarding is difficult to understand and where it diverges from being a sport. Professional athletes and umpires don't fraternize, as umpires are the enforcers of rules, whereas skateboarding has no rules, and there is nothing akin to cheating, so in some ways the judging is the result of a negotiation between the skaters and the judges. In fact, this process involves highly nuanced communication in which the skaters are also testing the judges to ascertain whether or not they understand exactly how hard and complicated their tricks are. The judges, riders, everyone is committed to skating as something larger than themselves, and as a result, so far, the integrity of skating far outweighs any consideration for personal gain.

"The Star-Spangled Banner" is sung, the skaters are introduced, and the contest begins. In the Control Section, on his first attempt Shane O'Neill tries a switch heelflip to feeble grind and misses. On the telecast pro skater Geoff Rowley comments, excitedly, that that is a "really hard trick." On the second try Shane makes it and stares up at the scoreboard waiting for his score to appear. He receives an 8.5. His face shows he wishes it was a bit higher, but he seems pleased. Upon closer scrutiny it was exactly as Aaron said, a high 8, a 9 if he had gotten on the rail sooner and grinded longer, which Shane knows he failed to do. And this was not only Aaron's assessment; the score shows that all of the judges were in agreement.

The contest proceeds as expected with the top riders, Paul Rodriguez, Nyjah Huston, and Chris Cole, swapping the lead back and forth until they get to the final section. The final section of the course used to be called the Big Section but is now the Impact Section, and it features the most difficult obstacles and requires the riders to take big risks. The skaters say this section is about "commitment." For most skaters the mental anguish of attempting something scary and potentially harmful is as challenging as the physical skills required. In these instances, skaters say that you have to commit to do the trick and attempt it with the confidence that you are going to make it. What makes these guys so good is that they rarely ever hesitate; they fly at the obstacle and attempt their trick, and surprisingly there have been no serious injuries in the four years since the contest began. In a street skating session even with top pros, it is not uncommon for riders to stop short of the obstacle 5 to 10 times before even making their first attempt.

The riders get six tries to post four scores, so that riders must choose four tricks they can land but will also garner high scores. It must also be said that the Impact Section is daunting, and that this is the section that Nyjah Huston has dominated over the past three years. He is young and fearless and seems to be able to execute extremely difficult tricks, when the pressure is most intense. He holds the record for the highest scores ever handed out, scoring 9.9, 9.8, and 9.7 in past contests to win. He has also made over a million dollars from Street League wins.

This Impact Section is a little smaller than others in the past, and Aaron tells me that this fact slightly levels the playing field, as Nyjah is clearly the rider who can go the biggest, but with the risk factor slightly decreased, the riders have more trick options.

For the fans, the Impact Section is the most exciting and requires the least amount of technical knowledge to appreciate. Because the obstacles are big, less technical tricks go down, but the only thing that really matters is landing the tricks. When a rider lands a trick, the noise from the crowd gives an indication of its difficulty, and in seconds he gets a score. As a result, the leaderboard is constantly fluctuating, and before each attempt the scoreboard shows what score skaters need to get into first place.

When the Impact Section begins, Chris Cole (17.8) is in first place, followed by Malto (17.7), Rodriguez (17.7), and Huston (16.9). They go in reverse order of their placing, so Nyjah is the first rider with a chance to win to go. He lands a nollie heelflip, backside lipslide, to fakie. He gets an 8.5 and takes over the lead. Paul misses. Next up is Cole; his strategy is to do his hardest trick first and he does a frontside halfcab, frontside bluntslide to fakie, which essentially means that he cannot see the obstacle through the entire trick. As he lands it, the TV announcer Felix Arguelles says, "Never done before." This is the first time any skater in the world has seen this trick done, and the crowd goes wild. Cole gets a 9.3 and reclaims first place. Nyjah follows with a backside 270 noseblunt on the rail and gets a 9.0, again thrusting him into first place. Cole then fires off a 360 flip to 50–50 grind, for an 8.0 and is again in first place. On his fourth attempt Cole falls, creating an opportunity for Nyjah Huston to do what he always does: land insane tricks under extreme pressure.

But to everyone's surprise, Nyjah falls. The crowd is confused. On Cole's next attempt he only needs a 5.7 to take over the top spot and he does a trick that he is well-known for, a perfect backside 270, noseblunt, which scores a 9.1 and widens the gap slightly.

It has come down to the sixth and final attempt. Nyjah needs to score a 9.8 to win, and his body language says that he expects to do just that. He heads toward the rail and attempts a kickflip, frontside hurricane, but the announcers say that he "failed to really lock his trucks in." Nyjah knows it's probably not enough and he shrugs his shoulders while he waits for his score. He gets a 9.3, a great score but not enough.

Now the only rider who can overtake Cole is Paul Rodriguez, and the tension is thick. Just yesterday Paul injured his back in practice and all morning the word was that he wasn't going to even compete, and now he is poised to take home the championship. He needs to score an 8.1 or better, and he is entirely capable of this. He goes through his routine: he prays into his hat and places it backward on his head so that it feels perfect, he tugs at his pants leg, he shuffles his feet back and forth, sweeping away the dust. He is visibly nervous as he waits for the buzz of the crowd to die down. The crowd is poised to erupt at the possibility of this great story, but Paul misses, making Chris Cole the winner.

Chris Cole is the oldest rider in the contest at 31, and also one of the most likable. His son and daughter run up and jump into his arms, and Chris beams with pride as he kisses his wife. This is a touching moment, and one not normally associated with the public's long-held perception of skating as an "extreme" deviant activity. He is this year's Super Crown World Champion and $200,000 richer.

Street League Revisited: October 2, 2016

While Street League may have garnered some strong opinions when it was first introduced, there seems to be general agreement that it has not destroyed skateboarding. Even those who still grumble at the corporate sponsorship either tune in to watch or show up to see it live. The reason? The level of skating that goes down during a Street League contest, especially the Super Crown, which ends the season and features the top eight skaters from the year, is mind-boggling.

Contests in general were frowned upon for many years, mostly because skateboarders in general (especially in the early days) don't like to think of skateboarding as a competition. But also street skating became such the dominant form of skateboarding that even skating inside skate parks became looked down upon. It was *all* about street skating. But Street League has changed that for two reasons. The course designs in street league more closely resemble street obstacles, and the top pros all have constructed their own personal courses on which to hone their tricks. What five years ago you would see only in a video part now takes place in the course of a contest.

Leaders of the event have tinkered with the format over the years and seem to have settled on a system that is efficient and showcases the skaters and the course. In section 1, the Run Section, skaters take two "runs" in which they have 45 seconds to perform consecutive tricks over the entire course. Skaters are judged on quality of tricks, creative use of the course, and speed and style. In section 2—Best Trick—skaters have five attempts to perform their best tricks on any obstacle of their choosing. Here skaters are judged on the difficulty of trick performed, taking into account the difficulty and danger the obstacle poses and of course style. The top four of the seven scores count, and the skater with the highest score wins. It is very simple and efficient, and most importantly it fits nicely within the 60-minute television slot.

This format has been successful and has attracted a global audience as well as participants. While all of the details have yet to be worked out, the thinking is that when skateboarding debuts at the 2020 Tokyo Olympics, the format will be very similar to Street League. Currently Street League has partnered with the International Skateboarding Federation as the "official qualification for world championship street skateboarding."[11]

✳✳✳

It is 2016 and I am in LA for my last Street League event for this book. This is the last contest of the year and features the top eight skaters in both men's and women's divisions. Last year was the first women's event, with Leticia Bufoni winning. The eight women selected to compete are Lacey Baker, 25, Leticia Bufoni, 23, Mariah Duran, 20, Pamela Rosa, 17, Alexis Sablone, 30, Alana Smith, 15, Monica Torres, 22, and Aori Nishimura, 15.

Leticia, Pamela, and Monica are Brazilian, while Lacey is from California, Alana from Arizona, Mariah from New Mexico, Alexis from Connecticut, and Aori from Japan. The course design is much smaller than a usual Street League course, and this is because it has to accommodate both men and women, or to be fair, men and girls. But make no mistake the course is challenging, and during the men's practice on Saturday they were loving the course.

Among these eight women are three who stand out: last year's winner Leticia Bufoni, who skates fast and takes big risks; Lacey Baker, who is technical and consistent; and Alexis Sablone, who has a combination of technical proficiency and pop. All of the women are excellent skaters, and the younger ones show that there is a very promising future for women's skating. I was curious about the scoring, and Aaron informed me that they were instructed to grade on a curve for lack of a better term. The tricks that the women perform are fairly basic compared to those of the men; for example, Leticia's winning trick in last year's contest, a 360 flip over a relatively small gap, would have received a 5 if done by a man, but in this instance she received a 7. But the judges and the male skaters are not interested in a direct gender comparison; they're interested in good skating, and these women are good.

Lacey Baker scores 6.6 and 7.2 on her first and second runs, and is followed closely behind by Leticia Bufoni and Alexis Sablone. Alexis misses her last attempt, leaving only Leticia with the possibility of overtaking Lacey for the victory. Knowing she needs a huge score, Leticia sets up on the far side of the deck and flies down the course toward the bump to rail, an obstacle that only three (Nyjah, Joslin, and Decenzo) of the eight male pros have even attempted. I watched all of her practice on Saturday and Sunday, and she never once attempted anything on this obstacle. However, during the practice session she did fly at it once but just ollied it. As Leticia flies at the ramp, there is a hush in the arena and then a gasp and dead silence. Leticia launches into the air and attempts to land the middle of her board on the rail, but the moment she hits the rail she gets pitched forward and slams face-first into the concrete. She tries to get up but is clearly woozy, and Chase Gabor, the filmer who was closest to her, guides her back down. She can't get back up. The medics take their time getting to her, but they bring out a stretcher and stabilize her head and neck before carting her off. Meanwhile, while this is going on, Lacey

Baker, who has effectively just won the contest, is crying in horror over what just happened to her friend.[12]

I should also note that Leticia attempted a trick that was clearly out of her depth, which shows an amazing amount of courage. But there are also some gender issues in the background of this discussion. Leticia, in addition to being an amazing skater, also gets the most attention because of her appearance. She is a beautiful woman and is not opposed to throwing a little sexiness into her videos.[13] But having watched Leticia all weekend, it is clear that she is the hardest worker. She puts in the most work and falls, a lot. Her back has bruises and scabs, and it may be that she wants to show the world she is more than just a pretty face, though, in that moment, what is most likely is that she wants to win and is willing to put it all on the line. However, anyone claiming that Leticia is just a pretty face has just been proven dead wrong. On her Instagram post from her hospital bed, she gives the "thumbs-up" sign, but she has an IV in her arm and a brace around her neck. She writes, "Just want to tell everyone I'm ok and say thanks for all the support and messages. I'm stoked on 2nd place on SLS it was all worth it!"

As to the men, the tricks being done have progressed so far that each time a new course is created, the tricks done far exceed anyone's imagination. For example, in the past five years skaters have gone from trying to be consistent to trying to do the hardest tricks possible, and they're not only doing tricks that have never been done in contests; in some cases they're doing NBDs in the contest.

At this year's contest, rookie Chris Joslin, comes out on fire and puts down two runs scored 9.0 and 9.2. This immediately wakes up the other skaters who now have to change their strategy to compete. Joslin makes a strategic mistake, and instead of attempting some of his hard tricks that will garner high scores, he falls three times attempting to land a dangerous trick on the quarter pipe. This allows some of the other skaters back in the game. Shane O'Neill then proceeds to take advantage of the smaller rail and puts down a switch 360 flip, lip slide, NBD in a contest, for a 9.0. Next a switch big spin kickflip, frontside board slide. Shane is the only person in the world to have done this trick and scores a 9.2. For his final trick, he does a nollie 360 flip, frontside board slide for a 9.4. This trick has been done only once in the streets, and no one has ever seen one in a contest. These tricks, combined with Shane's 9.0 in the run section give him the victory. As Shane receives the trophy, everyone in the arena and the folks around me are buzzing over what they just saw, equivalent to a progressive video part, and instead we watched someone land three impossible tricks, in five tries, which is nearly incomprehensible to most folks. Shane O'Neill is widely regarded as the best skateboarder in the world.

Skateboarding and the Subculture Career

In the second decade of the 21st century skateboarding is currently undergoing a tense moment when skaters feel like the corporate influence in skating is taking away some of what they've created. There is an emerging discussion among skaters who accept corporate sponsorship versus those who remain independent and skater-owned, but many skaters, like Paul Rodriguez for example, are actively balancing their sponsorships between the two. The skaters use the terms "core versus corporate" to describe this predicament, and many are actively attempting to reclaim independently owned companies by and for skaters. This is felt most seriously in skate footwear, as well-known brands like DVS and Lakai lose riders to Adidas and Nike, but despite the emergence of corporate sponsorship in skateboarding brands, most of the board companies (except Zoo York) remain skater-owned. This questions some long-held tenets of subculture theory, and suggests that the creation of culture is an opportunity for both co-optation and community (more on this later).

Skaters play with and in public space, thereby resisting attempts at spatial control.[14] However, their creative use of space for their own purposes should not be read purely as a critique of urban space; professional street skateboarders perform tricks on subcultural landmarks for the purpose of progressing the discipline of skateboarding and furthering their careers. The quickest way for a young amateur to go pro and make a living at skating is to "land" progressive tricks that have never been done on the well-known spots throughout the culture, like the Hollywood 16 stair at Hollywood High in or the stage at the West LA Courthouse. Or as Jake Phelps of *Thrasher* magazine writes, "Lincoln [high school in San Francisco] has made some people quite rich."[15]

Since subcultural activity has been interpreted by sociologists and cultural studies scholars as "symbolic resistance" for over 30 years, the fact that folks make careers out of it is an issue that is often difficult for many theorists to accept.[16] My research has shown that skateboarders participate in the subculture for fun, but many also hope to make a living doing what they love. Many of course fail, but the fact that skateboarding, along with numerous other careers in the distribution of skateboarding content and products, is now a legitimate career option is significant. In addition, these are careers in which the only education required occurs entirely within skateboarding.

This idea runs counter to the theory of the Birmingham School, which argued that British working-class youth solved the problem of a consumption imperative by creating spectacular subcultural styles that tried to "win space" from the larger society. They did this by mocking, reshaping, and resisting postwar capitalism's attempt to impose an identity upon them. These working-class youth became teddy boys, mods, and punks by "bricolaging" together a pastiche of styles, which shocked mainstream sensibilities and amounted to an act of fleeting, symbolic political resistance.

In the early 21st century, a new generation of UK scholars, many of whom had subcultural experiences, reassessed subcultural theory from a postmodern perspective. These "post-subculturalists" took many of the Birmingham tenets to task, specifically the notion of working-class homogeneity and symbolic resistance.[17]

However, for all of the attention the post-subculturalists have devoted to reassessing and dethroning the Birmingham project, their focus is almost exclusively on music subcultures, like punk and goth, which participants build an identity around, with a requisite spectacular uniform. Subculture studies is still mostly about spectacular fashions, and researchers have for the most part neglected subcultures that don't revolve around a specific type of music. However, the most significant blind spot of current subculture research is that it fails to consider the impact of subcultures on youth as they become adults.

In *Resistance through Rituals* Hall and Jefferson argue that subculture resistance is merely symbolic; it does not have an actual effect on the lives of the participants because they cannot ever escape their class position. They write:

> The problematic of a subordinate class experience can be "lived through" negotiated or resisted; but it cannot be resolved at that level or by those

means. There is no "subcultural career" for the working class lad, no "so-lution" in the subcultural milieu, for problems posed by the key structur-ing experiences of the class.[18]

They argue for example that being a teddy boy, mod, or punk rocker, while exciting and resistant for a moment, is ultimately tragic because working-class youth will be forced back into the limited choices that their class position affords them. Hence, even though they had spec-tacular youths, their adult lives will in all likelihood be similar to their parents', rife with occupational boredom and class exploitation.

Angela McRobbie often gets less credit than other Birmingham schol-ars, in part because she is a woman and because she has consistently defended young people's attempts to make their own lives.[19] Rather than claim an authentic political purity to subculture participation, she argues that all subcultures have an "entrepreneurial dynamic [that] has rarely been acknowledged."[20] This was a fact that most of her col-leagues in the Birmingham School denied or ignored because they were beholden to a Marxist political ideology in which any sort of commer-cialism was evidence of capitalist co-optation. McRobbie took seriously young people's ambitions and desires for success *"on their own terms,"* and argued against those who want to judge young people as "sellouts" for their complicity with capitalism and consumption.[21]

It turned out that McRobbie was the only person associated with the Birmingham School who was right about the lasting impact of subcul-ture. The "entrepreneurial dynamic" in subcultures has in fact sustained them over the past 30 years and can be attributed in part to a reaction to the boring career choices many young people face.[22]

Subculture researchers need to do a better job of considering if, and how, young people turn their subcultural experience into careers. While not every subculturalist achieves upward social mobility, it is equally narrow-minded to assume that those who do have material success should be deemed selfish, complicit, apolitical, or amoral.

The Birmingham scholars anticipated that resistance would be short-lived and that the culture industry would market punk style as a com-modity for mass consumption.[23] Therefore, subcultural symbolism, in the service of corporate interests, was no longer resistant. In the case of punk rock, this corporatization quickly led to its so-called "death" as a resistant subculture.[24] Sociologist Dylan Clark argues, however, that this "death" inspired punk's rebirth, where new followers were in constant dialogue with the forces of commodification. In this way, punks and other subculturalists learn the ways of the enemy and practice their "kung fu" in this context, constantly trying to outmaneuver their captors.[25] Clark argues that the commodification of stylistically resistant punk led to the actual politicization of punk, whose consequent forms of resistance were no longer merely symbolic. As Clark writes, "contemporary punk has forgone these performances of anarchy and is now almost synonymous with the practice of anarchism."[26] Punk has evolved in places like Seattle and elsewhere into a powerful political force, leading the antiglobalization and culture-jamming movements worldwide.[27]

Certainly there are punks who have put on the costume, and for reasons that are complex and often personal "step and fetch" for money, just as there are those who don the dress, only to remove it at the first sign of trouble, such as the need to get a "real" job. But there are also punks committed for life, and whose lives are being supported by a DIY punk subculture career and their politics and ideologies continue to challenge the mainstream, even as they appear, stylistically, to be no longer resistant. Clark argues that the experience of witnessing the commodification of one's own culture politicized punks to the point where the spectacular was replaced by the actual.

Graffiti writers responded similarly to negative media campaigns by creating their own media, which in turn allowed them to find their own voice as well as lay the entrepreneurial groundwork for subculture careers.[28] In skating there are those who are sponsored by Mountain Dew, Red Bull, Target, Axe Body Spray, and the like, and there are also those who would never dream of riding for those companies. While the choices individual pro skaters make about their own image and economic situation contribute to attitudes others might have about whether they are "sellouts" or "real" subculturalists, none of this makes pro skaters any more or less skateboarders, unless of course they stop skating. For example, some skaters have decried the success and the comments made by Ryan Sheckler when he was the 16-year-old star of MTV's reality show *Life of Ryan*, as well as his sponsorship by Panasonic and Axe

Body Spray. However, one thing you can't say is that he's overrated as a skater. As most will tell you, and as I have witnessed firsthand, he is an unbelievably talented skateboarder who takes incredible risks. This is to say that despite his commercial choices, his skating, which is to say his creative and courageous feats in and on public spaces, remains in keeping with the dictates of skateboarding subculture. It should also be noted that Ryan is a philanthropist, whose Sheckler Foundation (shecklerfoundation.org) gives away millions of dollars to support kids and those disabled by action sports injuries.

Social and political activism is starting to become a part of skateboarding culture. This is linked to the subculture career; as skaters have increased their social and economic capital, they have begun to translate this into political capital. Skateboarders' experiences being criminalized out of public spaces have led to discussions and activism surrounding the use of public space and the building of skate plazas. Some, like Billy Rohan and Steve Rodriguez, have long been engaged in activism and successfully won spaces for skaters in New York City.[29] While the commercialization of skateboarding style has not led to the type of activism that Clark recounts in punk subculture, the criminalization of skateboarding spaces has in many ways forced skaters to become political, taking part in community meetings and becoming active in the discussion of how public space resources are used, as chapter 9 makes clear in regard to the liberation of the West LA Courthouse.

The Street Not Taken: Robbie McKinley

Robbie McKinley was once a highly regarded amateur for Girl Skateboards who seemed to be on the fast track to the life of a professional skateboarder; however the fast track was a bit too fast for Robbie and at 24 he had a serious midlife crisis and decided that he wasn't going to make it as a pro skater. He quit skateboarding, went to college, and now has a job in graphic design.

Robbie's parents are both architects and were born in Poland. Their original last name was Warchawski, but upon moving to LA in the early 1970s they decided to change it to McKinley. Robbie was born in LA, and he and his family originally lived in Silver Lake, but they eventually moved to a city 60 miles east of the Pacific Ocean in a vast area known as Inland Empire, which comprises Riverside and San Bernardino counties.

Robbie started skating in the sixth grade and began to take it more seriously when he was introduced to a well-known skate spot at Chaffey High School in Ontario, California, which produced numerous pros, including Richard Mulder and Joey Brezinski.

At first Robbie got sponsored by his local shop, then by Grindking Trucks, and when Grindking decided to launch a board company called Society, he was put on the team as an am. He started skating a lot with a prominent filmer Tim Dowling and had a part in his *Listen* video, which garnered some attention. Robbie then got an offer to skate for Blind Skateboards, a much more prestigious company. In the summer between Robbie's junior and senior years of high school the recession hit the McKinleys hard and they decided to move to Florida, just north of Tampa. Robbie had no choice but to go and soon found himself in Florida, with no skaters in his high school or the entire town. Robbie had no interest in school since discovering skateboarding and learned he would have to stay an additional semester to graduate.

Meanwhile, Blind Skateboards was in the process of filming for a video and in October flew him out to LA to shoot some tricks. Robbie never got on the return flight home. He called his mom, who "freaked." Luckily Robbie's dad just happened to be in LA on business and reluctantly helped him find a place to live. They settled on an apartment in West LA near the Courthouse, and Robbie started to skate there with better and better skaters.

Around this time Robbie also began to enjoy the nightlife, partying at all the "go-to" Hollywood spots. One night out at a bar he ran into Girl Skateboard's team manager Tony Callaway, who suggested that Girl, universally recognized as the most important board company in skating, was interested in putting him on the team. This was an opportunity Robbie couldn't pass up. Robbie met Rick Howard, pro skater and Girl owner at a trade show in Long Beach, and Rick invited Robbie to go skate, which in essence was an audition.

Robbie won't really say what this felt like, but Girl had yet to add a single new amateur to the team. This opportunity also came with enormous pressure, but when Rick finally offered him a position on the team, Robbie accepted. This was akin to becoming a "made man"; the most prominent dudes in skating had deemed Robbie good enough and cool enough to be part of their gang.

At this point Robbie also began to develop a reputation for his drinking, and he admits that he wasn't working as hard on his skating as he should have been. He also says that he didn't really realize that being on Girl also meant that he had to hang out with those guys and skate with them. Had that been the case he probably would have received much-needed mentoring. In an interview by Tim Anderson for the website *Bobshirt*, Robbie put it this way:

> I guess you could say I had a mid-mid life crisis. Questioning what I was doing with my life etc. . . . . I was labeled the "Man Am," got kicked off DC and just felt like I was in this stand still not advancing in skating or in life. I wasn't focused at the time and that's the way it went down. Can't sit around and fuckin' cry about it you know, sometimes you just gotta man up and do what's right. At the time I felt like I was disrespecting Rick, Mike, Megan and everyone else, so it was time to move over and let the new guys have their chance. I talked to Rick and asked him if he could help me out for a few more months pay until I figured out what I was gonna do, he was cool with it and that was that. I would much rather have it go down like that then get a call from Rick telling me they had to let me go, you know?[30]

Robbie didn't produce skateboarding tricks for Girl at the level that he had been, and there are a bunch of factors that contributed to this. The easy answer is that he partied too much and skated too little, but this was also a time when skating was changing and people started skating bigger and bigger rails. Robbie tried to change his style to keep up, but the change didn't suit him and skating ceased to be fun.

Many folks would have just gone on with the party skate lifestyle until they got dropped from their sponsors and found themselves lost, but Robbie decided he would quit skating, go to college, and study graphic design, and he deserves credit for going down that road. Robbie has worked a regular job for nearly 10 years but has started to get restless. Even with the stability of a good job with health care and benefits, Robbie bemoans the grind of the "nine to five," and hopes somehow to find a way to work and be creative, which will include lots of time to surf, as skating has become less of a priority.

Pro skating is a difficult prospect for anyone and requires talent and luck, yet it also rarely combines self-reflexivity. Robbie's story is an example that for some it's okay to simply be practical.

5

The Production of Skateboarding Tricks

While skateboarding is an individual activity, it cannot be understood without also appreciating that the process of professional skateboarding is a production, requiring logistics, planning, and a diversity of talents to bring the product (tricks) to the people. To grapple with the scale of this production process is to be humbled first and foremost by the sheer audacity of skateboarding subculture, which has created its own infrastructure and industry to facilitate the dissemination of products and information (news, tricks, gossip, knowledge) on a massive scale. This business generates billions in currency, exists globally, in real time, in digital as well as physical space, in the past, the present, and way into the future, and it was made, created, managed, and, for much of its history, owned by skaters. The term "subculture career" barely scratches the surface of how this form is practiced.

Esteemed sociologist Howard Becker begins his second most famous book, *Art Worlds*, by doing a detailed analysis of the credits of a Hollywood film, to make the point that "art" is a collective process made by a diversity of people. In homage to Becker, and by way of hyperbole, I have scrutinized the credits of the most recent large-budget skateboard film, *Away Days*, released by Adidas Skateboarding. The production staff is made up of 25 people, including 3 executive producers who work for Adidas, 11 cinematographers, and 4 editors, in addition to 71 contributing cinematographers (filmers) and 21 contributing still photographers, all working toward producing the "video parts" of 23 separate skaters into a film. Of the 119 people involved in this production, only 3 are not skaters. In an effort to further explore how skateboarding produces content, in this chapter I highlight some of the more codified positions within the industry.

The Skater

For skaters, the process of building a skateboarding career starts when they amass a portfolio of documented tricks, sometimes called "clips." In the past skaters who had the goal of being sponsored documented their tricks on VHS video, edited them into what was called a "sponsor-me video" (similar to a musician's "demo tape"), and sent them to their favorite companies in the hope of getting "flow," free product from a team. Today skaters make their tricks public, either via social media sites or by sending footage directly to a board company. For young kids with talent, flow is usually the first step in the process and occurs when skateboard company owners (who are mostly skaters) offer promising young skaters free product to help them along with their development. The idea is that they will continue to skate and if they improve enough and are well-liked enough, will become sponsored amateurs, or "ams." However, in the skate-board world ams are not amateurs in the true sense of the term. They are officially on the team and try to get tricks in magazines, produce parts for videos, receive as much product as they need, and receive a small sti-pend ($500–$1,000/month). Ams also usually have additional sponsors for shoes, wheels, trucks, and so on, each of which pays the "amateur" a small amount of money.

Ams are expected to represent the company at "demos" (demonstra-tions) and contests, but mostly are supposed to continue to produce skateboarding tricks, all with the hope, and in many cases the expecta-tion, that their skating will progress to the point where the team will turn them pro, which means giving them signature boards, from which they receive royalties on the sales. This is analogous to the academy, where an am is an assistant professor getting hired for a tenure-track position. If she produces well-received scholarship, she will turn pro, or get ten-ure. This also leads me to say that ams as well as pros have PhDs in skateboarding.

Professional skaters have signature boards or "decks" with their name on it and some graphic artwork that may have something to do with their personality and style, and the board companies will usually release two or three pro models a year.[1] Pro skaters receive royalties based upon board sales in addition to a monthly salary. From a top-tier board sponsor, other sponsorships follow. Most of the top pros also have a signature shoe, as well as truck, wheel, clothing, and hardware sponsors from whom they are also paid. Top pros today begin making around $100,000 a year, with a few making well over a million. The website celebritynetworth.com is hardly a reliable source, but it provides a relative sense of the net worth of famous skaters/company owners: Rodney Mullen is worth $30 million, Tony Hawk $150 million, Chad Muska $16 million, Ryan Sheckler $16 million, and Paul Rodriguez $6 million.

While pro salaries are not usually a matter of public record, they are fairly easy to estimate based on a pro's status and number of sponsors. Top pros usually have between 10 and 15 sponsors, all of whom pay a monthly salary to riders to represent their brand. Most of the top board companies provide their riders with health care and benefits, however pros for smaller companies struggle to make a living. For example, when Billy Roper was a pro skater for a small company called Goldstar Skateboards, he supplemented his income as a stuntman in Hollywood productions.

Highly skilled skateboarders—those trying to get sponsored, the kids on flow, the ams and the pros—produce documented skateboarding tricks. For them, "skating" means to perform tricks in public spaces on obstacles that meet specific requirements for self-expression and to contribute to what they call the "progression of skateboarding." This essentially means to understand what's been done before and to improve upon it.

Similar to scholars who stand on the shoulders of giants, skateboarding tricks are done in the context of generations of skateboarders. Each obstacle and skate spot has a history of tricks, and any new trick must be original and more challenging. For most pro skaters and up-and-coming ams, the tricks they film are NBD. Consequently, skaters who do tricks that have previously been performed on certain obstacles will be ridiculed for unoriginality and for not recognizing the ABD (already been done) list at certain spots.

Progression is achieved by doing tricks with greater degrees of difficulty on existing skate spots or by discovering new spots and performing "legitimate" or difficult tricks on them. But skateboarders cannot achieve these feats alone; in order to contribute to this progression, they need photographers and filmers to document their tricks. Skateboarding in its current form would not be possible without the documenters.

The Photographer

Photographers and videographers are so important to subcultures like skating that it is important to look closely at how their role has shaped the history and production of skateboarding. The skateboard photographer has existed since the beginning of the skateboarding movement. Some of the early skate photographers like Craig Stecyk and Glen E. Friedman were surfers and skateboarders in West LA who hung out with the legendary Z-Boys.[2] They documented the early history of modern skateboarding and wrote articles on the emergence of the Z-Boys in *Skateboarder* magazine in the 1970s.[3]

However, skate photography is not simple documentation. To convey the difficulty and energy of a trick as well as the uniqueness of a spot, skateboard photographers must understand skateboarding, and this knowledge comes from their experience as skaters. There are also technical skills required in order to properly light a spot, and to use the appropriate lens and shutter speed to capture a fast-moving skateboarder, and not least of all to know the best angle from which to document a specific trick.

Skating as a fad began to fade in the late 1970s, leaving only the hardcore, committed members of the subculture. Skating became less of a sport based upon contests and competition, and more of an all-consuming lifestyle in which progression was documented on film and showcased in various subculture media outlets.[4] The first of these outlets were magazines. Fausto Vitello, who owned Independent Trucks, started *Thrasher* magazine and hired some of the best photographers of the day.[5]

Thrasher and *Transworld* have been the main outlets for skateboarding for more than 25 years and have shaped the style and culture of skating.[6] Today the main skateboard magazines are *The Skateboard Mag*, *Thrasher*, *Transworld*, and *Skateboarding*, all of which employ photographers and designers who are also skaters. These magazines are located in California and attract the best talent from around the country and the world. The story of Atiba Jefferson and his twin brother Ako, relayed in chapter 6, shows how skaters' personal histories are tied into the history and growth of the subculture.

The Filmer

The history of skateboarding is the history of skateboard videos. This history is well-known to all skaters, who can easily rattle off videos and reference specific "video parts" as well as groundbreaking tricks at spots that are subcultural landmarks. This history would not exist without a competent "filmer."

The job of the skateboard filmer and the role of the skateboard video part as the medium of skateboarding expression were among the last elements of skateboarding culture to emerge. In fact, the current process of skate production with skaters, photographers, and filmers has been codified for only approximately the past 15 to 20 years.

In the early days, those who did try to capture skateboarding on film used 8-millimeter, sometimes even 16-millimeter movie cameras. However around this time, video cameras began to replace film as the medium for documenting skateboarding. Consumer VHS cameras, which became a staple of middle-class homes, were easy to use and didn't require sophisticated lighting or developing. Kids encouraged their parents to let them use the family camera, and within a few weeks the 10-year-old became the family video expert (as was the case in our family). While not every kid had access to a family VHS camera, someone in the crew always did, and kids took turns filming each other's tricks.

In 1988, H-Street Skateboards (started by pro skater Tony Magnusson, who today owns Osiris Shoes) featured such stars as Matt Hensley, Rick Howard, Sal Barbier, Mike Carroll, and Danny Way. H Street's 1988 video *Shackle Me Not* was the first skateboard video to be shot entirely on videotape. While it did not have the aesthetic qualities of film, it was a document of each rider's skating that could be disseminated to the entire subculture, which encouraged other skaters to do the same. For some skaters at the time like Pete Lehman, "Matt Hensley's part revolutionized the public sidewalk as a site for the performance of flatground tricks."[7] From then on skaters were documenting their tricks and amassing video footage to edit into a "part." Those in the crew who were the best at documenting tricks eventually became full-time filmers.

H Street followed up *Shackle Me Not* with *Hocus Pocus*, but it was also in 1993 when Josh Friedberg started *411 Video Magazine*. These

hour-plus-long videos came out every other month and showcased rid-
ers from all over the country. This created a need for tons of footage, and
Friedberg encouraged skaters to send in the footage that they had shot.
If it got used in the video, they would be paid.

Soon the skateboard video began to dominate the culture. Each year
board companies would put out videos, which became integral in establishing their reputations and popularity. After the H Street videos,
Blind Skateboards released an amazing video called *Video Days*, which
featured Mark Gonzales, Jason Lee, Guy Mariano, and others. The video
was shot and edited by Spike Jonze.

Skateboard filming requires a very special combination of artistic
and athletic skills. Filmers must be able to compose shots while riding a
skateboard next to a performing skater. They must be good enough skaters to keep up with the pros, and in some cases come to a screeching
stop right on the precipice of a set of stairs, all the while avoiding the
skater's space and keeping the shot framed up. Filmers also are required
to have a vast knowledge of tricks so as to know what angles are best for
certain tricks, and to make sure skaters don't do tricks that have already
been done. Of course, there are also technical aspects involved that require knowledge of lighting, shutter speed, and the latest technology.
While many skaters become filmers, only the best, like RB Umali, Ty
Evans, and Greg Hunt, actually make a good living. Of course film and
digital video skills easily translate to other industries, including film,
television, and web content.

By the mid-1990s one could go pro as a skater, photographer, or filmer.
RB Umali, a Filipino American who began skating in Houston in the
early 1990s, was a sponsored amateur for Screw Skateboards. However, as
high school began to draw to a close his parents, both actuarial scientists,
convinced him to apply for college. For RB the idea of becoming a full-
time filmer meant that he could continue to skateboard and be creative
without having to constantly risk injury. He used his skate videos (and
excellent SAT scores) to get accepted at NYU Film School, and the move
to New York proved to be one of the best of his life. Today RB is a very
successful skateboard filmmaker with five highly respected skateboard
films to his credit. He now runs his own production company and shoots
skating and music videos as well as other commercial work.

RB Umali: The Filmer's Toolkit

One way to understand skaters' relationship to innovation and technology is to look specifically at the tools that filmers have used to document skating for over 20 years. What follows is an oral history of the technology RB has used throughout his years in skateboarding, ending with a staggering list of his current gear.

> I was crazy into skate videos and skate media and I liked taking still pictures too, and I was like, this is a subject I like and I'm having fun doing it. I never thought it was going be a profession, my parents are mathematicians and I thought I was going to crunch numbers and make money in a boring way like everybody else. And then I was like wait I'm having more fun and making more money filming than I am with my own skateboarding. I ended up taking it more seriously.

Innovations

> I saw a fisheye lens in a magazine and it was like 40 bucks and I talked my parents into getting it for me and I screwed it onto my dad's VHS camera, and I was starting to mimic the H Street videos; once you started seeing how technical the H Street skaters were, you really wanted to progress and show the new tricks that are coming out.
>
> Fisheye lenses are important because you see a wider picture and you can get right up close to the skater, it keeps everything in frame and it makes everything look bigger and faster, especially if you use it in the right way. And it makes the viewer feel like they're right next to the skater. It's also easier to keep steady if you're moving with the camera.
>
> The next big thing was the birth of the video magazine *411VM*, instead of waiting for paper magazines to come in the mail, we would wait for a video to come in the mail, which came out every other month, and they needed content and encouraged kids to send in footage of their local scenes, and by like the fifth issue I was filming for them also. It was a way to see what was going on around the world.
>
> It was started by Josh Friedberg out of Giant Skateboard distribution which owned New Deal Skateboards and Element Skateboards. [Side note: Friedberg is now the executive director of the International Skate-

boarding Federation, the team responsible for negotiating with Tokyo 2020 to have skating in the Olympics.]

In 1992 the Plan B Questionable video came out and I saw that they used a Sony 3 chip, Hi8 camera called the VX-3. We called it "The Terminator," it was silver, and it just looked so tech at the time. And I wound up selling enough copies of the first video I made [*Heads—A World Premiere*] to buy it. I was psyched, I used the money that I made from a video I made my senior year of high school, to buy a Sony VX-3. Kind of like a graduation present for myself.

And then I go to NYU and I'm in New York with the terminator camera. I was already shooting for *411VM* and I had the best video camera at the time and because I had been a sponsored skater, New York skaters were down to shoot with me, and boom, history was made right there.

Digital

Then I got hired by Zoo York to make the *Mixtape Video* and while I was making the mixtape video, my terminator camera started going a little haywire, and Zoo York bought me my first digital video camera which was the Sony VX1000, and I think they were about $5,000. And this was in 1996, right when it came out, it was the first digital video camera with a FireWire port, and the quality wouldn't depreciate when you were editing. You weren't losing resolution when transferring from video tape. (So suffice to say that in part the digital revolution was in editing.)

Side note: Before digital when you were working with tape, each time you edited, you would transfer the original footage from the camera onto a video tape, edit that to a master tape, and from the master tape you'd make copies, so by the time your copy got out there it was a fourth-generation copy. So you're losing a lot of quality. As soon as you went digital you could edit and make multiple copies without losing resolution.

The next innovation that really changed things was when Century Precision Optics released the Ultra Fisheye Adapter, better known as the "death lens." This was probably 1997–1998 and Dan Wolfe was the first to film a trick in a skate video with this lens. It was Jeremy Wray doing a frontside 360 down the Santa Monica Triple Set (1999 *The Element World Tour* video). And the first time you saw this footage you were like, something is different, it's so wide, and there are barely any black corners. Dan had discovered this lens from a small Century Optics advertisement in *Video Maker* magazine and bought it and it was $700 or $800, which was an astronomical amount of money for a skateboard filmer to spend on a lens, and now it's the industry standard.

Century Precision Optics still makes it, but they also make motion picture lenses, so like a little $800 lens is nothing for them, they probably don't even know how much it revolutionized the skateboard industry.

Then HD flat-screen televisions came out, and every skate video was getting either cropped with black bars on the side or the image was getting squeezed. So it was inevitable that we were going to have to start using high definition cameras to fit the aspect ratio of the screen.

High Definition

Panasonic came out with the DVX100 which was the first camera to shoot at 24 frames a second which made it look cinematic, and a lot of filmers were using this camera which was more cinematic but it couldn't capture the fast motion of skating, which requires higher frame rates for smooth slow motion.

I first went to high definition with the Panasonic HVX200, but it only shot at 60 frames per second and only at 720p, which is not full high definition, full high definition is 1920 × 1080p. Soon after that DSLR cameras came into play, and you could shoot video on them. I was the first person to get the Canon 7D which shot at 60 frames per second. And the previous one, the 5D Mark II, was already changing the role of the independent movie maker, by giving a video camera with a full-frame sensor that you could put great lenses on, and it shot well in low light, which the other high definition cameras were terrible with.

As soon as the Canon 7D was announced I preordered it, and I was definitely one of the first people to shoot skateboarding on a DSLR camera, which everyone is using today. And to this day I've been a fan of DSLRs over the big motion picture cameras, partly because I live in New York City and I need to have my kit very compact, because I don't usually have a car, also because the image quality is great at low light, and I'm trying to utilize as much natural light as possible, because I don't want to be lugging lights around.

The Red Camera

Today lots of the high-end filmers shoot with the Red Camera, which shoots at 6k, which is triple the amount of pixels that a regular high definition camera shoots at, which is 2k. But at the end of the day I've always said that it's about your content. And with color correcting I can make footage from a DSLR camera look very comparable to a Red Camera. And that's why I've always vouched for the DSLR kit, because it's a quicker work flow, not only to just pick up the camera and shoot but it's also low-key, and I'm a one-man production team when I'm skating and shooting in the street.

Advances in Editing

The first nonlinear digital video editing program I used after the primitive days of using two VHS VCRs and a Sony Walkman was an editing software from the 1990s known as Media 100. After Media 100, I used an early version of Adobe Premiere. Then Final Cut Pro came out and I used that for many years from FCP 3.0 up until FCP 7.03. Apple then updated Final Cut Pro to Final Cut X about five years ago and ruined the software for a lot of us by removing many of the professional features that Final Cut Pro 7 had. The new Final Cut Pro X also made older versions of the software obsolete, so a lot of us have reverted back to using the current Adobe Premiere software, which is what I am currently editing on.

Explain the Dynamics of Editing: What Were the Computer Requirements of a Filmer?

Back in the day you needed an expensive (preferably a Mac) computer with a lot of external hard drives and extra RAM to make a video. Even with the top of the line G3 or G4 Mac computer it would be really slow and always crash in the middle of editing. These days every low-end laptop comes with editing software, and you can even edit professional video on your iPhone using free apps like iMovie.

HD—How Did This Change Editing?

The introduction of HD video in the skate world changed the process of editing as you needed faster computers and more hard drive space to store your footage. This was also the beginning of showcasing your videos online via YouTube and Vimeo instead of making physical copies on DVD or VHS to send out.

Early Adopter: Explain Your Relationship to Technology

I have always considered myself an early adopter. My father has also always been into technology and has been a regular attendee at the CES (Consumer Electronics) show in Vegas for over 20 years now. He is always bragging to me about the new gadgets he has seen and played with at the show. I guess it has always run in my blood. I have a love and hate relationship with technology. I love having new toys but hate how necessary they have become a part of my everyday life. The fact that I cannot function without a Wi-Fi signal and a charged phone in my pocket is ridiculous. At the end of the day these gadgets are all just tools used to tell your story or to showcase skateboarding, which should not be as important as the subject itself.

What Is Your Current Kit?

Panasonic GH4 Camera with Metabones Speedbooster XL
Sony A7S Camera with Smallrig DSLR Cage
Canon XA30 20x Zoom Lens HD Camera
Eazy Handle Camera Support
Canon 8–15 mm Fisheye Lens
Rokinon 8 mm Fisheye Lens
Tokina 11–20 mm Wide Angle Lens
Canon 24–105 Zoom Lens
Rode Videomic Pro
Sennheiser Wireless Lavalier Mic
Azden Shotgun Mic
Seculine LED On-Camera Light
2 Aputure LED Light Panels with Stands and Batteries

Edelkrone SliderPLUS
Extra Batteries and Memory Cards
GoPro Hero 4 Silver Camera with Tripod Mount
Samsung Gear360 Camera
Sony VX1000 with Century Precision Optics Ultra Fisheye Adapter
Glidecam Devin Graham Signature Model Stabilizer
Beholder DS1 Handheld Gimbal
Defy G2X Gimbal
DJI Phantom 4 Drone
Manfrotto Carbon Fiber Tripod with Fluid Head
Calumet CK7102 4 section Monopod with Manfrotto Quick Release Plate
iPhone 7 Plus
Black Gaffers Tape
Cinebags CB25B Revolution Backpack
Zoo York Skateboard with 60 mm 80a Soft Cruiser Wheels

Mike Marasco's Tool Kit

In California the game is a bit different; in addition to being a skateboard filmmaker, some skate filmers transition their talents outside of the skateboard industry. Mike is currently a one-man production studio. He owns a Red Dragon camera, which is the standard-bearer in digital film. The camera, with lenses, batteries, sound attachments, etc., is worth nearly $50,000. He also has tripods and all the necessary gear to produce, shoot, and edit all types of short films. Today Mike shoots music videos and ads for corporations, and he drives a 2009 Porsche 911 Carrera, an accessory, he says, that is necessary in the Hollywood game, for giving off the impression that he deserves the fees he's charging.

This new model of cinematography birthed by skateboarding, where the director is also an owner/operator of all the equipment, challenges the old Hollywood model of having a director, a cinematographer, and a camera operator. Mike's current job is filming Beyoncé's Formation World Tour.

The Skateboard Team

In addition to all of the folks involved in magazine and video production, there are also numerous careers in the skateboarding industry that have to do with the designing, administering, and selling of skateboards and skateboarding-related products.

On the commodity side of skateboarding are board, shoe, apparel, watch, sunglass, truck, wheel, grip tape, and hardware companies. Of these, boards and shoes are the most lucrative. In the past 10 years, skate shoe companies have begun to compete with the major brands, and since skate shoes are also sold as "lifestyle" sneakers, they produce a lot of revenue, a fact not lost on Nike, Adidas, New Balance, and Converse, who are now making inroads into the business of skateboarding shoes. This has become a big issue within skateboarding as more and more skater-owned businesses cannot afford to pay the biggest riders in the industry to endorse their products, while these larger corporations can.

Still some companies are owned by corporations and sell skateboards in the toy section at Walmart; however, the most successful and influential skateboarding companies are all owned by professional skateboarders. For example, Jamie Thomas owns Zero, Mystery, and Slave Skateboards; Rick Howard, Mike Carroll, and Spike Jonze own Girl Skateboards and Chocolate Skateboards; Andrew Reynolds owns Baker Skateboards; Jim Greco and Eric Ellington own Bakerboys Distribution; Stevie Williams owns a portion of DGK Skateboards; and Ed Templeton owns Toy Machine. These skaters also own shoe, clothing, truck, and in some cases distribution companies.

There are however some companies that are owned outright by large corporations. Zoo York, for example, is owned by Iconix Brands, which also owns 32 other lifestyle brands including Joe Boxer, Danskin, Ecko, and Ed Hardy.

The model of the skateboarding industry is one known by every skater. The distribution companies, like Dwindle, Crailtrap, Diamond Supply Co., and Bakerboys Distribution Company, are umbrella companies under which other brands—of boards, shoes, clothes, and other accessories—are sold. For example, Kayo distribution owns and distributes DGK, Element-One, and Organika skateboards and Gold wheels.

One of the most successful skate company owners is Jamie Thomas, who is referred to by his peers as "The Chief," as in chief executive officer. Thomas was a top pro for Ed Templeton's company Toy Machine in the 1990s and later went on to start his own company. Today Jamie owns Black Box Distribution, which includes Zero Skateboards, Mystery Skateboards, Slave Skateboards, and Fallen Footwear. Black Box Distribution has 160 employees and a 120,000-square-foot warehouse in Carlsbad, California. The company has grown 200 percent during the past seven years, and in 2006 he was awarded Ernst & Young's entrepreneur of the year for San Diego County.[8] In 2014 however he sold his two major brands, Zero and Mystery, to Dwindle Distribution.[9]

Skateboarders retain ownership in their companies' distribution and media, and in doing so they create opportunities for themselves in the form of subculture careers and for future skaters by providing a subcultural enclave for skaters to flock to. This subcultural activity constitutes so much more than simply riding a skateboard, illegally, on a city street. Professional street skateboarders are engaged in the process of producing content (tricks) for the various subculture media outlets, which provides opportunities not only for skaters who are talented enough to accept the challenge of progression but also for many young people who flock to California in the hopes of making a career out of something they love. The skateboarding subculture has provided California with a ton of talented people who have impacted the state culturally, economically, and even politically, at least on the local level. While an economic impact study is beyond the scope of this book, it is clear that skateboarding is significant in ways that are rarely considered. This is clearly big business.

6

Skateboarding as a Career

The City and the Subculture Career

Skateboarding as a culture advances and codifies the idea of the subculture career, by both fixing it to a place and also honing the practices that make subculture participation profitable. The role that skateboarding plays in attracting skaters to cities like Los Angeles, San Diego, and San Francisco to participate in the skateboard industry and to skate the most famous spots sheds light on some of the more classic theories of the role subcultures play in the city. Early urban sociology bemoaned the city for its break with pastoral idealism, where farm and family made for close personal bonds and supposedly emotionally rich, happy lives. The city tore those ties asunder, and the costs, according to theorists of the decline of community like sociologist Louis Wirth, would lead to depravity and social disorganization, making cities dangerous, scary places. In his 1975 article "A Subculture Theory of Urbanism," Claude Fischer dispelled Chicago School sociologist Wirth's notion that citizens in large, dense, diverse populations no longer had emotional connections to each other, as they once did in the rural countryside.[1] For Wirth, the lack of close, emotional social interaction made cities scary, lonely places, with high levels of social disorganization and crime. Wirth suggested that the modern city produced extensive urban anomie, a concept he borrowed from founding sociologist Émile Durkheim that suggests a dearth of social solidarity.

Following Georg Simmel, Fischer recognized that releasing individuals from the conformist pressures of the small town might have a positive impact. The city may cause some form of estrangement, but Fischer argued that this "estrangement permits people in the city to spin the wildest fantasies and to act upon those fantasies whether they result in feats of genius or deeds of crime and depravity."[2] Urban ethnographers showed that in some form or another, community existed in many places and in vastly different forms and could be used to debunk the anomic myth of the city. Chicago School ethnographies showed that urbanites, even deviant ones, had lots of personal ties and felt connected to something larger than themselves.[3]

Fischer argued instead that "the more urban a place, the more intense its subcultures."[4] He challenged the notion that large, metropolitan cities lead to individual atomization and increased levels of individual anomie (deep feelings of exclusion) and showed that large populations produce diversity, which results in greater numbers of subcultures with higher levels of subcultural intensity. He also understood that when subcultures become large enough to achieve a "critical mass," it allows for the emergence of a subculture career, although Fischer did not use that term. When the subculture achieves "critical mass," the members act as both consumers and creators of subcultural content. "Sufficient numbers allow them to support institutions—clubs, newspapers, and specialized stores for example—that serve the group; allow them to have a visible and affirmed identity, to act together on their own behalf, and to interact extensively with each other."[5]

Fischer and others defined subcultures as those smaller cultural groups that exist within a larger cultural setting.[6] Cities were a "mosaic of subcultural worlds," which included not only deviant groups, but all groups that exhibit some sort of common interest and shared worldview, like youth cultures, professional organizations, and ethnic groups. This way of looking at subculture as an outgrowth of population increases, internal immigration, and folks' shared specificity of interests failed to generate much interest in post-1960s American sociology.

Even though many American urban sociologists have accepted Fischer's ideas as a counter to urban anomie, few have asked whether and how subcultures matter to cities beyond individual psychology. The influence of the Birmingham School essentially stopped the discussion surrounding subculture and cities that Fischer had begun.

What impact do subcultures have on the makeup of a city, and how does their success and popularity attract others? Certainly sociologists and others know that New York City Latinos differ from those in LA, or that Detroit has a large Muslim population and that Boston has the Irish. Each one of these groups is an essential component to its city and contributes culturally, politically, and economically to the life of that city, and thus draws future generations of those groups to the city. And, just as it would be difficult to imagine New York City without Puerto

Ricans or Los Angeles without Mexicans, it would be equally difficult to imagine San Francisco without hippies, Seattle without grunge rockers, New York City without punk rock, hip-hop, or graffiti, and Los Angeles without skateboarding.

The subcultures that exist in a particular city matter in ways that are often neglected or ignored by politicians and scholars alike. Today when many young people think about their futures and where they want to live, the subcultures they identify with is often a key factor in drawing them to a particular place.

One example of the way in which skateboarding draws talented people from different parts of the country to cities where the industry flourishes is the case of Atiba Jefferson and his twin brother Ako. Atiba and Ako grew up skateboarding in a section of Colorado Springs, Colorado, called Acacia Springs. In the late 1990s when they were 18 years old, they loaded up a U-Haul and moved to San Diego. They arrived with no jobs, but they knew skateboarders and skateboarding and thus looked to the subculture for survival. Ako used the graphic design skills he learned from making a zine to get a job assisting Tim Newhouse, then art director at *Transworld* magazine. Soon Atiba convinced skate photographer Grant Brittain to let him assist in the office. Now the twins had jobs and mentors. It was not long before Atiba, with his newfound access to film, was displaying his skill with the camera and began publishing more and more photos in the magazine, and he soon became a staff photographer for *Transworld*. He rapidly became one of the most respected young photographers of his generation, and today he is the photo editor for *The Skateboard Mag*, and his brother Ako is the art director.

Subcultural Enclaves

One way to think about how subcultures attract talent and sustain a presence in American cities is to borrow from some of the work done in immigration studies by urban sociologist Roger Waldinger.[7] He has shown that the persistence and success of specific ethnic groups in the United States depend upon a group's ability to develop an economic enclave or niche in a specific sector of the economy. This niche then creates opportunities for other coethnics. Opportunity for individual immigrants comes not from how quickly they can assimilate into the mainstream, but from how entrenched and cohesive their particular ethnic group is in the urban economy. Waldinger calls these cohesive immigrant groups "ethnic enclaves," and his studies of Irish firemen, Eastern European Jewish tailors, African American health care workers, and Korean grocers suggest that it is cultural retention, not individual assimilation, that creates opportunity and social mobility for immigrant populations.

Ethnic enclaves are a key factor contributing to upward social mobility of a particular group and explain why that group draws more and more people from the home country, creating not only strong personal ties, but also opportunity for more and more newcomers.

Just as the ability to speak Korean and having connections in the produce industry are helpful for newly arriving immigrants in New York, the ability to skateboard and all of the requisite knowledge the subculture requires are helpful for a newcomer to Los Angeles or San Diego. Subcultures like skateboarding create self-sustaining enclaves that attract more and more people to a city to capitalize on the opportunities that the subculture creates. While it's well-known that Hollywood attracts talent to LA, skateboarders from around the world have moved to Los Angeles, and other California cities, to skateboard the famous spots and to hopefully participate in the industry. There are approximately 50 board companies, each of which has on average 10 pros and 5 ams. Of these 500 or so professional skateboarders, half struggle to make a living, while the riders at the very top are millionaires. The subculture nurtures career opportunities and helps some individuals achieve economic self-sufficiency, and this means that despite all the negative attention that skating receives, it plays a significant role in the California economy by drawing people to the state.

Subcultures are critically important for understanding cities, and yet aside from the work done by Fischer (1975) and Fine and Kleinman (1979), US subcultures have received very little attention from urban sociologists. One of the reasons that subcultures matter to cities is because those that exist in a particular city influence many young people's career and living choices. Even though sociologist Sharon Zukin does not describe these groups as subcultures, she has shown that certain groups of young people, specifically artists and foodies, many of whom grew up in suburbs and are college-educated, are drawn to cities to take part in something that fuels their interests and imaginations.[8] In his book on bike messengers, Jeffrey Kidder describes the ways in which the bicycle messenger scenes in New York, San Francisco, and Portland draw bicycle enthusiasts from all over the world to work and play on the streets of major American cities.[9] Similarly, I have shown that graffiti writers from all over the country gravitate to New York City to participate in the subculture.[10]

While most scholars agree that spatial disadvantage and diminishing public space decrease both life chances and democratic freedoms, skateboarders have discovered spatial advantage in less conventional ways, where spaces that are good for skateboarding provide opportunity to progress the discipline of skateboarding and, in many cases, make money. Professional street skateboarders (along with graffiti writers, bike messengers, and parkour practitioners) use city spaces in unintended, creative ways that are transgressive, but also allow them to make lives for themselves.

Graffiti writers, bike messengers, and skateboarders all look at urban architecture from a different, more creative perspective. Ferrell and Weide, in their excellent article "Spot Theory," have shown that graffiti writers choose spots to write by employing a sophisticated understanding of the spot's meaning to the subculture, and to the city at large.[11] Similarly, skaters are constantly on the lookout for spaces that can be skated or be manipulated to allow for skateboarding.

Since the point of street skateboarding is that it can be done anywhere, it seems a little odd to argue that skateboarding could be so attached to a specific place. However, San Francisco, Los Angeles, and San Diego continue to be the centers of the skateboarding world because they are home to the most famous spots, the weather allows year-round skating, and the spots don't change too much over the years, so they act as a sort of proving ground for younger skaters and have become part of the history of the subculture.[12]

The Model of Subculture Profitability

The spatial activities of subcultures that use public space for their own creative and financial reward, which include graffiti writers, parkour traceurs,[13] bike messengers, and skateboarders, have received relatively scant attention from scholars who study resistant activity in public space.[14] Sociologists of sport who have studied skateboarding describe it as a site of masculine identity formation and treat skateboarding as an "alternative" or "action" sport in which professional skateboarders compete in contests for prize money. This model treats skateboarding simply as an individual sport based on freedom and creative expression. In the view of sociologist of sport Becky Beal and her colleague Belinda Wheaton, casual skateboarders (and surfers) gain subcultural "authenticity" not from actual board skills, but from reading the skateboard magazines and learning the language, which inspires a "real" subculture identity, as opposed to an inauthentic identity proffered by mainstream media and corporations not affiliated with skateboarding.[15]

While this mainstream view of skateboarding is not wholly incorrect, it is not how the practice of professional skateboarding actually operates. Professional street skaters would consider it false to be merely "contest skaters." While skaters who do well in skate contests will likely be well compensated, their contest winnings must be supplemented by video parts in order to ensure their reputations. Skateboarding contests are about performing the tricks you know you can land; for a video part skaters push themselves to do the most creative, most challenging tricks they can imagine. Hence a skater's reputation comes more so from the tricks that he produces on film and video. The most prestigious and successful professional street skaters produce "video parts" and get magazine coverage of their tricks on existing elements of urban architecture. Said another way, even though it is possible for very talented skaters to make a good living from skating contests and representing their various brands, if they don't produce video parts, the skateboarding community will not recognize their efforts as contributing to the progression of skating. Case in point, the first video part for Ryan Sheckler since he was a kid was his part in *Plan B: True* (2014, dir. Erik Bragg) and it *was* highly regarded and solidified his reputation as one of the gnarliest skaters in the world. (Although his part was largely a coronation for past achievements, that same video crowned a new king, in Chris Joslin.)

Without the documentation of skateboarding tricks disseminated through subculture media, it is tempting to interpret skateboarding as a risky act of spatial appropriation with significant political implications, as Borden's insightful work makes clear.[16] However to focus solely on symbolic resistance would be to miss out on the fact that subcultures sustain themselves through what McRobbie called their inherent "entrepreneurial infrastructure."[17] When Hall and Jefferson wrote in *Resistance through Rituals* that there were "no subculture careers," they were bemoaning the tragedy of subculture participation whose resistance they felt was merely symbolic. They held that symbolic resistance was essentially pointless if it didn't change your life. But even as they wrote those words, punk groups like the Clash were singing about the dearth of legitimate "career opportunities," which actually showed young people a way out and inspired them to find alternative ways to turn their play into work. For top-level skaters, skateboarding is something far more important than youthful mischief, as it provides an opportunity for a legitimate adult career. And because you can make a living out of it, many people are inspired to make skateboarding their lives. Even for those who don't make skating their lives, skateboarding can be a great teacher, especially for filmmakers and photographers, as evidenced by the careers of RB Umali and Atiba Jefferson, which include documenting skateboarders as well as making films and videos for other outlets. (Atiba has directed videos for the bands TV on the Radio and Dinosaur Jr.)

The contemporary model of subculture profitability uses digitally documented evidence, disseminated to a worldwide audience, to increase one's subcultural reputation, which is then translated into real capital both inside and sometimes outside of the subculture itself. Skateboarders pioneered this model early in their history, and it has since been borrowed by almost every other subculture of note since the digital turn.

Skaters began to utilize this model of profitability in the late 1980s when VHS video cameras became a staple of middle-class homes, but today with the ubiquity of digital recording devices and the Internet, the amount of illegal subcultural activity posted on the Internet is overwhelming. In addition to graffiti writers, street artists, skaters, BMX bikers, and the like, there are also numerous subcultures that involve using public streets to race and perform stunts. Urban motocross riders, street stunt bikers, as well as a huge contingent of illegal drag racers can all be found online with a simple search.[18] And each of these groups engages in the same set of media practices established by skaters. However, rather than making magazines and distributing videos to skate shops all over the world, these groups all use social media and YouTube and other sites to garner subcultural fame.

The model is generally the same for all of these groups. Do something illegal and exciting, record it, post it, get fame, translate fame into fortune. Once a fortune is made, travel, expand your reach, get more fame, get more money. Don't get caught. Go legit, bank on street cred. Make money doing what you love. Repeat. Enjoy. Obviously this is much harder in practice, but the basics remain the same.[19]

As Pierre Bourdieu explained with respect to subfields, producers produce for other producers to consume, not for the general public at large. Or as I've been saying throughout this book, contemporary subcultures have folks who are both producers and consumers of subcultural content. Bourdieu believed that in these realms of "restricted production" products were imbued with "symbolic capital." Here is where I depart and suggest that items invested with symbolic capital, which is to say that those in possession of subcultural capital, can turn this capital into actual capital.

The Ethnographic Imagination

Skateboarding creates commodities that are sold in the market and make a lot of money for people who are not skaters. On 13th and Broadway in New York City, next door to NYU Press, and in malls around the country, there is a Zumiez, one of the biggest retail outlets in the country, devoted to selling skateboard and surfing brands. On their website they describe themselves as "a leading multi-channel retailer of action sports related apparel, footwear, hardgoods and accessories."[20]

While anyone can purchase these commodities and look like a "skater," they will not be part of the community of skateboarding subculture if they cannot skate. This means that even though the products sold by Zumiez are commodities that may lead to the co-optation of a subculture, the way in which those products are used potentially leads to the creation of culture, and thus the community and solidarity fostered by those skateboarding commodities are also real.

As Paul Willis articulates in *The Ethnographic Imagination*, subcultural commodities are complicated by the fact that they are a function of both fetishism and in his words "de-fetishism."[21] There is the thing itself, which comes out of a capitalist system designed to reap profits from products invested with subcultural cache, and yet these "products" are also supported by an actual community of skaters who continue to imbue these products with new meaning.

A good mainstream example of this tension between commodity and community is exemplified by the case of the National Football League's Green Bay Packers, the only sports franchise in the world not organized as a for-profit corporation. Nonetheless, Packer fans are an established demographic who provide the franchise and the NFL with a deliverable audience ready to spend and to consume and keep consuming. Recently, the Packers, who are owned by the city of Green Bay, Wisconsin, needed to raise money, so they held a "stock" offering, where fans could purchase "shares" of Packer stock for $250, but the value of the stock was purely symbolic. It had no value beyond the paper it was printed on, and clearly this is an undisguised effort on the part of the board of directors (they don't have an owner) to raise money by exploiting the people's special relationship to their team. For the stockholders the fake stock has worth in the very fact of monetary worthlessness; it has no value other than as a symbol of one's fandom, a highly abstract and individualized act of community making. It is fake and real, fake as a stock, but real as a symbol and thus worth more than its exchange value, which is effectively nothing. But to say that Packer stock is worthless would smack of sacrilege to a Packer stockholder, and the community that people share as a result of this investment in pure symbol is real.

This complexity goes far beyond the simplistic assessment that subculturalists and fans are mere dupes of the profit machine. Willis's main argument is that it requires an ethnographic imagination to understand the nuances involved in how groups "use" the stuff they're given. From teddy boy bricolage to worthless Packer stock and specific skateboard brands, the meaning making of the group is a creative act of culture making even as it reproduces the capitalistic fetish, although *not* as it was originally intended.

Many would respond that it doesn't matter how consumers consume; their consumption is proof of their co-optation. This was the conclusion of the Birmingham School with the added notion that capitalists would figure out how to sell the commodity in its new form to an even greater number of people. But punks understand this, as do graffiti careerists and pro skaters; yes, their subcultural work is exploited and sold as a commodity, but the subculture as a real group of people in the process of constantly creating culture, as Willis suggests, remains and persists over time, thus strengthening the bonds of subcultural members and reinforcing their community and thus their political and social power. The subculture career exists on numerous levels simultaneously; it is both fake and real, co-optation and creation in the service of resistance and capitalistic persistence. The rub is in the tiny way that lives are made, material and otherwise.

Willis uses the term "symbolic work" to describe how people expand the use value of an object, which makes it culturally more useful, and "decreases the fetishization of the commodity."[22] Symbolic work in this case is an authentic practice of appropriation. Here there might be blissful recognition rather than ignorance: "I can't believe they actually pay me for this." And while it is true this is certainly a slippery slope, it is nevertheless one that subculturalists have made for themselves.

While Willis talks about "creative consumption," subcultures are also engaged in creative production (documented skateboard tricks, photos of graffiti pieces), which then becomes a commodity that other subculture participants creatively consume. Only ethnographic inquiry into the lives of subculture practitioners can reveal the both/and nature of these practices. This is not to say that the subculture career escapes the traps of commodity fetishism, but ethnography, as Willis argues, offers a more complete descriptive picture of how people's everyday lives are filled with acts of "symbolic creativity."[23]

Subculture Media and the Digital Turn

The subculture of skateboarders has one of the most highly developed and professionalized media, where former skaters make very successful careers from their ability to artfully document the form. Some skateboard photographers, like Spike Jonze, have gone on to become Oscar-winning filmmakers. The list of skaters who have achieved great success both inside and outside of skateboarding subculture as successful musicians, artists, and actors is long: Jason Lee, Mike McGill, Thomas Campbell, Tommy Guerrero, Matt Hensley, just to name a few.

Skateboarders' use of media makes technically illegal public performances of skateboarding tricks profitable. Skaters find places to perform tricks, photographers and videographers document it, and the edited content appears in magazines, on DVDs, on iTunes, and on the web; the tricks are then viewed and consumed by the rest of the subculture, thus adding to a skater's subcultural capital, which translates into real capital in terms of board sales and more sponsorship dollars. It is important to note here that skaters in general do not profit directly from the dissemination of their tricks; the published material increases their reputations, which can lead to increased sponsorship and hence greater profits, although this model is changing. Where formerly the skateboard brands reaped the monies from a skateboard video, now skaters are beginning to release individual videos available for download on iTunes, and the money gets divided between the skater and the sponsor.

Skateboard media are not simply about profit but are essential for the continued progression of the subculture. Even though pro skaters do not buy skateboard products, they do consume skateboard media, perhaps more so than the casual skater whose career isn't premised upon keeping abreast of the latest achievements. Subculture media are essential for pro skaters to keep up with the visual literature of their subculture, as skaters, like academics, must publish or perish, what skaters call "getting coverage."

In the context of subculture media, it is helpful to distinguish between the casual consumer and the active consumer. Recreational skaters read the magazines because they like to keep up with the latest tricks and read about the accomplishments of the top pros. Professional skaters, on the other hand, are active consumers of skateboarding magazines. They read or decode skateboarding feats with the intent of producing original skateboarding tricks themselves, so that they too can be in the magazines, and thus contribute to the discussion of what makes for great skateboarding.

This model is similar to the craft of scholarship. Academics read scholarly journals and books in the context of their discipline in an effort to improve their own research and to contextualize their work within the literature. We read so that we can write, in an effort to contribute to the important discussions taking place within the discipline. Skaters read magazines so that they can contribute to the progression of skating.

In addition to the salaries they receive from their sponsors, pro skaters receive royalties from the sale of their signature boards and shoes. They also often receive a small amount of their income from subculture media directly. Sponsors provide their riders with "photo incentives," which are cash payouts for the number of pages of "coverage" they receive in the four main skateboard magazines in which a sponsor's logo can be clearly identified.[24]

The editorial content of a skateboard magazine usually comprises an interview along with a number of tricks. Skaters will also shoot tricks with photographers to use as ads, which the board, shoe, and other companies pay to put in the magazine but are critical for establishing a skater's reputation. For magazine readers, therefore, advertisements are just as important as the editorial content because they often showcase a rider's most important accomplishments. The ads are also often used as teasers to show what can be expected from a forthcoming skateboard film, which are simply called "videos."

In essence one could also say that all professionally documented street skating is advertising. Whether tricks are used explicitly in advertisements or not, every skateboarding trick riders put out is intended to increase their reputation and hence their "brand." Skaters themselves are aware of this dirty little secret and editorialize often that the best skating is motivated by passion and the challenge of progression, rather than mere money.

Pay Scales

Skateboard "filmers" (videographers) get paid by the companies that are putting up the budget for the video. Top filmers usually have deals with specific companies in which they are paid salaries to shoot the team's riders. In addition to shooting skateboarding, filmers are usually also video editors, from which they earn additional income. For example, RB Umali is a very successful skateboard filmmaker with five highly respected skateboard films to his credit. He has also earned a yearly salary from both Zoo York Skateboards and Red Bull to film their skateboarders. More recently RB is expanding his reach by starting his own production company, which will focus on skateboarding but also other video content.

Skateboard photographers get paid by the magazines when their photos are used as editorial content and by the skate companies when their photos are used as ads. The best photographers also work directly for the magazines as photo editors and play a major role in selecting content. For example, Atiba Jefferson is one of the most sought-after skateboard photographers, in addition to being a founding member of *The Skateboard Mag* and its current photo editor. Atiba also shoots the NBA for *Slam Magazine*, in addition to numerous other well-known brands.

The Vulnerable Careerists

Yet despite all of these efforts, the subculture career should not be seen as a solution to any of the real problems that young people face. Such careers tend to be in fields in which there is often no health care and very little job security. Many people work freelance as independent contractors, and yet in many ways these are the careers young folks actually want.

Since the 1950s commentators on economic life have focused attention not only on the alienation of the laborer, but also on the alienation, despair, and dissatisfaction of managers. C. Wright Mills's "white collar men" led lives of quiet desperation, in which their own individual wills, imaginations, and intellects were subsumed by bureaucracies and the ethos of the group. In *The Power Elite*, he expanded his critique to include corporate executives, offering a scathing account of the type of conformity necessary for executive success. He writes:

> Be the tolerant Maybe-man and they will cluster around you, filled with hopefulness. Practice softening the facts into the optimistic, practical, forward-looking, cordial, brink, view. Speak to the well-blunted point. Have weight; be stable: caricature what you are supposed to be but never become aware of it much less amused by it. And never let your brains show.[25]

Many young people today seek a career where they can utilize aspects of themselves that facilitate some affirmation of their identities, one that they may have cultivated through youth subculture participation. In part, this is because the dream of a company job, with good health care, stability, and a clearly defined corporate ladder to climb, has in many ways vanished.[26] The guarantee that a well-paying, rewarding job awaits those who play by the rules and excel in school is becoming a thing of the past. The glaring inequality that exists in the United States today has impacted the less fortunate extremely hard, leaving folks with few opportunities and crushing student loans.

More and more the rewards for going mainstream seem mythical, and as a result, subculture participation, and the promise of working in a competitive field one enjoys, becomes a way of finding oneself and like-minded others. This tends to be the case in music, fashion, graffiti, and skateboarding.[27] Careers in these fields are highly competitive and draw many people from all over the world, and while many fail, those who succeed inspire others to keep trying.

In most cases the training for subcultural careers comes from a series of mentoring relationships, and DIY motivation that occurs entirely within the subculture. But even for those who don't succeed, the training provided by the subculture can often be utilized in other industries. This is clearly the case with skateboarding. Because skating relies so much on documentation, skaters are incredibly familiar with filming and being filmed, and in many cases this experience can be transitioned into other industries. Many skaters are able to work in film and television production as actors, camera operators, editors, stuntmen, and even directors.

But careers in subcultures that foster creativity might not be all that they're cracked up to be. McRobbie, in her 2002 article "Clubs to Companies: Notes on the Decline of Political Culture in Speeded Up Creative Worlds," argues that these careers, while offering fulfillment, also make young people more atomized and depoliticized and thus more vulnerable to the cruelties of capitalism. McRobbie's study of what she calls the "cultural sector" of the UK economy, which includes fashion, film, and other creative careers, shows that the turn toward creative cultural work has undergone a process of individualization where young people seek jobs they hope will be fulfilling, contribute to their sense of self, and "pre-empt the conscription into 9–5 dullness."[28] I would argue however that successful subculturalists are beginning to understand that they may indeed have some political clout.

McRobbie believes that young people are paying a significant price for this fulfillment. She argues that the transition away from a workplace of class solidarity and toward a self-fulfilling and ultimately self-exploiting individual creative career makes young people more vulnerable to the brutalities of capitalism. This is the case with many in the skateboard industry, who work as independent contractors, receive no health benefits, and skate with the knowledge that one injury could mean a mountain of debt. Only a small percentage of pro skaters make enough money to have a comfortable retirement, but professional skateboarding also teaches a set of what McRobbie calls "transferable skills."[29] Many therefore spend their late 30s trying to figure out how to remain part of skating sub-culture after they're done skating, which provides an infrastructure of current and former skaters, creating an industry of extremely talented and creative people, all of whom share one thing in common above all else—a commitment to skateboarding.

PART III

Skate Spots

7

Skateboarding and Architecture

Skaters' Response to Defensive Design

Skaters have responded to their diminishing spaces in numerous ways. In some instances, they've simply moved to a different city. Philadelphia, for example, was once a thriving skate city that nourished the bourgeoning careers of some of the best skaters in the world, including Ricky Oyola, Josh Kalis, and Stevie Williams, as well as Chris Cole, Tom Asta, and Ishod Wair. Philly's prominence was due mainly to the John F. Kennedy Plaza, better known as Love Park because of the famous sculpture by Robert Indiana. This plaza, through complete accident, was, according to skaters, absolutely perfect for skating, and when the skaters discovered it in the mid-1990s, Philly displaced New York and Washington, D.C., as the hub of East Coast skating. However, in 2004, exactly one year after hosting and profiting from the X Games, the city decided that skateboarding would no longer be allowed at Love Park, and anyone caught skating would be ticketed and threatened with jail. As a result, professional skateboarders, along with filmers, photographers, board companies, and designers, all moved away, leaving only a small number of skaters.

Richard Florida's concept of the "creative class," while problematic in many ways, is a good tool to understand how a thriving skate scene helps a city.[1] According to Florida new economic urban growth is fueled by an ever-expanding group of people who do creative work on their own terms. These folks are entrepreneurial by nature, and thus a city that caters to the needs of creative folks (in Florida's case this means bike paths and a music scene) will draw the most creative talent, and thus thrive. Florida never really defines the creative class as a class per se, meaning a group with similar economic power, nor does he think about subcultures or the role of race and diversity. However, despite the many conceptual problems with Florida's work, it is easy to see how a city with a thriving skate scene contributes to the economy when we start to understand all of the productive creativity that accompanies the documentation, dissemination, design, and distribution of skateboarding content and products. When skaters are not allowed to skate they leave, taking all of their young, creative, and entrepreneurial talent with them.

Conversely, when skaters are allowed to skate in public space, not only do they have a place that allows them to creatively progress skating, but this act produces a ripple effect of creativity and profit. When the trick is completed and the skating at the spot stops, the work does not end. When a professional skater is performing a trick, there is a filmer documenting it; the filmer then has to edit the video, add graphics, and deliver it to the website developer, who puts it on the site. Skateboarding in public space contributes to the economy in significant ways that most folks do not realize; it is, according to Ocean Howell, its own "circuit of capital."[2]

Many professional skaters have dealt with the crisis of diminishing spaces by going global. While many skaters live in LA or other areas on the West Coast, they travel the world in search of spots where they can skate and film skateboard tricks. Barcelona and other parts of Europe are extremely popular, as is Japan, and now skateboarders are intensely exploring the newly built cities in China and Dubai.[3]

Skaters have also been forced to get creative with respect to when and how they skate. Very often they will simply remove the anti-skate devices that have been put in their way. They use cordless saws and other power tools to return the spot to its original form. And they also fix spots by repairing cracks in the concrete with a product called Bondo, traditionally used in car body repair.

Night skating has also become one of the ways to skate high-traffic spots. Skaters arrive with generators and huge lights and skate until the cops come. Skaters have also been forced to seek more and more marginalized spaces where they engage in acts of guerilla architecture, or "concrete activism," to create their own skate spots.

Finally, skaters have also become urban activists, advocating on behalf of skaters for spots that they can actually skate. In New York, Steve Rodriguez, who owns 5 Boro Skateboards, went to community meetings and got the city to leave the Brooklyn Banks, a famous spot underneath the Brooklyn Bridge, open to skaters, and he and others such as Billy Rohan have set up all sorts of projects to get kids skating and provide access to what the folks at *Open Road* call "public art you can play with."[4]

In the past skate parks were designed as a place to put skaters and keep them away from the public. Architect Chihsin Chiu argues that street skating transgresses public boundaries, whereas park skating is about conforming to spatial and behavioral codes.[5] Howell writes that often these skate parks came with some sort of moral imperative, on the "right" way to behave, but the real problem according to skaters was that their design was bad.[6] None of the obstacles were things that contemporary street skaters actually skated, and professional skaters cannot film tricks at skate parks; it must be done in the streets. Today, skate plazas have improved tremendously, and they often reproduce those unintended aspects of architectural design that are good for skating. These design elements have names based upon their original location. A good skate plaza will have manual pads, which are similar to the stage at the West LA Courthouse, DWP-type marble ledges, Love Park granite, hubbas, pier 7s, a big 4, a Hollywood 10, a Rincon rail, a UC Irvine rail, and possibility even a Carlsbad-type gap, to name a few. It will feature some of the best skate architecture from around the world, but to the general public it will not appear to be specifically for skating, but a little plaza for rest and relaxation. These spots make a city attractive to skateboarders and serve as a destination spot for skaters all over the world. As stated, Stoner Park has become such an attraction that skaters are moving to West LA so they will have a place to practice, even if they have to live in their van.[7]

Resisting Arrest

Skateboarding enjoys worldwide popularity, and in many cases approaches mainstream acceptance, yet professional street skaters are frequently policed out of urban public spaces. In most cities in California, and other states as well, skateboarding is illegal, and many skaters have experienced various forms of mild and not so mild police harassment.[8] As a result, pro skaters are engaged in a set of practices to resist arrest for the purpose of progressing their skateboarding careers. These practices include reconstructing spaces to remove anti-skate devices, using cinematic lights to make spaces skateable in the dark of the night, engaging in guerilla architecture by creating their own spots, and most frequently casing a spot, figuring out the best time to make an attempt and complete a trick before the cops come.[9]

Some skaters, frustrated with the constant harassment, have simply made their own spots to skate. In secret locations skateboarders engage in DIY architecture, or what architecture critic Jeffrey Hou calls "Guerrilla Urbanism," in which folks reappropriate space in unintended ways.[10]

The complex network of freeways and other roads in Los Angeles creates an abundance of serendipitous opportunities for skaters in the spaces underneath overpasses. These spaces have no intended purpose other than as support structures for the roadway above them, and they are optimal locations for skaters looking to build their own spots (see the discussion of DIY spots below).

While it is illegal to skateboard in the entire state of California, not every session has the possibility of police activity. Skaters find out-of-the-way spots, where they can often skate for hours without hassle. This is the case with lots of California schools, which on the weekends are great skate spots, and most of the time free of cops. In these instances skaters might try to learn new tricks, which may require multiple attempts.

However, in many spots, time is not on the skaters' side. For some spots they have to accept the fact that the cops are going to come and that they'll be harassed and kicked out. So they set up and skate until they get kicked out, and they keep returning until the trick is complete. (Imagine if this was part of your job.)

DIY Urban Design

In the beginning of the 2000s, cities began to crack down more and more and many skaters found it increasingly difficult to skateboard in public spaces and thus began to seek out unused urban spaces. Many of the top pros who could afford it created their own indoor parks. Skateboarders searched the city for abandoned, underused spaces, which they might transform into skateboarding spaces through acts of guerilla architecture to remake a space to suit their needs.

One of the first of these skater-produced parks is under the Burnside Bridge in Portland, Oregon. Here, in the mid-1990s, skaters transformed what was once a classic junkie hangout into a concrete playground with deep bowls and ledges for skateboarding. At first, this concrete activism was transgressive, but when Portland authorities came to understand how well skaters' "eyes in the space" kept the seedier elements away from under the bridge, they gave Burnside their blessing, which is also why it remains the most famous.[11]

DIY Skate Spots: Fixer Uppers

One of the most common procedures that skaters employ to fix cracks in the "run-up" or approach to an obstacle is to use a product called Bondo. This car repair product became a staple of the skater's toolkit in the late 1990s. Sometimes a perfect rail will have a crack in the road or sidewalk leading up to it, which makes it unskateable. In these instances a skater will whip up a little Bondo and in only 15 minutes the spot can be ready to skate.

This was the case with the famous tennis court rail in LA, also known as the Owen Wilson Rail because of a skit in the 2003 video *Yeah Right.*[12] Today the rail is knobbed and can no longer be skated, but the evidence of its history is not on the rail, which is three inches in diameter, goes down nine stairs, is extremely sturdy, and exhibits no more than normal wear. The evidence is on the ground. There is a pinkish substance about 18 inches long by 4 inches wide covering a crack right before the rail.

What is also interesting to skate archaeologists is that when the rail became unusable, a different section of the ground was repaired with Bondo to allow skaters another level of creativity and a different part of the obstacle to skate. A close reading of the Bondo and the various elements designed to prevent skateboarding reveals the ongoing battle between skaters and agents of social control. Incidentally, the Bondo comes first, followed by skaters who come to get tricks; this gets the attention of authorities, who then add skate stoppers; the skaters then add more Bondo to skate the obstacle a different way, which then leads to more skate stoppers. The Bondo is the only thing remaining to suggest that this spot was once very famous in the skate subculture and tells the story of skaters being creative not only with the tricks they perform, but also with how they alter a space.

Over the course of this research we've been studying the Radisson Banks, in Culver City, California, to assess how a spot changes and progresses over time. This spot originally became famous in Natas Kaupas's

Tennis court rail with Bondo. Photo: Gregory Snyder.

video part for *Streets on Fire* in 1989. This was one of the first spots I photographed in 2008, and we've been returning every year to check on its continual evolution.

***

On this day in the summer of 2014, our view is obstructed by twelve-foot-high stacks of mattresses and dressers that are being discarded as part of the demolition of the Radisson hotel that will soon become a new hotel.

We climb over some dressers and are face-to-face with an ongoing slab of skateboarding history that I've come to feel a connection to. We notice that the spot has been transformed once again to allow for more skating progression. There is a bar that has been moved from the top of the fence to a position about two feet above the top of the bank, making it possible now to launch from the bank and grind the rail. Aaron is puzzled: was this here before? We look closer and upon critical inspection see the less discolored area of the metal fence post where the crossbar used to rest. This means someone came with wrenches to unbolt the bar and slide it down and then re-secure it in place. There are also shoelaces tied to the fence to keep it out of the skaters' way. (Shoelaces are an ubiquitous multipurpose item in skating, as skaters' shoelaces get worn out quickly from the grip tape. Thus every pair of skate shoes comes with multiple pairs of shoelaces, and skaters find many ways to repurpose them, including as belts.)

There is much to interpret in this terrain. The workers involved in the hotel's demolition however are visibly perplexed by our enthusiasm over this crusty chunk of concrete and gnarled chain-link fence. After at least 20 minutes we race back to Aaron's apartment to check my 2008

Radisson Banks. Photo: Gregory Snyder.

Radisson Banks 2.0. Photo: Gregory Snyder.

photo on my computer. It shows indisputable proof that the bar had been moved recently. We're ecstatic in an amazingly nerdy way at our discovery. Aaron texts one of his friends, "Do you know of any footage with somebody skating that bar above the Radisson Banks?" A half-hour later Sean McNulty sends back a link to a video. We didn't realize that he was responding to our question and think McNulty is sending a video of some hot new skater. We watch the video, *Gravis [shoe company] Presents Kevin Terpening*. This dude is good, but at the one-minute mark, 10 tricks in, Kevin does a front-side smith grind on the bar over the Radisson Banks. Such are the joys of studying skateboarding in the Internet age. We examined and imagined what the possibilities were, and then before the day was out witnessed the purpose of that effort.

"The only question left unanswered," says Aaron, "is: was he the fortunate recipient of someone else's labor, or did [Terpening] see the potential and manipulate the space for his own gain?"

Two months later, young up-and-comer Curren Caples does a backside tailslide, much more difficult and scarier than Terpening's trick, on the fence rail for his part in the *Flip 3 Video*, through which Flip Skateboards introduces their three new pros.

DIY Skate Spots: From the Ground Up

The first generation of street skaters spent a lot of time in parking lots skating the parking blocks. They have an approximately three- to four-inch top and then are angled, creating a sort of rounded top. This top is special for skaters because it allows for specific types of board manipulation that are impossible on a 90-degree ledge. However, for today's skaters parking blocks are simply too small to be a challenge.

Aaron decided he needed to change that. He tells me he had the idea for a long time but finally executed it when he saw on a recent skate DVD that someone else had made one in Arizona. Aaron found two parking blocks at a construction site behind his house in West LA and loaded them into his Honda Element, along with purchased cinder blocks, Quikrete, a gallon jug of water, and Bondo. He then spent the next three days driving all over LA to find the perfect spot to build his obstacle.

His desire to make his own spot was also a reaction to the city, which at the time (2008) refused to listen to skaters and consistently pushed them to the margins. He needed to find a spot totally secluded and yet accessible and also with enough smooth ground to be skateable. For this he used graffiti and signs of homelessness for clues to spots where the authority of the city is lacking. He looked for neglected areas of the city, what some have called loose space or dead space.[13]

Los Angeles's enormous tangle of freeways, highways, and byways, on-ramps and off-ramps, creates a complex by-product of spaces underneath overpasses, essentially forgotten spaces. These spots are ideal for graffiti writers who can take time to paint elaborate murals and for drug users who want to tie off and nod in peace. They are also ideal for skaters.

Finally, Aaron discovered his spot from the Fairfield on-ramp, and it took him another half hour to locate it. The spot is a little bridge over some sort of waterway. There are massive graffiti pieces on the surrounding wall, and despite the cars that can be seen overhead, no one can see the spot.

The first step was to lay out the cinder blocks and cement them to the road. On day 2 he returned and put the parking blocks on top of the cinder blocks, filled in all the cracks with Bondo, and then painted it white. He was absolutely thrilled with it, and for the first two weeks he kept it a secret until he filmed the tricks he wanted. Then he told the photographers that they were allowed to bring other skaters to his spot. He published his trick in a new digital video, and folks began to ask about it. He was interested to see what other people would be able to accomplish at his spot. When I suggested some sort of graffiti guest book, he replied that if somebody does something worthwhile, I'll see it, meaning it will be published somewhere. Aaron just wanted credit for making the spot.

Aaron's DIY spot. Photo: Gregory Snyder.

Two years later in the April 2010 *Skateboard Mag*, Eric Koston had a trick on a similar obstacle that two other skaters got credit for making, and in the next month Mike Mo had an ad at the same obstacle. Aaron's spot never was noticed, and soon enough it was discovered by the authorities and destroyed.

The most well-known DIY spot is Burnside, but recently in La Paz, Peru, with help from Levi's, kids built a skate park. There are also spots in Philly, and strangely Red Bull is currently offering grants for skaters to construct their own legitimate spaces.[14]

Even as skateboarding is tightly linked to social media as skaters' completed tricks are broadcast in near real time, skaters are still dependent upon relationships with humans in and upon physical space. The architectural impulse runs deep within skateboarding, so much so that the task of interpreting existing spaces has caused many skaters to create places of their own to perform tricks and create community, especially as their space diminishes.

8

Landmark Achievements

The Creation of Subcultural Landmarks

In order to discuss the importance of skateboarding landmarks, it is necessary to talk about public space, where the majority of skating takes place. From a sociological perspective space is not simply where we live and how, but a complex nexus of political, economic, and social forces that facilitate the maintenance and distribution of power. Space therefore constricts movement, grants or restricts life chances, regulates uses and users, nourishes culture, and even instigates political action.[1] Classical theorists of space argued that the city had a dual nature where larger forces of control attempted to impose order, on day-to-day life and spaces, ultimately to make space profitable. They argued that the late capitalist tendency to seek profit in every possible phase of social life applied to space as well; for urban economic elites space could no longer be neutral, it had to be profitable.

The most influential early theorists of space were Henri Lefebvre and Michel de Certeau, who argued that while space and power operate as constricting forces, people in their everyday lives do not fully accept space as it is and can engage in activity with transformative political potential. The resistance they cite is an outgrowth of how people actually live; thus despite the overwhelming constellation of forces designed to elicit submission, people's everyday lives are often unconsciously quite resistant.[2]

These ideas (often called the "spatial turn") have influenced scholars from a wide range of disciplines, and they have produced a vast literature that highlights an amazing array of "resistant" public space activities, included but not limited to dancing, busking, gardening, parking, walking, painting, selling, vandalizing, skating, biking, free running, and applying art. These public space actions fall into the larger category of people using space in ways that they're not supposed to, thus creating the possibility for a spatial politics that various scholars have called insurgent public space, everyday space, guerilla urbanism, loose space, DIY urban design, and urban space interventions, just to name a few.[3]

Most of this scholarship focuses on *the political*, and there appears to be significant evidence, from Tahrir Square to Occupy Wall Street, of burgeoning social movements with activists consciously employing spatial tactics. However, it is also the case that this literature has largely ignored the role of urban subculture members who use public space for their own enjoyment. These subculture practitioners aren't all that interested in "the political," and their acts of vandalism, from skating to graffiti to street art, are done for subculturally specific reasons (fun, fame, money), more often motivated by subcultural passion rather than a notion of the political.[4]

Professional skateboarders however are not just having fun and profiting at the expense of public space; their actions over time have created deeply meaningful subcultural landmarks that are revered the world over. Skateboarding therefore should be seen less as a political act and more as an act of architectural appreciation that transforms the mundane into the iconic.

Urban Public Space

Cultural criminologist Jeff Ferrell and others have argued that public spaces are everywhere diminishing. Citizens are being policed out of public spaces for all sorts of activities that were once deemed totally acceptable.[5] Other scholars have argued that public space has never been truly public, meaning open to all. True public space, as Don Mitchell claims, has never been guaranteed, it "has only been won, through concerted struggle." Making space public therefore, involves some sort of political action.[6] Ocean Howell takes that argument a step further. For Howell public space is an abstraction, a simulated fantasy meant only to *appear* public. Howell writes that "if it were plain that the exigencies of capitalism determine nearly every space that people inhabit, many would not accept it." Therefore, public space exists not as a right, but as a simulated fantasy of those rights, which upon close inspection, or citizen action, quickly reveals the "publicness of public space."[7] The act of designing security into the architecture of a space, what criminologist Oscar Newman proudly called "defensive design," must deter citizen activity while appearing to be humanistic. As Mike Davis wrote in *City of Quartz*, his well-known study of Los Angeles, public space "must not be transparently militaristic" because then even the selected public would resist.[8] As Howell writes:

> The corporate bureaucracies that have replaced the public service bureaucracies have indeed become more "sensitized" to the public; not for the purposes of creating a more democratic city of free associations, but for the purposes of narrowing the definition of who the public is, for accelerating the creation of an exclusionary city of rigid spatial hierarchies: a city of profit.[9]

That desire for profitable public space that Howell describes means that contemporary public spaces are indeed not for everyone. Rather, public space must select for consuming members of the public while attempting to filter out undesirables. This can be accomplished through a variety of defensive mechanisms first articulated by Oscar Newman in the highly influential book *Defensible Space*.[10] Others have since shown that spaces are regulated through surveillance and security, as well as through specific design strategies meant to deter the masses and prevent loitering, a strategy that Howell calls "poetic security."[11]

Public space is also controlled symbolically through a set of aesthetic codes (corporate logos, people in suits) that mark a space for a specific set of users and uses, namely the consumption of goods and services. Urban sociologist Sharon Zukin argues that the loss of manufacturing has led to a reliance on culture as a city's main "selling point." Postindustrial cities, she argues, engage in two interrelated processes, the production of space and the production of symbols. For Zukin culture is a creation of the people, yet the culture that people produce in the city—whether street art, ethnic cuisine, or a music scene—can also be repackaged to brand the city and fuel the tourist economy. In this sense she argues that a diluted "culture" is proffered to tourists looking to experience their own idea of the "authentic."[12] Urban sociologist Mark Gottdiener suggests that consumption involves not only purchasing but also behaving according to the dictates of a particular theme. He argues that spaces are "themed environments," encoded through the use of symbols that delineate the meaning and hence the uses of a particular space.

Folks replicate the theme of a space by consuming not only the goods and services but also the intended meanings of a particular place, which thus reinforce and regulate its use.

For Gottdiener, however, consumption—of stuff, of architecture, or of symbols—is an interpretive act, and thus we do not always consume exactly as we are told. This means that some activities actively reinterpret existing symbols, and create entirely new meanings in a particular place.

For Howell the question of whether or not "a destructive activity like skateboarding" should be allowed in public space obscures the issue. Howell writes that this idea "proceeds from an assumption that what we have is public space to begin with. If we recognize that what we have is commercial space, however, it becomes clear that skateboarding is not destructive of public space at all, but rather, productive and creative; it creates public space, if only for a moment."[13]

While much of the scholarship on ground-level spatial activity argues that reinterpreting the city is a political act, for skateboarding this act of collective meaning making leads to the creation of significant subcultural landmarks. Despite all of the constraints upon citizens in public space, skateboarders continue to use space in unintended ways, which over time marks a space as historically significant. The iconic spaces of skateboarding contain layers of subcultural history that makes them intrinsically important to the people who have participated in this culture. And when skaters talk about these spaces they sometimes engage in a quasi-spiritual discourse. For example, on the "freeing" of the Courthouse, Nick Tucker says in a recent video, "To be able to skate at such a legendary spot, and feel that old school energy, and to be able to skate here now is a blessing, I can't believe they blessed us with such an amazing place to skate."[14] In his "Yes Skateboarding" manifesto, Alec Beck writes, "They now understand that we deserve the privilege to skate this sacred spot."

Similarly, in a discussion of the famed Clipper Ledge in San Francisco, the writers on the *Thrasher* magazine website wrote about all of the tricks and the people "who made this lump of plaster and concrete the hallowed ground it has become." While this talk does exist, it should not be misconstrued that skaters believe that they are participating in something sacred in the traditional, religious sense of the term; however it is clear that there is a strong emotional attachment to the "lumps of plaster and concrete" that make up their history.[15]

The phenomenology of skateboarding at the highest levels is an experience that resonates on multiple layers of meaning, for the skater, for the community, and for the space. Certainly one aspect of this is about basic ambition, having the imagination, the courage, the skills, and the dedication to accomplish a seemingly impossible goal.

However, some skaters' goals are not only to accomplish a particular trick and increase their reputation, but to perform a trick at a place that will make them part of subcultural history. Much of the desire to skate on iconic spots is fueled by the possibility of progressing the discipline and becoming part of skateboarding history. To skateboarders these spaces are quasi-sacred grounds saturated with the accomplishments of a very select group, and therefore skaters are willing to sacrifice blood, sweat, and broken bones to become part of that history.[16]

Clearly musicians and professional athletes feel some sense of greater importance when performing on venerated stages. Yet it is also important to remember that skaters are making special something that was intended to be mundane. It is enticing therefore to view skateboarding as a political act, which bends, breaks, and blatantly says "fuck off" to all of the embedded overt and covert mechanisms of spatial control. However, the politics of skateboarding come from the community that this activity—seen mostly by outsiders as illegal, destructive, and stupid—fosters. In other words, skaters' acts of architectural transformation inform their politics. In many ways the community of skateboarding, much like that of graffiti writers, is informed by the experience of ground-level hypocrisy and arbitrary exercises of state control. Not only have skaters coalesced around the fact that outsiders misunderstand them, but they have developed a special knowledge when it comes to the administration and control of public space. Therefore, their sense of community comes not only from a belief in each other because of their shared experiences, but also from a maybe unspoken but nevertheless real sense that they are engaged in a struggle for spatial justice. Over time, skaters have turned this community and sense of injustice into collective power and have engaged in traditional political activism to reclaim local spots.

Skaters' first response to criminalizing their actions in the mid-1990s was the production of a literal bumper sticker that read "skateboarding is not a crime," a phrase that was later appropriated by other groups.

However, the real evolution of skateboarding as a culture with emerging political clout is that the current generation understood that there are specific reasons why it is a crime, and enforcing it as such reveals exclusionary control of public space. Therefore, the politics of skateboarding, while symbolically resistant as an act, stem also from the experience of being policed for an activity skaters believe to be just.

Ironically, skaters, even as they misuse a space, are also consumers. When they are skateboarding at a spot they spend money. They spend gas money to get to a spot and buy drinks and food from the establishments surrounding the spot, and thus while they are profiting from their public space activity (by documenting it), they are also contributing to the local economy. They contribute economically to outdoor spaces that were never intended to actually produce revenue. Skaters take over mundane spaces, making them special, but their constant presence also entails consumption. Consider this case in point: the ice cream truck operator, who now sells ice cream, Gatorade, and skate supplies and is parked next to Stoner Plaza, has revealed that his profits soared "over 200%" following the opening of the park in 2010.[17]

Spots help not only skaters but also filmers and photographers to advance their careers. Mike Marasco, a skateboard filmer, started going to the Courthouse when he didn't really know anyone in the skateboard industry; he developed a relationship with Aaron, and started shooting Aaron at the tail end of his career. But the Courthouse is also a place where skaters can forge a community, and that's how Mike met more skaters, did more filming, and eventually created a career within skating and beyond (he is currently working on the Beyoncé Formation Tour). The level of creativity and production going on at a skate spot like the Courthouse is incredible.

While more scholars are studying how folks use public space creatively in their everyday lives, many fail to appreciate the significance of subcultures whose opportunistic use of public space serves their goal of progressing their subcultures and building individual reputations. This is the case with graffiti writers, street artists, skateboarders, parkour practitioners, and bicycle messengers, to name a few, whose creative interpretations of public space earn them subcultural capital, which they transfer into real capital.[18]

This model of subculture profitability is used by a broad array of cultures, members of whom use video to disseminate their feats to their audience. As I have described elsewhere, skaters, writers, and others document their feats and "publish" them through subculture media to other members of their world, thus making participants both producers and consumers of the subculture media content.[19] Often but not always this process involves illegal activity, from graffiti to street racing, in which the subculture media sustain the subculture and turn illegal activity into a commodity. Thus not only urban elites profit from public space through a consumption imperative, but other groups like street racers, bikers, graffiti artists, and most notably skaters have also found a way to make public space profitable.

Spot Progression

Professional street skateboarders are motivated by what they call progression, increasing the degree of difficulty of tricks on a specific obstacle or performing basic tricks on more difficult obstacles. There is some wiggle room here as skaters who have appreciable styles can get away with doing tricks that others have already performed, but this is rare. This progression is driven and inspired by the available architecture. Tricks are done first on flat ground and then on smaller obstacles, and when mastered are brought to more difficult obstacles like handrails and ledges.

These days in Los Angeles, skaters use skate parks like Stoner Plaza and Hollenbeck Plaza to learn and perfect on smaller obstacles tricks that they then take to the street. In a sense then, skate parks and plazas don't keep skaters from "skating street"; however, they decrease the amount of time skaters spend in a spot, because they have essentially rehearsed the trick at a legal spot before attempting it "in the wild" or at an illegal skate spot. Architect Chihsin Chiu argues that street skating in New York City transgresses public boundaries, whereas park skating is about conforming to spatial and behavioral codes.[20] But parks and other spaces where skaters are allowed to skate, practice, and hang out increase the speed of progression and also foster community; remember that it was the "Stoner Locs," the locals at Stoner Plaza, who initiated and maintained the campaign to free the Courthouse.

Beyond the architectural specifications that make a good spot, the historical record of subcultural performance makes it a proving ground for future skaters. Highly skilled skateboarders produce documented skateboarding tricks and, for them, what it means to "skate" is to perform tricks in public spaces on obstacles that meet specific requirements to contribute to the progression of skateboarding.

Skateboarding tricks are done in the context of the subculture. Each obstacle, or skate spot, has a history of tricks that have been completed on it, and any new trick must be original and more challenging. Consequently, skaters who do tricks that have previously been performed on certain obstacles will be ridiculed for unoriginality and for not recognizing what they call the "ABD list," or list of tricks that have already been done at certain spots. However, this is not always the case. Tricks must be performed with great style, and sometimes just trying to "one up" the previous trick results in "circus tricks," those done only for the sake of originality, and these too will be met with disdain.

Skateboarders undergo a rigorous process of peer review. In skateboarding there are unwritten rules passed down by the gatekeepers, loosely composed of the top pros, filmers, photographers, and magazine editors, all of whom determine what tricks are cool or not. If you're a skater who does difficult, original tricks that have been deemed passé, you will not be recognized as a top skater contributing to progression.

Progression is achieved by doing tricks with greater degrees of difficulty on existing skate spots, or by discovering new spots and performing "legitimate" or difficult tricks on them. It is not enough to simply go to a famous spot and do what's been done before. As a result, some of the most famous and most dangerous skateboard spots may yield only ten or so completed tricks—*over a 15-year period.*

For example, the Wallenberg Big 4 is a massive set of stairs at a school in San Francisco. The first trick ever done on this spot was a simple ollie by Mark Gonzales in 1990, and since then only eleven tricks have been done here, each progressively more difficult and dangerous. In 2005 Chris Cole landed the first ever 360 flip down the Wallenberg 4 for his *New Blood* video part; it took him 66 tries. In 2015 Shane O'Neill successfully landed a nollie, backside 180 heelflip, thus reinvigorating the spot once again, and seriously raising the bar.

The Carlsbad Gap

While skateboarding talent is necessary to build a career it is also important to recognize the role that spots play in the creation of subculture careers. One of those iconic spots is the Carlsbad Gap.

Located at Carlsbad High School in Carlsbad, California, the Carlsbad Gap is one of the most famous spots in all of skateboarding and evokes awe from skaters.[21] The spot is a simple looking "grass gap" next to a set of stairs, but it has an "uphill roll away," which makes it deceptively difficult to skate, and as a result the tricks that have been done have become the stuff of legend. Carlsbad also has its own Wikipedia page, in addition to a plastic toy replica sold at Target and produced by Tech Deck.

Such spots play an important role in subculture lore, but they also serve the purpose of being the stages where young skaters go to prove themselves to the subculture. Even for Aaron who never skated the Carlsbad Gap, the spot is significant. He had this to say:

Hollywood High and Carlsbad Tech Deck. Photo: Gregory Snyder.

The Carlsbad Gap was an extremely famous spot for years. From Kris Markovich's first ever kickflip over it in 1993 which got him the cover of *Transworld* magazine, to Jeremy Wray's line in his Plan B video part, in which he ended a one-minute line with a frontside kickflip over the gap. Or how Tom Penny, from England, switch frontside flipped it, supposedly first try, and then nothing. For years the spot wasn't even touched.

By not touched, Aaron means not that skaters hadn't been going there and attempting to do tricks, but that no one had landed anything. The proof is that there was "no coverage," nothing in the magazines or videos of any new tricks on it, despite the fact that only basic tricks had been done so far. Chris Cole was an East Coast skater from the suburbs of Philadelphia, extremely talented and also unique in his style. This difference rubbed some of the skate tastemakers the wrong way, and it was only when he went out to California and stepped to Carlsbad that skaters began to change their minds about him.

According to Aaron,

Chris Cole had been struggling over and over to get a legitimate board sponsor. At the time he was only [getting free boards] for a company called enjoi, he wasn't even officially part of a skateboard team. Skaters had all sorts of criticism for why Cole was not a top pro prospect despite showing significant talent. He was criticized for his skating style, his gear, and even the way he pushed on his skateboard; no matter what he did he couldn't overcome it. But he did overcome it. In 2000, he went to the biggest stage in skateboarding at the time, the Carlsbad Gap, and switch frontside 180 heelflipped it. With that one trick Chris Cole sent shockwaves through the industry and crystallized how far ahead of the times he really was.[22]

As a result of this one trick, Chris's career began to take off. He got on Zero Skateboards and turned pro later that year. He is now a top respected pro, with multiple groundbreaking video parts and big-name sponsors, a two-time X Games champ, winner of Street League's Super Crown World Championship, and twice *Thrasher* magazine's Skater of the Year. He is also a husband and a father.[23]

This individual act was documented and disseminated through the subculture via *411 Video Magazine* issue 42, released in 2000. As a result of skateboarding media, Aaron says, "Skating is an individual act that is still experienced as a community." He reflects,

> When Chris Cole did his trick down Carlsbad, I got excited not only for him, but for all of skateboarding. With that one trick I felt the page turn to a new generation and sensed the possibilities that were right around the corner. And there's really nothing quite like believing something is impossible [like switch 180 heelflipping Carlsbad] to seeing it manifest right in front of you. Skating rules.

In order for Chris Cole to get the attention and respect of his peers, he had to do a trick on a famous spot, so other skaters could compare his skills to those of the skaters who had come before him. But Chris didn't only do a trick that had never been done; he did a trick that most people thought he was utterly incapable of landing.

This accomplishment was not spontaneous or improvised in any way. Chris did not discover the Carlsbad Gap while cruising through the city, critiquing traffic patterns or the use of public space. This event required much planning in order to achieve Chris's idea in practice. The process began in his mind when he thought to himself that he could switch front side 180 heelflip the Carlsbad Gap. Next, he needed to convince a photographer and two videographers to join him on this quest. And they needed to schedule a time when the obstacle wasn't in use by high school students. They all went there that day knowing that if Chris was successful, his career would likely be forever changed.[24]

The Carlsbad Gap is located at a school, and to perform tricks on school architecture is to use that space in new and creative ways that suggest that the ideological imperatives embedded in the architecture and landscape are not ones we have to accept. And while Chris Cole certainly had fun that day, he was there not to play but to work. He went to the Carlsbad Gap to make his career. And he profited not only creatively but also financially from this performance. His performance marked the beginning of a successful, extremely lucrative subculture career.

The act itself, in the moment, is defiant and illegal, while the document of the performance is a commodity that can be purchased by other members of the subculture. As a result, products (boards, shoes, clothes, energy drinks) are all sold with Chris Cole's name on it, and large sums of money, for subculturalists and corporatists alike, are generated from this performance of illegal activity in public space.

Profitable Spots

Angela McRobbie argued in 1989 that "subculturalists were inherently entrepreneurial"; however, the Birmingham School and many scholars hence have dismissed subculture entrepreneurialism with the simplistic assessment that subculturalists who make money are co-opted "sellouts."[25]

The large group of academics, architects, designers, and urban planners influenced by the spatial turn are interested in the tactical ways in which city dwellers creatively resist the strategies of urban elites in their everyday lives; and they have, for the most part, ignored the importance of the spatial practices of specific subcultural groups for understanding the city.

The actual tactical practices of professional skaters reveal that their "radical" fun is a for-profit enterprise. Skaters don't simply use spaces as a way of redefining the boundaries embedded in architectural design; they use public spaces to progress the discipline of skateboarding.

Since the Birmingham School invested subcultures with political promise, most accounts of subcultures have focused on the all-or-nothing bipolarity of resistance or co-optation, and have tended to ignore or neglect the economics of subculture, in favor of discovering the politics of postmodern identity formation.[26]

A deep appreciation of skateboarding subculture forces you to look at the built environment from a different perspective, where suddenly subtle elements of control become plainly obvious, which may inspire average citizens to pay closer attention to how their worlds are made, and for whom.

While traditional social and political activism is for the most part missing from skateboarding culture, as more and more skaters have had the experience of being treated like criminals in public spaces, they have become active in discussions about the use of public space and in the building of skate plazas. In California, Alec Beck, Aaron Snyder, and the community of West LA skaters recently assisted the Los Angeles Parks Department and the local municipal government with the building of an excellent skate plaza at Stoner Park. More and more, skaters today are taking part in community meetings and becoming active in the discussion of how public spaces and the resources devoted to them are used.

So, yes, skaters carve and grind their way through the city, as Borden notes, engaged in micro acts of resistance that seem to be putting into practice some of the ideas of critical postmodern geographers, spatial anthropologists, cultural criminologists, architectural critics, and others, which indeed suggests a politics that has the potential to reframe the spatial activity of late capitalist struggle. Yet skaters don't skate just because it's radical fun. Skateboarders who have accomplished challenging tricks at famous skate spots are also folks who through the subculture of skateboarding have used public space to achieve all of the trappings of mainstream success.

Defensible Space

Skateboarding is a controversial form of expression that has been criminalized as much for its style as for the destruction of property.[27] While it is the case that in certain instances skateboarding causes minor vandalism, its criminality is often exaggerated, as often moral entrepreneurs utilize "broken windows" and "quality of life" rhetoric for political and economic gain.[28]

Street skating is the act of performing tricks in and upon obstacles in the built environment, and its illegality is supposedly based upon the damage it causes to street furniture. Though skateboarding is illegal, arrest and jail time are not the main issues for skaters. The real problems come in the form of harassment, abuse, tickets, and constantly getting kicked out of spots by cops, security guards, and concerned citizens.

While skaters have certainly done much to cultivate a "skate and destroy" rebel image, part of skateboarding's public relations problem comes from the fact that what they do is difficult to understand and even harder to describe.[29] Even the simplest tricks are incredibly difficult to comprehend. And the American public remains generally unimpressed and oftentimes even offended at what skaters are trying to accomplish in the streets. Also, passersby rarely see the finished product and instead witness what seems to be a lot of falling and flailing around. In Europe and Asia, however, where the public has less knowledge of skaters and consequently has not been taught to disapprove of them, passersby often become an audience, actively cheering the performances of skaters.[30]

Skaters themselves are also not very good at articulating what they do. Many of them began skating as kids and have spent their entire lives within the culture of skating and have really communicated only with other skaters. If you ask skaters to describe a 360 kickflip, they will look at you sideways and just say, "it's a 360 shove it, combined with a kick-flip," which hardly describes the fact skaters are using their feet to get the board into the air and, while suspended, rotate the board 360 degrees simultaneously on both the x- and y-axes.

Edmund Bacon, the famous city planner from Philadelphia and de-signer of skaters' beloved Love Park, said, just months before his death, in the film *Freedom of Space: Skateboard Culture in Public Space*:

> I think sometimes that skateboarders are even a little bit modest about themselves and I think that they must realize that they are at the edge of a new perception of life for the young. And that in the long run they're absolutely bound to win because that's the way history works, there are a bunch of jerks that can't see the new vision at all and it scares them.
>
> I want to talk directly to the skateboarders, you really are the revolu-tionaries in sport and culture you should be proud of the resistance you've created and you must stick with it. You must not let the stick in the mud prevent you from continuing the great process that you've initiated.[31]

But it's not only the cops, the security guards, and the concerned citizens whom skaters have to deal with; the architecture itself clearly says "we don't like your kind around here." As many scholars have pointed out public spaces are becoming less accessible to citizens to engage in myr-iad forms of democratic community, and more and more are becoming privatized, selected for a specific type of activity, most notably middle-class consumption.[32]

Urban sociologists like Don Mitchell and geographers like David Harvey worry that we have lost our "right to the city" and without avail-able space to exchange ideas and to protest, democracy will be further weakened.[33] Cultural criminologists have shown that spatial control and surveillance are essential components of late capitalist crime prevention, yet despite huge expenditures, these methods have not proved effective in reducing major crimes.[34]

In addition to video surveillance, urban spaces today feature partitioned benches designed to prevent the homeless from sleeping and various metal knobs and bolts welded onto handrails and ledges to prevent skateboarding. In addition to the "no skateboarding" signs that skaters come into contact with, skateboarders must also confront the architecture itself, which says "no skating" in a different way. Despite the fact that anti-crime is the main goal, security also means designing spaces to prevent skateboarding. Spots are unskateable because of security and surveillance, as well as the strategically placed planter, the canted ledge, and various other design elements to prevent skateboarding. There are numerous companies that specialize in the skateboard-prevention business. A quick search revealed that it costs $437.29 for a pack of 20 skate-stopping devices. Clearly "No Skateboarding" also has a financial incentive.[35]

One thing that happens when urban planners make spaces unskateable is that often the spaces revert back to places for more illicit types of activity. Howell argues that many of the plazas that were designed in the 1970s failed to be successful urban spaces for a number of reasons, including lack of proper seating and also the fact that many of them were isolated from the city at large. William H. Whyte shows in his film *The Social Life of Small Urban Spaces* that good urban design should allow clear views of the street, to watch passersby, and have ample seating. Because many of the plazas built in the 1970s did not have these, they were taken over by skaters, who used them to hone their skills and confirm their communities.[36]

Skaters have always actively engaged in deviance; however, most often this is not because they savor criminal activity, but because of a constant need to explore and interpret a changing environment. Pro skaters seek out new spots to skate because so many spots in LA have been made unskateable, and because they have a tacit desire to explore urban space. It is also the case that many obstacles on the West Coast have accrued so much subcultural history that it is difficult to do anything new. Chris Cole describes in an interview in *The Skateboard Mag* that the "ABD list (already been done) is so long there's no tricks left to do."[37]

Skate stoppers. Photos: Gregory Snyder.

Very often these practices are described as "political" by scholars wishing to valorize a certain set of cultural practices. Often those people who are labeled political by scholars are unaware that they are indeed being political. There is an unconscious potential politics being suggested by scholars, and hence the activities of said subcultural group are reevaluated not as criminal mischief, vandalism, or childish folly, but as something important because they are in fact "political." But the task,

Skate stoppers. Photos: Gregory Snyder.

for many academics, stops once the political has been discovered. The technique usually involves applying a heavy dose of the latest theoretical turn to the everyday lives of youthful actors. There is no action, no attempt to have a dialogue on the politics of subculture practice with punks, writers, or skaters, no attempt to make political alliances with these folks, no effort to discover actual rather than abstract politics, no attempt to find common ground, in fact no actual effort to engage politically with a group whose practices you admire, but with whom you have no allegiances.

The spatial practices of skateboarders are enticingly political and certainly resistant, but that is not how skaters experience skateboarding. Getting tricks is dangerous, hard work with fun, camaraderie, and actual money as the payoff. The experience of being a part of a collective has led skaters to become activists engaged in collective action to "liberate" spots and effect real social change, and as a result they are starting to feel like regular citizens with a worthy claim over public space. This attempt, initiated by skaters, to change how they are viewed by the public

Skate stoppers. Photos: Gregory Snyder.

is beginning to have a positive impact on how skaters view themselves and their relationship to the public. Rather than skate and destroy, many skaters are looking to be good stewards of the public spaces that they hold in such high regard. The result is that adult skaters are asking to be included in the discussion of the use of public spaces.

PART IV

Resistance

Skateboard Activism

The Courthouse: A History

Between 1957 and 1965 the architecture firm Allison and Rindle built the West Los Angeles Civic Center, known to skaters as the Courthouse. This group of buildings with adjoining pedestrian plaza came out of a push in 1949 by the City of Los Angeles to streamline their administration to provide municipal services to Angelenos whose rapidly expanding city covered a vast geographic expanse. According to the LA Conservancy:

> The civic center reflects the postwar growth of municipal services and the general optimism of the period, exemplified by its eye-catching Mid-Century Modern design. The City Hall and court buildings are particularly notable for the decorative concrete grilles and geometric metal brise soleils, which ornament their front façades. The most flamboyant structure is the amphitheater, with a swooping, parabolic arch of a roof held aloft by tiled pillars and sheltering a small stage with curves to match. It looks for all the world like a miniature version of the famous Union 76 station in Beverly Hills.[1]

The amphitheater has some of the characteristics of what is called Googie design (named after a John Lautner–designed coffee shop called Googie's), reflecting the period's fascination with cars, jets, and space travel. (The most famous example of Googie design is the Theme Building at LAX, which I have seen every single time I've flown to LA, and now thanks to my study of the Courthouse, I know what this design is called.)[2]

Even though the Courthouse is listed as a "historic place" and garners appreciation from architects, in the early 1990s it had fallen on hard times. The lack of foot traffic in the plaza, except by those who had to appear in municipal court, created a nearly empty space in which an expanding homeless population, due to earlier deinstitutionalization, found a home. There is a stage surrounded by an upper level with concrete tables and benches, which the homeless folks use to store their belongings and to sleep. This spot is also desirable for its invisibility; the municipal plaza is nestled in between Corinth and Purdue avenues but does not join the two blocks. This fact, coupled with the overall lack of pedestrian traffic in LA, made the plaza rather deserted. The homeless encampment, which backs up to a public library and is close to a VA hospital, exists to this day, and the folks who live there have created a relatively nice living space, with mattresses and reading lamps. In general, and because they are hard to see, the civilian population tends to ignore these folks, and they conveniently make themselves scarce on Saturdays when a farmers' market is held.

The plaza has a smooth concrete ground, a small four-stair set, tons of ledges upon which to sit, an empty fountain, and a stage at the amphitheater. All of these elements, combined with the plaza's lack of use, made this an ideal location for skateboarding, in terms of both the varied types of obstacles that can be skated as well as the atmosphere of camaraderie

Homeless at the Courthouse. Photo: Gregory Snyder.

Homeless encampment at the Courthouse. Photo: Gregory Snyder.

The West LA Courthouse. Photo: Gregory Snyder.

West LA Courthouse, stairs. Photo: Gregory Snyder.

Nick Tucker, kickflip, West LA Courthouse. Photo: Aaron Snyder.

that comes from being able to spend all day at a particular space (free from police harassment) sharing ideas and pushing one another. From the early 1990s the Courthouse was *the* place to skate, and on any normal day it was host to some of the best skaters in the world.

The Courthouse came to prominence in the early 90s, but the first video to really showcase the versatility of the space for skating was shot by Girl Skateboards called *Goldfish*, directed by Spike Jonze. This video features now legendary skaters, all of whom had significant lines at the Courthouse. Rudy Johnson, Javontae Turner, and most notably Eric Koston, all had groundbreaking performances at the Courthouse that were documented and disseminated to the rest of the subculture, which only increased the Courthouse's fame. However, in this video only the ledges, the stairs and the fountain were skated. No one yet had the "pop" to step to the stage, until the 1996 video *Trilogy* where Ronnie Creager skates it as a ledge. Manual tricks in which riders had to ollie up onto the stage and ride on either the front or back wheels were still far off in the imagination.

Decriminalizing the Courthouse

On Monday June 16, 2014, Aaron calls to tell me that the one West LA homeowner who has consistently hated Stoner Plaza and the skaters who use it has somehow managed to get before the City Council a plan to build a "sound wall" around the park. This fence would effectively wall off the skaters from the street. We discuss the ways that urban planners consistently emphasize that when a space is no longer subject to "eyes in the street" it invites illicit behavior. In addition, Aaron says that this would be a giant "fuck you" to all the skaters who have worked so hard to make Stoner a success. He says that there will be a City Council meeting on the following Monday and that everyone would get one minute to voice their opinion. He jokingly says that I should write him a speech, which I do. This is what I write:

> First off I want to thank Jay Handal for all of his efforts to help get Stoner Plaza built.
>
> It has been an unqualified success. The park is in constant use by skateboarders, and is generally regarded as the best skate plaza in LA.
>
> Not only is the park a great place to skate, it has proven to be a place where young skaters' talents are nurtured, and many skaters have used Stoner to develop their professional careers.
>
> How amazing is this park? So amazing that a person would leave his hometown, and choose to live out of his van, just to be near it. There is no better example of this than Sebo Walker. When word of Stoner's brilliance reached him in Oregon, Sebo decided that he would move to California and live out of his van. He parked right on Stoner Avenue so that he would be able to skate the park every day. Sebo's intense practice paid off and he now has a shoe sponsor and a board sponsor and is on his way to making a pro career.
>
> Stoner has made skaters feel like they matter. Stoner has even turned some skaters into community activists, and because of Stoner, many skaters voted for the first time in their lives in the May 18th, 2014, municipal elections.
>
> Putting a wall around the park would be a symbolic attack against all of the positive things that Stoner has brought—decrease in gang activity,

increased sense of community among west LA skaters, mentoring relation-ships between older and younger skaters, pro careers nourished—and say to the skate community that despite all these gains, you are still outsiders, an eyesore to be hidden from the public eye. The reaction among skaters, I'm sure, would be to further entrench our sense that we are misunderstood and hated for no reason, and hence we see no reason to respect the community that has shunned us.

Not only would a wall be seen as an attack, but putting a wall around Stoner would make the plaza a place that cannot be seen from the street. Urban sociologists say that when activity is out in the open and can be seen by all members of a community, a space has a self-regulating potential. A wall around Stoner would make the plaza a place where illicit activity could take place without being seen, it would become an open invitation to crimi-nal activity, and a place where young people are no longer safe.

I implore this committee to see all of the good that Stoner has accom-plished, and all of the bad that would ensue by walling it off. Thank you. And thank you again to chair Jay Handal, I'm a West LA homeowner, and you've got my vote, again.

Aaron attends the meeting on Wednesday and is overwhelmed by the number of people who show up. The speakers, many not skaters, who argue for leaving Stoner Plaza alone are so numerous that Aaron is unable to give his speech in the allotted time, but only one person at the entire meeting, the angry lady, speaks negatively about Stoner Plaza. He says, "even members of the City Council talked about how positive Stoner has been."

On Thursday the energy directed toward Stoner Plaza changes as Aaron goes to the West LA Courthouse and notices work being done. Aaron sends me an email.

It started on Thursday when I was out skating with Nick and he wanted to go to the Courthouse to do another trick on the stage. Upon getting to the spot Nick and I discover that it's completely fenced off. We look a little closer and the whole place is getting a face lift—but not a regular remodel—a re-model that suggests skating. They have re-cemented the planters with metal edges and built ledges coming off of the stage—Holy crap.[3]

He posts a photo on Instagram of the apparently skate-friendly upgrades being made. (Note that metal edges on a ledge help skaters to slide better. A hubba, as you know by now, is a ledge that goes down a set of stairs.)

He follows it up with a phone call to me and says that the construction is clearly intended to facilitate skateboarding. After a few texts to industry insiders Aaron discovers that Nike is indeed behind this, and

●●●○○ Verizon 🔇   8:45 AM   ✳ 75% 🔋

← **PHOTO** ↻

💜 **74 likes**

aaronsnyder77 Yes those are metal edges, yes those are hubbas, but when asked if it's permenant the response was "doubtful". WTF is going on here and please don't tease us if you're just going to destroy it after your "shoot". #freethecourthouse

Courthouse getting a makeover. Photo: Aaron Snyder.

Aaron initially believes that Nike has embarked on efforts to make the Courthouse legal. "There is no way that they'd invest this much money if it wasn't going to be permanent," he says. "It's finally reached a tipping point, people are starting to understand that skateboarding is good."

However, his moment of naïveté is short-lived as the crushing truth becomes apparent. He learns that the intention of the city is to make the place unskateable immediately after the industry-created skateboarding holiday called "Go Skateboarding Day," which is every year on June 21. Aaron says that it would be a travesty to allow Nike to use one of their most cherished landmarks to garner goodwill among skaters on this holiday only to then reinforce the notion that skaters are a public nuisance by taking the spot away from them. Aaron sends off a series of passionate texts to Alec Beck suggesting that they should not allow this to happen.

In another email Aaron says:

> So anyways I finally get Alec to see the inherent crappiness of the situation and he gets in touch with city councilman Jay Handal—who is directly responsible for Stoner and has been a champion for skaters. Councilman Handal talks to the City Council and reports back to Alec that if Nike will agree to pay $10,000 per year for maintenance for the next 5 years, that the city will not knob the ledges and the space will be a legal spot after regular business hours and on weekends. Keep in mind the renovations Nike has already done to the space are in the hundreds of thousands of dollars. Alec drives directly over to the Courthouse—finds the top people from Nike that are there overseeing the project—pleads his case voicing the concerns of the local skaters—and gets an immediate (although tentative) "yes."
>
> Only time will tell if my activism has paid off but if it does I may be at least partially responsible for freeing one of the most legendary skate spots in the world. Fingers crossed!

Go Skateboarding Day, which was initially dreamed up by some skate companies in 2004 to promote skateboarding, has become a huge international phenomenon with events taking place all over the country and the world. In LA skaters gather at Hollenbeck Plaza and Stoner Park, where thousands of kids mob the pros for autographs. Paul Rodriguez gives a little speech about what the Courthouse meant to him growing

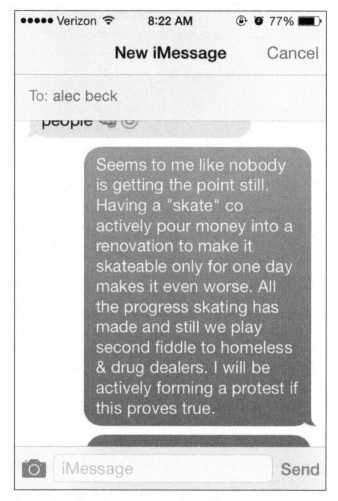

Screen shot of text from Aaron to Alec Beck. Photo: Aaron Snyder.

up, and directs all of the kids to head over there. The pros including Paul give a demo for the kids. Jay Handal poses for photos with the skaters; everyone is happy except Aaron and Alec, who know they need to keep the pressure on.

After the event Aaron and Alec start an Instagram campaign, imploring skaters not to skate the Courthouse until they get final approval from the City Council.

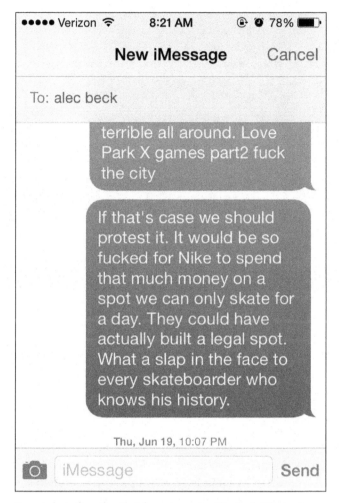

Screen shot of another text from Aaron to Alec Beck. Photo: Aaron Snyder.

WAIT! DON'T BLOW IT.

We got them to keep the knobs off . . . but please be patient as we, as skaters, work with the city to create a schedule of hours for us to LEGALLY skate here at the WEST LA COURTHOUSE.

They would entrust us to keep it clean, friendly and peaceful during certain hours and now is our chance to prove that we can handle it, by not skating yet.

Paul Rodriguez, Go Skateboarding Day. Photo: Aaron Snyder.

> If you skate through this you are blowing it for everyone.
> Just be cool. We might have a new legal spot if we are all patient.
> —Alec Beck, The Stonerlocs, and the West LA community of skaters.

This post goes up late Saturday evening, and nobody skates the Courthouse that evening, on Sunday, or on Monday. This is amazing. This photo gets "reposted" by famous pros and goes viral. (When Paul Rodriguez posted it to his 500,000 followers, he got 22,000 likes.)

***

On Monday, June 23, 2014, the focus is back on Stoner Plaza. The skateboarding community is being challenged again by a local homeowner who wants to build a sound wall around the plaza, so Aaron posts again, encouraging skaters to show up and voice their disapproval.

Aaron approximates that 100 skaters show up, and not only skaters but also regular citizens make speeches favorable to Stoner. In fact, the only person in favor of the "sound wall" is the woman who started the campaign and says that "kids shouldn't be allowed to voice their opin-

Screen shot of Instagram post, "Wait Don't Blow It." Photo: Aaron Snyder.

ion." The City Council says that it will deliberate and meet again on Wednesday for a vote on the proposed sound wall and the status of the Courthouse for skaters.

No one skates the Courthouse on Tuesday. No one skates the Courthouse on Wednesday. This spot has just been given a skateboarding makeover and has legendary ties to the subculture, and still everyone stays away, even as the desire to skate it is tremendous. The elder statesman

Screen shot of Instagram post, "Stop the Wall." Photo: Aaron Snyder.

of the skateboard community put the word out via social media to all skaters not to skate the Courthouse, and everyone obliged. This fact is almost unbelievable and certainly flies in the face of conventional wisdom about skaters' lack of empathy or responsibility. And it certainly says something impressive about their collective power.

On Wednesday, once again Aaron and Alec, via Instagram, implore their fellow skaters to show up for the City Council vote on the proposed plan to wall off Stoner and make the Courthouse legal. It reads:

Come out tonight and voice your opinion on both the Stoner sound wall and turning the West LA Courthouse into a legal skate spot for evening/night and Saturday hours. Do not skate at the Courthouse yet.

—Alec Beck, Stoner Locals & the West LA Community of Skateboarders

I wait by my phone while the council is in session. Around 11 P.M. Eastern Aaron calls and I can hear the pride and elation in his voice.

Screen shot of Instagram post, "Support the Courthouse." Photo: Aaron Snyder.

"They voted 13–0 against the wall, and 12–1 in favor of making the Courthouse a legal spot. We did it."

***

This development marks one of the first times that skateboarders have successfully lobbied their local government to allow them to reclaim a spot that was illegal. Skaters have engaged in other forms of "concrete activism" that they've been able to get approval for after the fact, but to successfully argue that skaters can be excellent stewards of public space and get approval for it is an amazing accomplishment.[4]

What is also amazing is how quickly kids nowadays can organize, using social media. This whole grassroots campaign took less than a week. No door-to-door canvassing, no petitions; just a call to skaters to stand together, and they did, for a month. This could be precedent-setting, and I'm very proud of my brother. Being able to skate the Courthouse not only gives skaters another place to practice but will also contribute positively to skaters' careers, because it will be a place where they can hang together and film tricks. Skate plazas where skaters can not only skate but congregate have been essential for skateboarding progression because skaters can push each other, in addition to forming close bonds.

On Thursday, July 24, I land in LA, and the next day, a month and four days since Go Skateboarding Day, we arrive at the Courthouse around 7 P.M. for its grand reopening, sponsored by Nike. I immediately recognize pros Luan Oliveira, Theotis Beasley, Shane O'Neill, Eric Koston, and Paul Rodriguez, all sponsored Nike skaters, but there are also tons of kids skating and enjoying the ledges.

Nike SB logos are everywhere, but the vibe is amazing. Skaters are greeting each other with joy and amazement that this is actually happening. The event planners have set up barriers around the stage, and this area is accessible only to those who were invited. We enter the invite-only area and go right to the bar for a free cocktail and some hors d'oeuvres.

I see two older non-skating gentlemen and assume that one of them is City Council Chair Jay Handal (the other gentleman is Daniel Tamm, Mayor Eric Garcetti's Westside Area Representative). I introduce myself and thank Handal for all of his hard work and I emphasize how amazing it is that they're trusting skateboarders to be good citizens of this public space. I tell them that I'm a sociologist working on a book and that they'll eventually get to read this story; we exchange cards.

As the sun goes down, more people fill up the stage area and are milling about black-covered cocktail tables chatting and enjoying Nike's largess. Every skater I talk to is in awe at the sureality of this moment. They used to get kicked out and ticketed and made to feel like criminals, and now they're relaxing in the glow of the setting sun being treated as if attending an art opening at which all of the assembled are gifted artists.

Then out of nowhere Luan (from Brazil) and Shane (from Australia) start attempting tricks on the stage. They've never skated this spot before and know it only from videos, and they are overjoyed to be getting this opportunity. Aaron told me he talked to Luan, who said that growing up in Brazil he would imagine that someday he'd get to skate this spot; he said he was "in heaven."

An emcee who works for Nike SB starts the proceedings and says, "the space we are at tonight is sacred ground."[5] The crowd roars. Then a video of historic tricks at the Courthouse plays; however, noticeably absent are any of the groundbreaking tricks from Stevie Williams, who is not sponsored by Nike. The host then passes the microphone to Jay Handal, who describes a bit of the process of resurrecting the Courthouse, claiming it to be the perfect storm of corporate sponsorship, community activism, and government cooperation. Jay then passes the mic to Alec Beck, and the skaters give him a lengthy applause. Alec begins:

So Nike brought out this event, they uncapped the spot, and everybody came out, it was an amazing Go Skateboarding Day. And two days prior we talked about how we could get this thing to work long term and Jay was on board, Nike was on board, and everybody was really going for it.

A couple things had to happen. After the Nike event it dawned on me that this place is open, it's absolutely skateable and now we had to keep it on the low as much as we could to make sure that it could get through the government in just four weeks, which is pretty unreal, so we needed to find a way to skate stop the spot. So a couple people got together and we printed out some fliers and said, "wait don't blow it" and capped the spot with some paper, and posted it to Instagram. Believe it or not, for me that's kind of the story. Of course it's about Nike bringing back this spot,

Skaters share the stage with municipal leaders. Photo: Gregory Snyder.

and the local government bringing back the spot, but the fact that the skateboarders in this community and in the greater Los Angeles community respected the concept. Everybody got together and nobody skated the spot. And this is one of those opportunities where with the help of the right companies, and the right people we have a new outlook for skateboarders, where we can go from being tolerated to being exemplary, and that's where we are right now. [applause]

And we all owe a special thanks to not only everybody who ever skated here and everybody who supported this but also to Mr. Aaron Snyder [applause]. Every project has a spark and Aaron was the spark for this project. [applause] He texted me in the wee hours of the morning trying to make sure this happened. His belief helped instill a belief in me, and in Jay and ultimately in Nike and the city, and now we're all here and we can skate this place. [APPLAUSE]

Social movement scholars have yet to fully address the impact of social media platforms like Instagram and Twitter. The Black Lives Matter movement, which started in response to the police killings of unarmed black youth, began as a hashtag on Twitter and is now a social movement.[6]

On further political organizing of young people in the area of immigration rights, Cristina Beltran writes about so-called "DREAM activists," who have borrowed much from the LGBTQ rights movement and have been using sites like YouTube to post videos and "come out" as undocumented and proud.[7]

Legalized Skateboarding: Day 1

On Monday, July 28, 2014, Aaron and I go over to the Courthouse to see if the spot is being used. Aaron, thinking out loud, says nervously, "Will I be super bummed if no one is skating it?" We arrive, and for the first time since this project started I (gingerly) ride on my skateboard alongside Aaron. I wanted to say that I too had skated the Courthouse. When we get close, a ton of kids in their 20s recognize Aaron and shout congratulatory "SNYDERS" as we approach. In attendance is the entire Plan B skateboard team, who are there with their filmer, trying to get tricks for their forthcoming video. Included in the group is Brazilian Felipe Gustavo, who Aaron judged the day before in the Street

League contest. They all want to know the same thing: "How did this happen?" Aaron relays the story to them and proceeds to join them skating. Sitting next to me is Mike Adalpe, better known as "Hoops," whom I've known for a while, and he just can't stop talking about how amazing it is to be at the Courthouse and how happy he is; he says, "this is absolute pure elegance, it makes me proud what we've done." (Notice that Mike played no role whatsoever in the unlocking of the Courthouse, and he still refers to the accomplishment using a collective "we.")

We leave after about an hour and Aaron texts Alec.

Courthouse 2.0, Day 2

The next day, Tuesday, July 29, Aaron gets a text from Nick, just before 3 P.M., that he is skating the Courthouse, so we jump in the car and head over. I'm rolling on my skateboard for the second day in a row now, and it feels good. The first person I see is my friend RB Umali, whom I saw only briefly at Street League on Sunday, and we give each other a warm greeting, but RB is working, filming pro skater (and street league contestant) Chaz Ortiz, so I sit down to watch the skating.

The spot is populated with black, white, and brown kids mostly in their 20s. The Courthouse plaza has only big ledges and a huge stage, which means it attracts a high level of skater. And because it has just been resurrected after such a long time, pro skaters are eager to skate it before the ABD list gets too long. Aaron says the Courthouse is not a place for kids to learn to skate, but a spot for masters. And there are plenty of them. Nick Tucker, Sewa Kroetkov, Chaz Ortiz, Sierra Fellers, and they're all trying to get work done by performing progressive tricks on the ledges. There are about 50 people total at the Courthouse, and the homeless folks have moved to the playground in the distance. There are also filmers with very expensive cameras.

Once again, skaters are asking Aaron to tell story of freeing the Courthouse. "How did this happen?" they ask a little puzzled, and Aaron is all too happy to relay the story again.

When Aaron was skating yesterday he had complained that his board had lost its pop. For skaters who get their boards for free, which Aaron still does because of his connections, changing boards is a quite common

Alec Beck and Aaron Snyder sharing a moment of pride on opening night. Photo: Gregory Snyder.

occurrence. The process requires putting grip tape on the new board, using a razor blade to trim off the excess, then removing the trucks from the old board and mounting them on the new one.[8] While Aaron was changing his board I started to chat with Andrew, a 14-year-old African American kid sitting next to me. He was there with his mom, who was sitting behind him in a lawn chair, taking in the scene. He told me that they were from Florida and drove cross-country to skate parks across America. They attended Street League on Sunday, and Andrew said he knew that the Courthouse was skateable because of the video that Nike played on the big screen during the contest. (The same one they played at the opening on Friday.) When Aaron has finished with his old board, I give it to Andrew who is overjoyed and so cute with his appreciation. Then Nick comes and sits next to me to change his board also, and I tell Andrew, "just sit tight, I think I've got a treat for you." I introduce Andrew to Nick and Nick is super nice, and Andrew is a bit starstruck. When Nick finishes with his old board, I ask him if he would sign it and give it to Andrew and Nick says, "Of course, but I don't have a Sharpie."

Andrew's mom says, "I do," and quickly runs off to the car to retrieve a marker. Mom comes back with two black Sharpies, in addition to her son's Primitive brand hat, which was exactly the same as the one Nick was wearing (smart). Nick signs the board and the hat as Andrew smiles ear to ear. Mom says, "Thank you so much, you've made his entire summer." Andrew jumps on his board and goes off to skate, and he is actually pretty good.

Nick gets on his new board and skates around a bit getting a feel for it. Someone does what is called a "bump jump" over a small crack in the sidewalk, as a joke trick, and while the skaters sitting next to me on the curb all discuss the various iterations and techniques of "bump jumping," Nick does one with power and grace that is no joke at all that silences the chatter. Aaron says, "Nick, you should film that."

These days there are so many more outlets to showcase one's skating other than subculture media, and skaters put out a ton of tricks, many of which would never have been seen. Skaters use Instagram to put out little tricks that might not be in their video parts but are cool nonetheless, and keep their followers satisfied. Nick asks Aaron to film it, but

Aaron says, "I don't have a 5, and you need to do it in slow mo." Someone else has an iPhone 5 and passes it to Aaron. Nick takes about three tries and executes a nollie bump jump, front foot kickflip. It looks very cool in slow motion, and within seconds it goes out for Nick's 110,000 followers. By the next day it has generated 6,100 "likes."

Aaron and Nick then begin a serious discussion of possible trick options for Nick to attempt to get on film. They finally agree that Nick should attempt a kickflip over the rail (which nobody has done before), back side nosegrind on the first ledge, and a nollie front-foot flip to back side 5-0 on the last ledge. Nick begins looking for "Spanish Mike," the Primitive filmer, but he's off shooting someone else. I ask Nick if he would like RB, one of the most respected filmers in all of skateboarding, to film it. Nick says meekly, "I don't really know him like that."

I say, "I do. Do you want me to ask him?"

"If you would be down to do that, hell yeah," Nick says.

There are a lot of complex rules of social interaction in the world of pro skateboarding, and in this case it would be perhaps thought of as a bit presumptuous for Nick to ask RB to film him. And since RB is being paid by Zoo York, Chaz Ortiz's sponsor, to shoot him, Nick also has to be sure that RB is finished filming Chaz for the day. But RB is a close friend of mine, and because I'm not a skater, these rules of social interaction don't apply to me. I walk over to RB who is enjoying an iced coffee and ask him if his work day is finished. He says yes, so I say, "Would you be down to film Nick Tucker?" RB jumps up to retrieve his camera and says, "Hell yeah, he's one of my favorites." I call Nick over and reintroduce him to RB, and Nick says to RB that he wasn't sure about asking him if it would be cool to film, and RB says, "No, it's totally cool, what are you thinking?" So Nick and RB skate off. Nick explains his plan, and RB concurs that it is a good choice, meaning that it is worth his while. (This is an example of how the filmers act as tastemakers. If RB didn't feel like Nick's trick was worthy, he would either not agree to film it or maybe suggest something else. The filmers and photographers, because they are witnesses to so much progressive skateboarding, are the repositories of history, and are always attune to how particular tricks fit into the subculture history.)

Meanwhile just as Nick and RB are getting ready to make their first attempt, a police officer, gun in holster, arrives at the plaza and comes right up to us and explains that he knows it's okay to skate here now, but that he has a youth group every Tuesday and Thursday from 5 P.M. to 7 P.M. and he needs the skaters to stop skating and vacate the premises. He was stern but cordial.

Some of the skaters are a little confused. Aaron immediately takes charge and goes over to the skaters and relays to them that they have to stop. Aaron explains that this is not a skate park but a public space, and that lots of different members of the public have access to the space. Aaron says, "If we want to be included as members of the public, then we have to share the space." Everyone seems cool with this explanation, and the skaters leave peacefully and head out to their cars. Nick gets in his Audi A4, while Chaz Ortiz and his friends drive off in his 2014 CLS63 AMG Mercedes-Benz. The engine makes a mean and expensive sound as they depart.

Aaron is extremely pleased that the skaters' first confrontation with a police officer at the Courthouse goes so well, and that skaters might someday come to be thought of as accepted users of public space.

Three days later Alec takes his role as public citizen and community leader even further and posts a set of guidelines that he created for his fellow skaters to follow; he puts a physical copy at the Courthouse and of course posts it on Instagram and Facebook.

YES SKATEBOARDING

This isn't a skate spot, it isn't a skate park, it's something new. The city has agreed to let us skate here because they believe we deserve it. They now understand that we deserve the privilege to skate this sacred spot.

Don't give them a reason to take it away.

–OPEN SKATING ONLY WHEN THERE IS NO EVENT OR PERMIT. If you are asked not to skate because there is an event, come back later.

–PICK UP YOUR TRASH AND RECYCLING. Keep this place spotless.

–IF SOMEONE IS WALKING BY, BE COURTEOUS AND STOP SKAT- ING. You may be able to skate around them easily, but they don't know that. We don't want to make anyone nervous.

YES SKATEBOARDING

This isn't a skate spot, it isn't a skatepark, it's something new. The city has agreed to let us skate here because they believe we deserve it. They now understand that we deserve the privilege to enjoy this **sacred spot.**

Don't give them a reason to take it away.

-Open skating only when there is no event or permit. If you are asked not to skate because there is an event, come back later.

-Pick up your trash and recycling. Keep this place spotless.

-If someone is walking by, be courteous and stop skating. You may be able to skate around them easily, but they don't know that. We don't want to make anyone nervous.

-Park on the street. Never park or skate in the police lot. They helped us get here, let's give them the respect they deserve for doing the job they do.

-No stickers. Ever. If you see a sticker, peel it off.

Let's work together to maintain the respect from the community and show them we deserve this spot.

If someone's blowing it, help them out.
(Make sure the kids get it)

We want to make it look like we aren't here (no trash, stickers, etc.) Since we are here, let's add value to the spot: Help people carry stuff, say hi, be cool. Thank them for letting us skate in their house. Give them every reason to continue to believe this is a good idea.

In short, be skateboarders.

Thank you
Alec Beck, Stoner Locs and the Los Angeles Community of Skateboarders

Yes Skateboarding. Photo: Gregory Snyder.

—PARK ON THE STREET. NEVER PARK OR SKATE IN THE POLICE LOT. They helped us get here, let's give them the respect they deserve for doing the job they do.
—NO STICKERS. EVER. If you see a sticker, peel it off.

Let's work together to maintain the respect from the community and show them we deserve this spot.

If someone's blowing it, help them out.

(Make sure the kids get it.)

We want to make it look like we aren't here (no trash, no stickers, etc.). Since we are here, let's add value to the spot: Help people carry stuff, say Hi, be cool. Thank them for letting us skate in their house. Give them every reason to continue to believe this is a good idea.

In short, be skateboarders.

Thank you.

Alec Beck, Stoner Locs and the Los Angeles Community of Skaters

For nearly all of 2015, Aaron worked closely with City Council and Nike on further restoration of the Courthouse plaza. (Alec got a job working for Tony Hawk's foundation and moved to San Diego, which therefore left Aaron as the sole liaison between the politicians, skaters, and Nike.) At the plaza was an empty water fountain that acted as an obstacle for doing tricks into and out of. However, despite much archival work with assistance from the City Council, Aaron could not find the original plans. Therefore, Aaron and some other skaters helped the designers reconstruct the fountain *from memory*. Again capitalizing on their Go Skateboarding Day success in 2014, Nike debuted the reconstructed fountain on June 21, 2015. I wait all day to hear from Aaron about the day's events, but he says he is too exhausted to describe them all. Instead he sends me an email on Monday morning with the following document attached.

Go Skateboarding Day 2015

So as I arrive at the Courthouse sometime around 4 P.M. Nike SB had been marketing a 3–6 P.M. event featuring Nike SB riders Eric Koston, Shane O'Neill, Sean Malto, and a slew of amateurs. As I arrive I survey the area; hundreds upon hundreds of kids. The fountain is roped off with security guards making sure it's not skated yet . . . the fountain looks awesome, other than the metal edged planter ledge inside it that has CLEARLY been misplaced and is about 10 feet closer to the wall than it should be, making going into the fountain from the front all but impossible. Also the big fountain ledge up top that has been knobbed for the last 5 years is still knobbed. The repainting of the ledges was clearly an afterthought or something they just ran out of time on because they painted the ledges with some extremely shitty red paint that is peeling off in large sheets exposing the blue underneath. As you mentioned the stage has a new painting that includes a Nike logo—I forgot to inquire whether or not this would be painted over after GSD. Other than that there are a total of 3 large Nike logos in the area. One at each entrance and one in the bottom of the fountain. Upon closer inspection these reveal themselves to be easily removable decals.

There is a DJ station set up in the corner on top of the "4 up 4 down" and a Wahoo's taco truck in an open area. I find Jason Cohn and am greeted warmly. Jason (being good at his job) immediately addresses everything that's already going through my mind:

- "We ran out of time painting the ledges and therefore will come back again to lay down a proper coat that won't peel off in the same way."
- "We still are going to unknob and resurface the big ledge up top."
- "The logos will be removed after today."

He requests that I go up into the offices of the Courthouse at 5:20 for a little pre-show meeting. I go upstairs and it's a mix of the Nike riders, local politicians and the workers making the event run. I am greeted by Andy Crahan with a new pair of super dope Grant Taylor shoes (which he knows I like) in the new color way (grey w/ yellow).

A couple of cool things happen before things get rolling that make me feel quite good and needed.

- Koston seeking me out to ask if I had looked at the fountain and inquiring if they put the metal planter too close to the wall? Just knowing that he knows I'm involved is nice in itself.
- Finding the new "Go Skateboarding" signs that will soon be placed around the plaza.
- Jay Handal takes me aside and asks if I'm available over the next week to come in and discuss "a few ideas" for the Courthouse. He mentions the desire to implement more community events such as concerts and movie or video nights. I enthusiastically agree and we have been emailing back and forth to find a time.
- Once we are all gathered up ready to go out Jason addresses the group and specifically singles me out as being an integral part of making this happen. Nice.

We walk out of the side door as a group and are escorted by security through a channel of kids to the fountain. Eric says a few words about how excited he is to have back a place that was so important to his career. Another Nike representative gets on the mic to list off the names of people to thank (of which I am one) and then City Council representative Len Nguyen says some words about how impressed they have been with the community and reinforces his general approval of what's been accomplished.

Koston is then given the honor of "first trick" into the fountain—essentially replacing a ribbon cutting ceremony. And after a few tries he backside kickflips over the wall in pure Koston fashion. Next there is a 30-minute demo of the Nike guys all skating the fountain. This ends up evolving into all of the Nike guys filming lines from doing a trick on the big curved ledge of the stage and then coming over and popping a trick into the fountain—just like people used to do.

Demo is nearing an end so I take my opportunity before it's too late to thank Jason for all his work on the project and ask him if he's available to get lunch in the near future because I have some exciting ideas I'd like to discuss with him. He enthusiastically agrees.

10

Matt Gottwig

Circle Complete

Thursday, May 12, 2016. It's been a cold spring, but today it is beautiful. I ride my bike into work for a department meeting. At 2 I leave, but I don't have to race home to pick up Luna/cook dinner/just be home, instead I've got time (shout-out to parents) to enjoy my city on my bike.

My Urban Sociology students have to do an ethnography of "mixed-use public space." This year Bryan Paternoster, a skater, is doing his on Tompkins Square Park, a spot skaters have referred to as the TF (training facility) for years. I decide I'll pass by on my way home, to see if he is doing some research. En route I get a text from my friend Niels that chef Mario Batali is doing a role on the *Gaffigan Show* and that I should come by and meet him. I think about it, but decline, and head over to Tompkins. As I'm straddling my bike checking out some skaters whom I don't recognize and looking for Bryan, I hear a familiar whir coming from the street behind me and I instinctively turn my head—that sound is inside me now—and I see this big blond dude with a shaved head and glasses, who looks familiar and I sheepishly say, "Uh, Matt?!" He stops and looks at me strange, like who the fuck knows me in New York, and more specifically who is this old dude. "It's Greg," I say. And he smiles a toothless ear-to-ear grin and we embrace in a giant hug.

We are both flabbergasted. No freakin' way? This is incredible. We haven't seen each other since May 2011, and in that time we've had relatively little contact. And now as this project comes to a close, the dude who opens the book is standing right in front of me. In the past two months Matt, as the skaters say, has been ripping. He's gotten on Huf, a very-well respected skate shoe brand, had a "welcome" video, and his star is on the rise. And here he is, and here I am, at this exact moment, to help me finish this book. I am self-consciously acting in a moment that I know is going to make for good writing, and it's thrilling. If I had done anything

Matt Gottwig and Greg Snyder. Photo: Gregory Snyder.

differently, like for example go meet larger-than-life chef Batali, this moment would not have happened and yet it did. I'm in glorifying disbelief at the skating gods, and just want to bask in this new Gottwig. First off, dude has grown; he's taller and wider and full of rock-solid muscle and he's happy and confident. Also Matt is my friend. He's crazy smart, was super giving of his time and energy at the beginning of this project, and I am overjoyed to see him.

I congratulate him on his recent successes and say, "So . . . what's your plan? Where are you planning to skate, do you have anything that you're trying to get?" (This, by the way, is a very common question; it's like asking actors or writers, "What are you working on?")

Matt says, "I'm just gonna skate the spot these guys [the pros like Brad Comer] go to. But there's only one thing I have to get, a varial heel over black marble. I've gone there like four times and gotten robbed every time and they already ran the photo so I *have* to get it."

Whoa that's serious.

Matt and I hang out Friday night and we have good food and mezcal, we go to Max Fish, meet up with RB, and have more good times. At the end of the night I ask if it would be okay for me to witness a skate session, and he says, "Sure, hit me up." For the next two weeks we text back and forth and I don't really have time so I don't ask where he's skating. But on Tuesday night, May 24, I text him, "hey have you been to black marble yet?" meaning, have you completed the monstrous task you set for yourself, and if not can I witness it?

Matt: "yeah, went yesterday. Going back tomorrow morning too." Meaning, failed yesterday, going to try again tomorrow to varial heelflip black marble for the fifth fuckin' time. Yes, no one has ever done it before, so it's worth it, but imagine the torture. You know you can do it. You've gotten so close it's ridiculous, so close it feels like the universe is just not on your side, so close. But close doesn't fucking count, and if the photo is already in the ether you cannot give up. You cannot lie. You cannot have a midair photo that isn't followed up with video evidence of a successful make. Matt has to land this trick, not only because if he does he will get closer to everything he wants to accomplish, but because if he doesn't, he's committed a cardinal sin of skateboarding, and absolution will be extremely difficult. Now, it wasn't Matt's idea to run the photo, and these scenarios are not completely unique, but still, to allow people to think you varial heelflipped black marble (NBD) when you actually didn't, well that would just be wrong.

***

I show up at black marble, which is a marble hubba, meaning a ledge that goes down stairs, which often anchor handrails, but skaters have removed the handrail, somehow, on one of the obstacles and the spot remains skateable. How and why I do not understand. Thomas Paine Park is located in the triangle between Centre, Lafayette, and Worth streets, across from the US District Court Building, next to City Hall. And the gaggle of lawyers and defendants strolling through have real shit on their minds, and could not care less whether some fuckin' kids are willfully throwing themselves at this aesthetically pleasing, but otherwise totally inconsequential in the larger scheme of things piece of architectural flourish.

I arrive on this summer-like spring day wearing a Primitive tiki shirt and Vans sneakers on my feet, quietly signaling some, but not actual, skateboard affiliation. (Primitive and Vans also sell to civilians.) I slowly approach two skaters sitting in the shade. When I hear the familiar sound again, it's Matt approaching on his board with iced coffee and a bagel from Starbucks.

Matt is not paying attention to people around him and he weaves by me. "Matt" I say. And he breaks out of his nervous, anxious, assassin mode for 10 seconds to greet me. "How you feeling?" I say, and he doesn't really respond with actual words, but the clear answer to that question is, "out of my fucking mind." The energy coming off of him is a mixture of nerves, excitement, focus, and control. And the same way I don't exchange many words with Reverend Vince before a show, I know to leave Matt alone. Matt introduces me to his friends as "Aaron Snyder's brother," which gets a "cool" nod. I say "I'm also a sociologist who loves to witness other people do amazing shit." This for me works as informed consent, and Matt already knows I'm going to write about this. But no matter what, to skaters I will always be "Aaron Snyder's brother"; this makes me both proud and humble. That one line, which RB has used thousands of times, has allowed me to have so many great and productive conversations.

I make small talk with Brad Comer, pro skater for Krooked skateboards whose name is on the bottom of the board Matt is riding, and Tyler the filmer. I discover that they are leaving today, 5 P.M. flight, JFK to LAX. (I do the math in my head: gotta leave by 2 at least, maybe they could get away with leaving by 3, but that's cutting it close.) But instead of casually spending the morning packing and reflecting on their trip, they are here to see if Matt can get this elusive trick that has beaten him now, four times in a row.

Matt skates around a bit breaking in the new deck he's just put on, adjusting the trucks, scraping the grip side of the board on the pavement. He does one flat-ground warm-up trick—a varial heel that he lands perfectly. He goes for a second one but misses, and for an instant it seems like his board is going to career into my ankles, but of course as he's falling he reaches out with his hand and stops the board before it can do damage. This is not uncommon; all skaters on this level have a very special relationship to their board and know exactly where it is at all times. They would never allow a board to go flying and hurt a civilian. Matt gets up and skates over to the obstacle and does a few tricks on it, but he is not yet flying over it.

Tyler sets up his camera and Matt begins. I'm not sure if he's going to warm up; maybe he'll ollie it first or just heelflip. Matt speeds at the obstacle and with his back foot pops the tail, while also pushing the board 180 degrees front side or clockwise on the y-axis, while at the same time letting the heel of his front (right) foot flip the board 360 degrees on the x-axis, all the while flying about 6 feet in the air over a 15-foot span, and landing with a controlled thud on the concrete, hexagonal-tiled plaza floor.

He rattles off four tries and each time he's forced to kick the board away in the air. He hasn't really committed yet to "catching" one and fully attempting to land it (understandably because this shit is petrifying). On the fifth attempt Matt flies at the obstacle and ollies right in front of a mother and toddler; he misses the trick, but nobody cares, the mom, the child, or the skaters. Only I was like holy shit the kid, but I kept my nervous dad act quiet.

Matt is in complete control of his board and his surroundings; he is not going to hurt anybody. Skaters on this level of professionalism have the ability to do something incredibly risky and amazing, while weaving their way through the civilian masses. In fact, with all the skateboarding that is available to view on the Internet, you would be hard-pressed to find instances of a professional skater injuring a civilian; that's how good they are at this. They are not simply good at doing tricks, they are good at riding, controlling, and being on a skateboard, as if it were an extension of their mind.

Attempt number six is close, and Brad, Tyler, and me (a bit) are clapping, trying to be encouraging, and then on the seventh try, he makes it, and just skates by us. Silence. I'm stunned like, what's wrong, wasn't that good? On all the videos I've watched when the dude makes the trick the witnesses go crazy. Matt is off taking a moment for himself, and now I'm thinking how come none of these dudes are cheering, is there a problem? I realize that they're sort of in shock. Tyler points the camera at Brad and says, "What did we just see?"

Brad says, "Gotti just varial heelflipped this thing." Seconds later Matt returns to us, just beaming. He jumps off his board and tackles Brad in a bear hug, nearly knocking the camera over. Then a huge hug for Tyler and then one for me. Matt is crushing me, and I am beside myself with jubilation and pride. I say something like that was fucking amazing. Matt is so relieved and so happy and he is relatively unscathed. He finally slayed this monster that had been fucking with him for the past six months. And now all of the negativity has been turned positive by a factor of a million with this one make. Matt says, "I think it's the pressure, I like it, the more there is the better I skate."

And so for the second time in my life I have witnessed an NBD (shout-out to Nick), and also for the second time in my life Matt has taken a potentially stressful situation, like impending police or missing a flight, and solved it all by just landing the trick. To think about how devastating it would have been if he didn't get it is also to understand the pure, un-adulterated, and well-earned joy. Congratulations Gotti, now I get to say I was there the day Matt Gottwig varial heelflipped black marble (NBD).

Coda

Every single skater whom I met on that first day at Stoner Plaza is now a current pro. Paul Hart rides for Cliché Skateboards and recently put out an amazing video part. Sebo Walker is a pro for Krooked and Lakai. Nick Tucker is a pro for Primitive. In addition, Matt Gottwig, who was one of the first skaters I met, now rides for Krooked and Huf Shoes. Diego Najera I met only a year ago, and in that short time I've watched in awe as his career has skyrocketed. In 2016 he turned pro for Primitive Skateboards.

Aquil Brathwaite recently became head of Footwear Operations for Diamond Supply Skate Footwear brand. He lives in Silver Lake with his dog, and is eager to put his entrepreneurial mind to work. Atiba Jefferson continues to shoot all of the top skaters, as well as the NBA greats and legends. He has shot photos of musicians from Lil Wayne to Public Enemy, Bad Brains, Battles, and Arcade Fire. Atiba has also directed a video for TV on the Radio, and started a backpack company Bravo, which makes backpacks for photographers. RB Umali has started his own production house, RB Umali Film and Video Production, and already has a list of over 50 clients. He's done commercial work as well as music videos, for up-and-coming rappers. RB also got married on October 26, 2016.

Nick Tucker is now 26 years old and a highly respected professional skateboarder. He rides for Primitive Skateboards, one of the top companies in the industry, as well as the newly formed skate footwear brand from Diamond Supply. Nick is currently working on his video part for the second season of the highly acclaimed Berrics series *Push*, which will follow eight pro skaters for eight months, capturing the process of filming a video part. This series also goes in-depth into how skaters got their starts as well as interviews with the skaters' families. When I saw Nick last I asked him about filming with his family; I said, "Did your mom cry?" He laughed and said, "Oh yeah, tears of joy." Nick's part will be highly anticipated, and the series begins on October 25, 2016. There will be five 10-minute episodes, followed by the premiere of the video part. Most of the part is done, and Nick has yet another NBD at the Courthouse stage. This will be Nick's first part since his *Golden Hour* part that announced the beginning of his professional career. Nick is also working on a signature shoe with Diamond. Nick has also matured and constantly asks me what he calls "life questions," which include financial management and how you buy a house. I'm very lucky to have met this young man, and look forward to all of his future successes.

Since 2008 many spots have come and gone. The sand gaps in Santa Monica are no longer skateable, though the Triple Set continues to see action, most recently Diego Najera's nollie 360 flip. The Hollywood 16 remains a site of progression, and an NBD can be a career-cementing move, case in point Paul Hart's backside blunt slide, to fakie, in his most recent video. The Radisson Banks spot remains skateable, though it's waiting for its next upgrade.

Many of the classic spots are gone: Carlsbad, Hubba Hideout, and even Love Park in Philadelphia have all been demolished. However, the Courthouse continues to be a success. The skaters have developed a symbiotic relationship with the municipal workers and have been able to share public space while also progressing in their skating. On a recent trip there I counted about 30 skaters, many of whom were out-of-towners who had made the pilgrimage to skate the Courthouse, though when they see how high the stage is in real life, they quickly head over to the ledges.

Finally, Aaron Snyder. Aaron got married in Mexico in the spring of 2016, and I'm honored to say I was his best man. Recently he and his wife Michelle sold their condo and purchased a fixer-upper home in the Inglewood section of LA, and it's exciting to see what they will make of it. Aaron will be 40 the year this book comes out, which is incredible to me. He continues to work as an editor both in skating and in television; however, he has yet to really find a career that fuses all of his interests and talents. I'm sure that by the time you read this he will be well on his way. I consider this book as much his as my own.

During the course of this project we have learned from each other, grown together, annoyed each other a bit, and became closer than ever. I am so overjoyed that this project allowed me the opportunity to develop and hone a working relationship with my brother, and I hope it continues. I love you so much. Similarly, to all the skaters who shared their time and their stories, I am thankful and humbled by your patience and your kindness. I will forever be fascinated by your culture and am so excited to see where it goes. Thanks skateboarding for letting me hang. #skateboarderscanchangetheworld

APPENDIX

INTERVIEW WITH ALEC BECK, *TRANSWORLD* MAGAZINE
REPRINTED WITH PERMISSION FROM MACKENZIE EISENHOUR
So let's go through the whole story. When did you guys get involved in
this?

Thursday (GSD—2 days)

Basically, Go Skateboarding Day was June 21st, which was a Saturday. On
the Thursday night before GSD (Aaron) Snyder started texting me. He
was pissed. Understandably so. He texted me a whole bunch. He had just
found out that Nike was going to bring back the Courthouse ledges
for one night only.

Was that true though? I mean this wasn't just a rumor?

Yeah. They had a crew on the way to re-knob the spot at 5:30 P.M. on that
Saturday of Go Skate Day.

Wow. That's insane.

Right? So Snyder was bummed. He was really pissed about it. He thought
that it made skateboarders look like second-class citizens.

Yeah. His brother showed me the texts he wrote and it was pretty well
written—arguing that skateboarders were once again playing second
fiddle to homeless people and junkies. He was going off.

Exactly. In my personal opinion, I could see where he was coming from,
it's not that I don't care, but to me, if somebody wants to help us skate
something cool, no matter how long we get to skate it for—like you
could open up a handrail somewhere for half an hour I'd be psyched—I
was just looking at it that way. But I know Snyder and a ton of other
people have had a real personal involvement with the Courthouse for
a long time. So I understood why he was pissed and he made a bunch
of good points.

So how did this translate into actually getting it liberated?

So basically, as this was going on I was also knee deep in trying to rally
people and get support against this sound wall they want to build at

Stoner. (—Ed note: Stoner Skate Plaza was supposed to have a massive non-transparent wall built around the skate portion which Alec and the West LA Skate Org. have successfully fought against up to present. Alec was also the person responsible for the creation of Stoner Plaza.)

So you already had your hands full.

Yeah. I was knee deep in that and at first I just didn't feel like I could deal with Snyder and the Courthouse. But he kept on texting and explained that he was just venting too. He wasn't really asking me to do anything. So finally I started thinking like, "Well, actually, maybe there is something worth looking into here. Let's get back on it tomorrow." This was still all Thursday night.

Friday morning (GSD—1 day)

The next morning I called Jay Handel, the Chair of the West LA Neighborhood Council—he was the one who had originally hired me to get Stoner built. I called him up and was like, "Hey, I heard there's this Nike thing going on at the Courthouse, this might sound crazy but what do you think our chances would be of keeping the Courthouse as an open skate spot?" It was really just one of those where you figure, "I'll just call and see what they say." He came back and said, "I think it's a good idea. Definitely a long shot, but I see the value in it." He loves skateboarding. He gets it. At that point I asked him, "What do you need?" He said, "Well, we probably need an agreement from the skateboarders. Some type of show of solidarity and an agreement to take care of the space. On top of that we would need some type of maintenance money." So I was like, "Okay, how much would you need?" He said, "Probably $10,000 a year for the next five years." I told him I would call him back.

I went from my house straight to the Courthouse. I was just going to see if there was anybody there I could talk to. As I park my truck these two guys are walking out—walking to pretty nice cars and they look like they might be involved. So I ask them, "Hey, are you guys involved with what's going on here?"

They kind of looked at each other, "Depends who's asking." I started laughing and introduced myself—told them my involvement with Stoner and things like that. They were really nice and said, "Congratulations. We've heard about that" and we just kind of chatted for a second. Finally, I just came out with it, like, "I just got off the phone with the Neighborhood Council, I want to see if we can find a way to keep this thing open."

They turned out to be Jason Cohn, who is the Action Sports Brand Director for Nike West, and Travis Trick who is the Marketing Specialist for Action Sports at Nike. They said, "It's funny, we were just talking about the same thing but it's scheduled to be closed and re-knobbed tomorrow evening." I told them that the City Council would be willing to look into it if they were willing to donate $50,000 over the next five years. They looked at each other and just said, "Done."

Jesus. That's amazing.

At that point they said that it was obviously still a tentative "Yes" but "We think this is a great idea and we'd like to support it." We chatted a little bit more, they left and I called Jay (Handel) back and told him the news. He was blown away.

You had just talked to him. Like; "Fifty grand?" . . . An hour later, "Got it."

Yeah (Laughs.) Definitely right place, right time. A lot of serendipitous timing. So I let Jay know and he said, "Great, I'll start talking to some of the people involved and see what we can do." We talked some more a little bit later in the day but the point was that it would take some time. I thought to myself, "Well, we don't really have much time. We have until tomorrow at 5:30." I told the Nike guys I would see them the next day.

Which brings us to Saturday (GSD 2014).

Exactly, so by Saturday the Courthouse was ready to go. Nike had spent X amount of money and gone in and resurfaced all the ledges, de-knobbed the stage, built the hubbas, rail, and stairs, bondo'd the cracks, painted it blue, all ready to go for just for that one day—GSD.

I saw it Friday night and they had put a ton of work into it.

Yeah. I think they had taken out something like a hundred trash bags full of debris and garbage. So I saw everyone there the next day. We started out at Stoner. We had something like 2,000 people at Stoner, it was amazing. P-Rod made his arrival like Cher or something skating up to the park, he gave his speech, rolled around a bit, and then we skated through the streets to the Courthouse. I had never done any of those Wild in the Streets type things and it was just so electric. It felt like you were in like whitewater rapids or something. (Laughs.) All moving together. Great vibes.

So you get to Courthouse.

Yeah. So we got to Courthouse. The whole thing went down. It was really fun. Really smooth. They did a good job. And then it got to be about 4:30 P.M. and I was kind of stressing by then waiting to hear back from Jay. Like I said, Nike had made their agreement with the Courthouse to put the knobs back on at 5:30. That was just the extent of the agreement, nothing on Nike. And while I understand the arguments against it, I still think that even if it was only for that one day—a lot of kids that never got to skate there would still have had an amazing opportunity. That said, one day was rad but having it stay open forever was obviously even better.

4:30 GSD.

So it's 4:30, the clock is ticking and I haven't heard back from Jay, the City Councilman. So I just decide to just make the call. I just decide I'm going to make this call and deal with the fallout. At the time it wasn't really thought through or anything, but I just told them like, "Look, just call them off. Call off the knob crew."

It sounds like a movie thriller, "Call them off! Stand down knob crew!"

(Laughs.) Yeah. That's basically what it felt like. I was really stressed out. In my mind, if we didn't stop the knobs then, it was never going to happen. I told the Nike guys that we would explain to the city on Monday why they had to break the agreement and hadn't re-knobbed it. In the meantime, I told them, just call off the crew.

So amazing.

So they called the crew and told them to cancel the re-knobbing. But then it dawned on me; everybody has seen this—these pristine new ledges and beautiful open spot. What the fuck are we going to do to keep people from skating this for however many months it takes us to get an agreement worked out? I talked to the Nike guys for a minute and to them it was kind of in my hands now. I understood that they were already nervous about not putting the knobs back on and didn't want to be responsible any further than that. So it dawned on me that the only way we could make this happen now, would be if we made an effort from the skate community side to try and convince people not to skate it yet.

Pretty ironic. After finally liberating the spot you now have to be the one that makes sure nobody skates it.

(Laughs.) Yeah. It was pretty interesting to be on the other side of that. So I went home that night and drafted a little paper sign saying like, "Wait, don't blow it." That went on social media, Koston, P-Rod, and a bunch of other people re-posted it and then I also went and physically knobbed the ledges basically with the paper signs. Saying essentially, "If you grind through this paper, you are blowing it for everybody."

Two months later.

Two months passed, and in those two months nobody skated Courthouse. Nobody. It was amazing. I'm kind of a Pollyanna optimist most of the time, but I know my hunger for skateboarding. If there's a spot that I want to skate, nothing can stop me. So I really didn't know if the signs would work and people would get it. But everyone respected it. I was seriously surprised and stoked. There wasn't a single grind mark. The cop who works the desk at the Courthouse said he would see skaters constantly roll up, read the signs and leave. How rad is that? We had an opportunity to prove that we deserved this spot.

And we proved it.

We did prove it. We finally had a rally meeting with City Council after all that time and the motion was to pursue the possibility of this project. Not even to do it. But just to pursue it, and that passed 12–1. One member thought it was turning into Nike branding because of the color of the ledges. That was just over five weeks ago. Four or five meetings later, we talked to Nike; they appropriated the funds for the "minimal maintenance fee," and then all of the sudden I get this call from them telling me they are ready to do the grand opening. They wanted it to coincide with the Street League event that weekend. So July 25 we had the grand opening. Geoff McFetridge did that really cool mural on the stage the night before. At one point we were up in the Neighborhood Council office with the whole Nike crew, and Koston gave this moving speech about how much the Courthouse meant to him.

GLOSSARY

AM. A sponsored "amateur" skateboarder.

BANK. A skate spot. Usually a wall angled at 45 degrees.

BENCH. A skate spot.

BIG FOUR. Large steps, usually in a stadium format but not always. The big four at the Museum of Contemporary Art (MACBA) in Barcelona is one of the most famous, along with Rincon and Wallenberg.

BOLTS. The hardware that is used to attach the trucks to the deck.

BOWLS. Pool-like skate spots, usually made specifically for skating.

BUMP. Any obstacle from which a skater can launch into the air.

DECK. The wooden top of a skateboard.

DIY SPOT. "Do it yourself" spot. Any spot that skaters have constructed themselves.

DOUBLE SET. Two sets of stairs joined by a flat in the middle. Skaters say "four flat four," meaning four stairs, eight or so feet of flat concrete ground, and four more stairs.

EURO GAP. A bank to gap that ends on a higher plane than the bank. An uphill gap as opposed to a downhill gap.

FAKIE. To ride backward.

FLAT. A flat skateable surface.

FLAT BAR. A bar usually a foot or more off the ground that can be skated like a handrail.

FLAT GROUND. Level ground. Concrete, asphalt, marble, or wood that can be skated.

GAP. A space to be ollied over.

GNARLY. A word used to describe something dangerous. Or a description of a skater who skates dangerous obstacles.

GOOFY-FOOTED STANCE. Riding a skateboard with your right foot on the front of the board and pushing with your left foot.

GRIP TAPE. A sheet of black sandpaper-like material that adheres to the skateboard and allows the rider's feet to grip the board.

HALF PIPE. Any wooden, concrete, or metal obstacle that contains transitions to vertical walls composing half of a circle, or a giant "U" shape.

HAND RAIL. A rail that accompanies a set of stairs that can be skated.

HIP. An obstacle found in skate parks usually with multiple banked sides and a flat top.

HUBBA. Traditionally referred to the famous angled ledges that accompany the stairs at Hubba Hideout in San Francisco. Today refers to any angled ledge.

LEDGE. Any raised flat surface that can be skated.

MALL GRAB. A derisive term. Holding the skateboard by the trucks, which immediately signals that one is not a member of the subculture.

MANUAL PAD. An elevated surface on which to do manual (wheelie) tricks.

MELLOW. A word used to describe something that for skaters is not very dangerous.

MINI RAMP. Small half pipe usually only about four feet high, made specifically for skateboarding.

PICNIC TABLE. Obstacle found in many school yards that can be skated in multiple different ways. Since they essentially have the same dimensions throughout the country, they can be a litmus test.

PIER 7. The famous ledge and plaza at Pier 7 in San Francisco. Generally any ledge on which the distance from the ground is greater at the end of the ledge than the beginning.

PLAZA. An open public area with architectural components that were not made specifically for skateboarding but can be utilized as such.

PUSHING MONGO. Pushing forward on a skateboard with your front foot, contrary to the more accepted back-foot push and immediately signaling non-membership in the subculture. It also looks awful.

QUARTER PIPE. Any wooden, concrete, or metal obstacle that contains transitions to vertical walls composing one quarter of a circle.

REGULAR-FOOTED STANCE. Riding a skateboard with your left foot on the front of the board and pushing with your right foot.

SICK. A word used to express something good, e.g., "a sick style."

SKATE PARK. A place specifically designed for skateboarding.

STAIRS. Architectural component that can be skated as a gap.

STANCE. The positions of the feet for riding a skateboard.

STOKED. A word used to express emotional excitement, e.g., "I'd be stoked if I could ollie."

STREET. The entirety of the built environment that can be repurposed for skateboarding.

SWITCH STANCE (SWITCH). Riding a skateboard opposite your normal stance.

TECH/TECHNICAL. A word used to describe something complicated, or a description of skater who does very technical tricks on less dangerous obstacles.

TRANSITION. Curved transition to a vertical wall.

TRIPLE SET. Three sets of stairs joined by a flat in the middle of each set. Double sets and triple sets are more difficult to skate because they are longer and hence require the skater to fly in the air a greater distance at greater speeds.

TRUCKS. The metal axles that attach the wheels to the deck.

NOTES

INTRODUCTION

1 Higgins (2006).
2 Vivoni (2009); Borden (2001).
3 On the use of social media in social movements, see Beltran (2014) and Garza (2014).
4 On symbolic resistance, see Hall and Jefferson (1975); Snyder (2009).
5 You can find this video here: www.youtube.com/watch?v=5ZU5K3y7QhU.
6 Many of the top skaters have foundations dedicated to providing water to impoverished people around the world or providing kids in underserved communities with skateboards, gear, and skateboarding lessons. See www.skateistan.org.
7 Hall and Jefferson (1975: 47).
8 McRobbie (1997 [1989]: 197).
9 Lombard (2010).
10 See Hebdige (1979).
11 Graffiti writers also refer to their places as spots. Snyder (2009); Ferrell and Weide (2010).
12 Gottdiener and Hutchinson (2006).
13 Massey and Denton (1993); Feagin (2000); Kozol (1991); Brisman (2009).
14 Feagin (2000); Beeman (2015).
15 Lefebvre (1991).
16 Gieryn (2000); Gans (2002).
17 Hou (2010); Chase, Crawford, and Kalinski (2008); Franck and Stevens (2006); Chappell (2010).
18 Malone (2002); France (2007).
19 MacDonald and Shildrick (2007: 344).
20 Ilan (2013; 2015); Snyder (2009).
21 Borden (2001); Willard (1998).
22 Woolley and Johns (2001); Vivoni (2009); Beal and Wheaton (2003).
23 Howell (2001; 2005); Beal and Wheaton (2003); Vivoni (2009); Lombard (2010); Kelly, Pomerantz, and Currie (2005).
24 Borden (2001: 233).
25 Willis (2000).
26 On ethnic enclaves, see Waldinger (1995). On subcultures achieving "critical mass" and thus becoming self-sustaining, see Fischer (1975).

27 Five trips were made possible with grants from the PSC-CUNY Research Foundation. One trip was financed by the Eugene Lang Junior Scholar's Fund, and two trips and ongoing research were funded by the Whiting Fellowship.

28 On access, see Polsky (1969) and Hammersley and Atkinson (2007).

29 On research with family members, see Rambo-Ronai (1996).

30 On ethnographers fumbling with their pickup lines in the field, see Whyte (1947); Fine (1993).

31 Rose (1987; 1990); Venkatesh (2008).

32 See Seymour (2007); Pitts (2003); Bunsell (2013); Wacquant (2004).

33 Snyder (2009); Ferrell and Hamm (1998).

34 Most of the work on place as a site of knowledge formation deals with a single revered space. See Borer (2008).

35 On techniques for developing trust, see Polsky (1969).

36 On photo elicitation and other methods of visual sociology, see Collier (1967); Harper (2001).

37 Troy Turner originally made me aware that the way a well-executed trick sounds is just as pleasing as the way it looks (author interview, summer 2014). On sensory ethnography, see Pink (2009).

38 Becker (1963); Sanchez-Jankowski (1991); Duneier (2000); Wacquant (2004); Venkatesh (2008); Bunsell (2013).

39 See Wynn (2011); Kidder (2011; 2012).

40 Duneier (2000).

41 Collins (1990).

42 See Hayward and Presdee (2010). "Interactive device" comes from Ferrell and Hamm (1998).

43 See Ocejo (2012).

44 Shortell (2016).

CHAPTER 1. SKATEBOARDING AND THE CITY

1 Brooke (1999).

2 Brooke (1999).

3 Brooke (1999); Weyland (2002).

4 *Wheels on Fire* (1987, dir. Skip Engblom); *Streets on Fire* (1989, dir. Skip Engblom). See also *On Video* (Winter 2003, dir. Kirk Dianda).

5 Mullen and Mortimer (2004).

6 Mullen and Mortimer (2004). Also see the documentary film *The Man Who Souled the World* (2007, dir. Mike Hill).

7 This insight comes from former skater and current scholar of comparative literature Pete Lehman. Email, April 10, 2016.

8 Letter to the author, summer 1992.

9 *Man Who Souled the World*.

10 Higgins (2006).

11 See *Epicly Later'd*, Andrew Reynolds episode (July 5, 2010), www.youtube.com/watch?v=mxjLs3VGjcg.

12 You can find the video here: http://houseofhammers.com/videos/detail/973690f-3982e89?ucd=1. See also "Jaws vs. the Lyon 25," *Thrasher*, www.thrashermagazine.com/articles/videos/jaws-vs-the-lyon-25/.

13 See Girl Skateboards, *Mouse* (1996, dir. Spike Jonze).

14 This description is for explanatory purposes only; it is not the case that lefties ride "regular footed" and righties ride "goofy footed."

15 Shepard and Smithsimon (2011).

16 Newman (1972).

17 The film can be viewed on a number of platforms on the Internet.

18 Howell (2001).

19 See Howell (2005).

20 Howell (2001: 35); Jacobs (1961).

21 See the video blog *Epicly Later'd*, James Kelch episode (2009), www.youtube.com/watch?v=U70KO8zSl4.

22 Howell (2001: 13).

23 To learn more about hubba hideout, see the video on YouTube, www.youtube.com/watch?v=V-MpdrdAYL8.

24 Park (1915).

25 Thrasher (1929); Anderson (1923); Cressey (1932).

26 This transition is also represented in the HBO series *Boardwalk Empire*.

27 Burgess (2005 [1925]: 78).

28 Du Bois (2010 [1899]).

29 Dear (2005: 107).

30 Massey and Denton (1993). See also Coates (2014).

31 Soja (2002).

32 Davis (1990); see also Weide (2015).

33 Weide (2015).

34 My use of the term "beauty" is strictly phenomenological. I do not intend to enter into a discussion of aesthetic form, or beauty as a philosophy or worldview, but mean it subjectively and simply in the eyes of the beholder.

35 Fischer (1975). I too was seduced by the Birmingham School's spectacular punk Marxism and did not include Fischer's insights in my earlier subculture work, though all of the elements of the subculture career were present in Fischer's work.

36 Fischer (1975: 1329).

37 On the changing nature of subculture values, see Fine and Kleinman (1979).

38 Snyder (2009); Hodkinson (2002).

39 Dougherty (2016).

40 Kelly, Pomerantz, and Currie (2005).

41 See www.exposureskate.org for a description of an organization that seeks to "empower women through skateboarding."

42 Alexis Sablone is currently studying architecture at MIT, and I think that her insights would be perfect for this project. I've sent many emails and Instagram messages, but she hasn't replied.

43 Fuel TV produced a reality television show on Camp Woodward.

44 The stereotype of the skater as some combination of stupidity and brazenness is still rampant in mainstream media, despite skateboarding's corporate appeal. On skater "boi" as a sex type, see Alana Massey's 2015 horrific *New York Magazine* article, "The Enduring Appeal of a Skater Boi," in which she calls skaters "flaccid losers." When I decried her characterization on Twitter, she responded, "what if your hobby was taking jokey articles on the internet seriously." November 24, 2015.

45 On subculture media, see Duncombe (1997); Atton (2002); Snyder (2006).

46 Subculture was an antidote to urban anomie (Fischer 1975).

47 Hall and Jefferson (1975).

48 Lombard (2010: 475–76).

49 For a detailed critique of the Birmingham School, see Snyder (2009).

50 Nemeth (2006).

51 "LOVE Story," in *On Video* (2004, 411 Productions).

52 Howell (2005); Florida (2003).

53 See the film *All This Mayhem*, directed by Eddie Martin (2014).

54 The most notable and heroic are Andrew Reynolds and Jim Greco. Also see the short film *The Way Out*, directed by Jim Greco (2016). You can find the video at http://theridechannel.com/news/2016/02/jim-greco-the-way-out.

55 Author interview, July 2009.

CHAPTER 2. SKATE SPOTS

1 For one list of these spots see, Phelps (2008). See also Skatemaps.com.

2 Peter Lehman, email, April 10, 2016.

3 This point comes from the combined knowledge of Ocean Howell and Peter Lehman. Howell offered Westgate and Tershay as examples of skaters who don't always skate the most pristine spots, whereas Lehman pointed out that for Jordan Sanchez skating the unskateable is a stylistic choice unto itself. Howell, email, winter 2010; Lehman, email, spring 2016.

4 Many of my contacts have brought this up, though it is also articulated in Louison (2011).

5 See skateistan.org for more information on the organization.

6 "Process: The Technology Behind *We Are Blood*," Berrics, www.theberrics.com.

7 "We Are Blood: Interview with Ty Evans," *CCS*, http://shop.ccs.com.

8 Thornton (1996).

9 Email, April 2016.

10 Koerner (2015).

11 Koerner (2015). See also the Innoskate initiative sponsored by the Smithsonian at http://invention.si.edu/innoskate.

12 Koerner (2015).

13 Mullen (2012).

14 Wentzle Ruml confirms this in the documentary film *Dogtown and Z-Boys*.

15 "Master of manual skating" comes from Pete Lehman. Aaron's quotes come from author video, summer 2008.

16 Filmers and photographers are on the cutting edge of technology, and the gear described in text is already outdated. Today's filmers are using cameras twice as expensive.

17 This is not to suggest that there are no skaters who have been flipped and participated in the process of creating anti-skate devices for a profit.

18 See the film *Man on Wire* (2008, dir. James Marsh), where random, dangerous, pointless beauty can be transformative. Many of the citizens who witnessed Pettit's illegal death-defying act thought it was one of "the greatest things they'd ever seen."

CHAPTER 3. SKATEBOARDING BASICS

1 Because Brian Emmers was 16, a fellow skater became his legal guardian.

2 Author interview, summer 2014.

3 Author interview, summer 2014.

4 Gladwell (2008). Although the 10,000-hour rule is imprecise as a sociological concept, it does work for explanatory purposes.

CHAPTER 4. PROFESSIONAL STREET SKATEBOARDING

1 Again, this insight comes from Peter Lehman's close reading of this book.

2 There are add-on devices, including a fish-eye lens to attach to an iPhone, from companies like olloclip.

3 *Pain Is Beauty* (2013, Primitive Apparel), www.youtube.com/watch?v=oJe62B367fE (see the trick discussed here at the 00:50 mark).

4 The Berrics was purchased by the Wasserman Group after being rated one of the top 500 websites in the world.

5 Zitzer (2014).

6 Nick has a "Trickapedia" video on the Berrics website, where he does switch inward heel flips over and over, so one can get a real sense of what's happening. www.theberrics.com/trickipedia-switch-inward-heelflip.

7 Putting one's best tricks, the "hammers," after black was invented by Baker legend Jim Greco.

8 Understandably, Nick does not want this information public.

9 The fact that Aaron included a clear reference to Jane Jacobs shows how this project has impacted his own thinking.

10 Aaron provided me with a copy of the document.

11 See www.streetleague.com/faq.

12 You can watch the slam here, but beware it is gnarly. www.youtube.com/watch?v=zK9DEGqco3A.

13 For an instance of this technique in her videos, see videos such as this one: www.youtube.com/watch?v=XuJO4iAW6LU.

14 Borden (2001).

15 On the relationship between urban spaces and consumption practices, see Hayward (2004).

16 Hebdige (1979); Hall and Jefferson (1975); Muggleton and Weinzierl (2003).

17 Hodkinson (2002); Muggleton and Weinzierl (2003); also see Snyder (2009).

18 Hall and Jefferson (1975: 47).

19 McRobbie (1997 [1989]; 2002).

20 McRobbie (1997 [1989]: 197).

21 McRobbie (2002: 518, emphasis added).

22 McRobbie (1997 [1989]); Thornton (1995).

23 Hebdige (1979).

24 Clark (2003).

25 On "kung fu" as a political metaphor, see Prashad (2001).

26 Clark (2003: 233). For more on the relationship between symbols and political activism, see Ferrell (2007).

27 Klein, N. (2000).

28 Snyder (2006; 2009).

29 This comes from a discussion with Billy Rohan on the corner of Broadway and 17th Street in New York City, August 2010.

30 Anderson (2010).

CHAPTER 5. THE PRODUCTION OF SKATEBOARDING TRICKS

1 Skateboard art has been featured in galleries, books, and film. The California Heritage Museum had a show in 2008 called "The Evolution of Skateboard Art."

2 See also the award-winning documentary film *Dogtown and Z-Boys* (2001, dir. Stacy Peralta).

3 Friedman and Stecyk (2000).

4 Mullen and Mortimer (2004).

5 Brooke (1999).

6 Phelps (2006).

7 Email, April 10, 2016.

8 Higgins (2006).

9 See *Jenkem* magazine on Jamie Thomas's decision to sell one of his companies and the state of the skateboarding industry. www.jenkemmag.com.

CHAPTER 6. SKATEBOARDING AS A CAREER

1 Fischer (1975); Wirth (1938).

2 Fischer (1975).

3 Whyte (1947); Becker (1963).

4 Fischer (1975: 1320).

5 I'm embarrassed to say that I did not discover Fischer until after the publication of *Graffiti Lives*, as I, like the rest of academia, was under the spectacular spell of

the Birmingham School. Even though Fischer didn't call it a "subculture career," all of the elements are in place in this sentence. Fischer (1975).

6 Becker (1963); Berger (1972); Fine and Kleinman (1979).

7 Waldinger (1994).

8 Zukin (2009).

9 Kidder (2011).

10 Snyder (2009).

11 Ferrell and Weide (2010).

12 Friedman and Stecyk (2000); Phelps (2008).

13 Parkour traceurs are folks engaged in the practice of "free running" and performing quasi-gymnastic, athletic, and dangerous feats on urban obstacles. Although they do not appreciate the phrase, they have often been likened to "skaters without skateboards."

14 On graffiti, see Snyder (2009); on parkour traceurs and bike messengers, see Kidder (2012); and on skateboarders, see Borden (2001) and Snyder (2012).

15 Beal and Wheaton (2003).

16 Borden (2001); Vivoni (2009).

17 McRobbie (1997 [1989]).

18 On the practice of urban motocross, see the film *The 12 O'Clock Boys* (2014, dir. Lofty Nathan).

19 I recently learned that there is an entire subculture of folks who are highly skilled with a wooden toy called Kendama. The best of them post videos on YouTube and receive endorsements and sponsorships. (It's a bit silly though.)

20 See www.zumiez.com.

21 Willis (2000).

22 Willis (2000: 56).

23 Willis (1990).

24 The four main skateboard magazines are *Thrasher, Transworld, The Skateboard Mag*, and *Skateboarder*.

25 Mills (1956: 143).

26 McRobbie (2002).

27 On music, see Hodkinson (2002); on fashion, see McRobbie (2002).

28 McRobbie (2002: 521).

29 McRobbie (2002: 520).

CHAPTER 7. SKATEBOARDING AND ARCHITECTURE

1 Florida (2003).

2 Howell, email, spring 2012. The term "circuit of capital" comes from Lefebvre (1991).

3 See the amazing skateboard film *We Are Blood* (2015, dir. Ty Evans).

4 Rodriguez relays this story in *Freedom of Space: Skateboarding and Public Space* (2009, dir. Steve Olpin and Tim Irvin). See also the blog *Open Road*, http://playgrounddesign.blogspot.com.

5 Chiu (2009).

6 Howell (2005).

7 Sebo Walker famously lived in his van until he could afford an apartment.

8 Keith Hufnagel tells the story of the San Francisco police handcuffing a group of skaters, placing them in the back of a van, and slamming on the brakes while driving the city's streets. See www.youtube.com/watch?v=WhyDxPgkb70.

9 This can be seen in Trevor Colden's *Push* part on theberrics.com.

10 Hou (2010).

11 See the film *Freedom of Space: Skateboarding and Public Space* (2009, dir. Steve Olpin and Tim Irvin).

12 Owen Wilson plays a skater in *Yeah Right* (2003, dir. Spike Jonze). See www.you tube.com/watch?v=WGYGhAPlsVM.

13 Franck and Stevens (2006).

14 "DIY Spot Supply," www.redbull.com.

CHAPTER 8. LANDMARK ACHIEVEMENTS

1 On segregation, see Massey and Denton (1993); on politics, see Mitchell and Staeheli (2007); on culture, see Low (2000); on regulation through use and users, see Zukin (1995) and Gottdiener (2001).

2 Lefebvre (1991); de Certeau (1984).

3 Ferrell (2001); Hou (2010); Chase, Crawford, and Kalinski (2008); Franck and Stevens (2006).

4 Douglas (2014).

5 Ferrell (2001; 2007).

6 Mitchell (2003: 5).

7 Howell (2001: 3).

8 Newman (1972); Davis (1990: 22).

9 Howell (2001: 19).

10 Newman (1972).

11 Howell (2001). See also Shepard and Smithsimon (2001).

12 This is similar to David Grazian's argument in *Blue Chicago* (2003). See also Greenberg (2008).

13 Howell (2001: 21).

14 "Nick Tucker's Process: Golden Hour Ender," *The Berrics*, www.theberrics.com.

15 Jake Phelps, "Bust or Bail 2: The Ripper at Clipper," *Thrasher*, May 26, 2015, www .thrashermagazine.com. On other spaces that evoke quasi-spiritual awe, see Borer (2008).

16 On the actual activity of making sacred space, see Pena (2011).

17 Author interview, summer 2014.

18 See Snyder (2009); Young (2014); Kidder (2012).

19 Duncombe (1997); Atton (2002); Snyder (2006).

20 Chiu (2009).

21 There is an entire video on the mystique and legend of the Carlsbad Gap. See *On Video Skateboarding* (Summer 2002).

22 Email, 2010.
23 Chris confirmed this story in a 2016 discussion with me at Street League in Los Angeles.
24 For a fascinating look at Chris Cole's career, see the recent documentary *Motivation: The Chris Cole Story* (2015, dir. Adam Bhala Lough).
25 McRobbie (1997 [1989]).
26 Hall and Jefferson (1975); Muggleton (2000).
27 I have argued elsewhere that graffiti employs an "illegal" aesthetic, meaning the act of writing your name a certain way will signal to law enforcement that you are doing something bad, rather than, say, street art. See Snyder (2016).
28 See Howell (2005) and Kramer (2011).
29 "Skate and Destroy" was initially the rallying cry of *Thrasher* magazine, the first skater-owned media outlet.
30 See the Brian Lotti interview above, as well as the Vice Sports video on pro skaters in China, with cheering Shenzhen citizens in the background. The video can be found at www.youtube.com/watch?v=VFrxFeIYAVc.
31 *Freedom of Space: Skateboard Culture in Public Space* (2009, dir. Steve Olpin and Tim Irvin).
32 Hayward (2004).
33 Mitchell and Staeheli (2007).
34 Ferrell and Sanders (1995); Hayward (2004).
35 eMedCo, "Skateboard Prevention Devices," www.emedco.com.
36 Howell (2001); *The Social Life of Small Urban Spaces* (1988, dir. William H. Whyte).
37 *The Skateboard Mag*, November 2009.

CHAPTER 9. SKATEBOARD ACTIVISM
1 Los Angeles Conservancy, "West Los Angeles Civic Center," www.laconservancy.org. "The Union 76 station was designed by architect Gin Wong and completed in 1965. The design came earlier, though, and was meant for a very different location: in 1960 Wong designed the building to be part of Los Angeles International Airport."
2 Los Angeles Conservancy, "West Los Angeles Civic Center."
3 Email, June 2014.
4 Technically this is the second time. New York city skater Steve Rodriguez was able to get the city to recognize skaters' attachment to the Brooklyn banks, although skating was not heavily criminalized there. See Olpin and Irwin (2005).
5 "It is important here to understand that Nike is resacralizing the spot in an effort to make it profitable." Pete Lehman.
6 Garza (2014).
7 Beltran (2014).
8 Skateboarders can do this blindfolded, as they were asked to do so on episode 1 of season 3 of the *Thrasher*-produced series *King of the Road* (2015).

REFERENCES

Anderson, N. (1923). *The Hobo: The Sociology of the Homeless Man*. Chicago: University of Chicago Press.

Anderson, T. (2010). "Robbie McKinley Interview." *Bobshirt*. www.bobshirt.com.

Atton, C. (2002). *Alternative Media*. London: Sage.

Avramidis, K., and Tsilimpounidi, M., eds. (2016). *Graffiti and Street Art: Reading, Writing and Representing the City*. London: Ashgate.

Beal, B., and Wheaton, B. (2003). "'Keeping It Real': Subculture Media and the Discourses of Authenticity in Alternative Sport." *International Review for the Sociology of Sport* 38 (2): 155–76.

Becker, H. (1963). *Outsiders: Studies in the Sociology of Deviance*. New York: Free Press.

———. (1982). *Art Worlds*. Berkeley: University of California Press.

Beeman, A. (2015). "Walk the Walk but Don't Talk the Talk: The Strategic Use of Color-Blind Ideology in an Interracial Social Movement Organization." *Sociological Forum* 30 (1): 127–47.

Beltran, C. (2014). "'No Papers, No Fear': DREAM Activism, New Social Media and the Queering of Immigrant Rights." In A. Davila and Y. M. Rivero, eds., *Contemporary Latina/o Media: Production, Circulation, Politics*, 245–66. New York: New York University Press.

Berger, B. (1972). "On the Youthfulness of Youth Cultures." In P. K. Manning and M. Truzzi, eds., *Youth and Sociology*. Englewood Cliffs, NJ: Prentice Hall.

Borden, I. (2001). *Skateboarding, Space and the City: Architecture and the Body*. Oxford: Berg.

Borer, M. (2008). *Faithful to Fenway: Believing in Boston, Baseball, and America's Most Beloved Ballpark*. New York: New York University Press.

Brisman, A. (2009). "Food Justice as Crime Prevention." *Journal of Food Law & Policy* 5 (1): 1–44.

Brooke, M. (1999). *The Concrete Wave: The History of Skateboarding*. Toronto: Warwick.

Brown, E., and Shortell, T., eds. (2016). *Walking in Cities: Quotidian Mobility as Urban Theory, Method and Practice*. Philadelphia: Temple University Press.

Bunsell, T. (2013). *Strong and Hard Women: An Ethnography of Female Body Builders*. London: Routledge.

Burgess, E. (2005 [1925]). "The Growth of a City: An Introduction to a Research Project." In Lin and Mele, *Urban Sociology Reader*, 73–81.

Chappell, B. (2010). "Custom Contestations: Lowriders and Urban Space." *City and Society* 22 (1): 25–47.

Chase, J., Crawford, M., and Kalinski, J., eds. (2008). *Everyday Urbanism*. New York: Monacelli Press.

Chiu, C. (2009). "Contestation and Conformity: Street and Park Skating in New York City Public Space." *Space and Culture* 12: 25–42.

Clark, D. (2003). "The Death and Life of Punk: The Last Subculture." In Muggleton and Weinzierl, *Post-subcultures Reader*, 223–38.

Cloward, R., and Ohlin, L. (1961). *Delinquency and Opportunity: A Theory of Delinquent Gangs*. New York: Free Press.

Coates, T. (2014). "The Case for Reparations." *Atlantic*, June.

Cohen, A. (1955). *Delinquent Boys: The Culture of the Gang*. New York: Free Press.

Collier, J. (1967). *Visual Anthropology: Photography as a Research Method*. New York: Holt, Rinehart and Winston.

Collins, P. H. (1990). *Black Feminist Thought: Knowledge, Consciousness and the Politics of Empowerment*. New York: Routledge.

Cressey, P. (1997 [1923]). "The Life Cycle of the Taxi Dancer." In K. Gelder and S. Thornton, eds., *The Subcultures Reader*, 35–45. New York: Routledge.

Davis, M. (1990). *City of Quartz: Excavating the Future in Los Angeles*. New York: Verso.

Dear, M. (2005). "Los Angeles and the Chicago School: Invitation to Debate." In Lin and Mele, *Urban Sociology Reader*, 106–16.

Dear, M., and Flusty, S., eds. (2002). *The Spaces of Postmodernity: Readings in Human Geography*. Malden, MA: Blackwell.

de Certeau, M. (1984). *The Practice of Everyday Life*. Berkeley: University of California Press.

Dougherty, C. (2016). "Brian Anderson, Skateboarding Star, Comes Out as Gay." *New York Times*, September 28. www.nytimes.com.

Douglas, G. (2014). "Do-It-Yourself Urban Design: The Social Practice of Informal 'Improvement' through Unauthorized Alteration." *City and Community* 13 (1): 5–25.

Du Bois, W. E. B. (2010 [1899]). *The Philadelphia Negro*. New York: Cosimo Classics.

Duncombe, S. (1997). *Notes from Underground: Zines and the Politics of Alternative Culture*. New York: Verso.

Duneier, M. (2000). *Sidewalk*. New York: Macmillan.

Ellis, C., and Bochner, A., eds. (1996). *Composing Ethnography: Alternative Forms of Qualitative Research*. Walnut Creek, CA: Altamira Press.

Feagin, J. (2000). *Racist America: Roots, Current Realities and Future Reparations*. New York: Routledge.

Ferrell, J. (2001). *Tearing Down the Streets: Adventures in Urban Anarchy*. New York: Palgrave.

———. (2007). "For a Ruthless Cultural Criticism of Everything Existing." *Crime, Media, Culture* 3: 91–100.

Ferrell, J., and Hamm, M., eds. (1998). *Ethnography at the Edge*. Boston: Northeastern University Press.

Ferrell, J., and Sanders, C. (1995). *Cultural Criminology*. Boston: Northeastern University Press.

Ferrell, J., and Weide, R. (2010). "Spot Theory." *City Journal* 14: 48–62.

Fine, G. (1993). "Ten Lies of Ethnography: Moral Dilemmas of Field Research." *Journal of Contemporary Ethnography* 22 (3): 267–94.

Fine, G., and Kleinman, S. (1979). "Rethinking Subculture: An Interactionist Analysis." *American Journal of Sociology* 85 (1): 1–20.

Fischer, C. (1975). "A Subculture Theory of Urbanism." *American Journal of Sociology* 80 (6): 1319–41.

Florida, R. (2003). *The Rise of the Creative Class*. New York: Basic Books.

Foucault, M. (1986). "Of Other Spaces." *Diacritics* 16: 22–27.

France, A. (2007). *Understanding Youth in Late Modernity*. Maidenhead: McGraw-Hill.

Franck, K., and Stevens, Q. (2006). *Loose Space: Possibility and Diversity in Urban Life*. London: Routledge.

Friedman, G. E., and Stecyk, C. (2000). *Dogtown and the Legendary Z-Boys*. New York: Burning Flag Press.

Fyfe, N. (1998). *Images of the Street: Planning, Identity and Control in Public Space*. London: Routledge.

Gans, H. (2002). "The Sociology of Space: A Use-Centered View." *City and Community* 1 (4): 329–39.

Garza, A. (2014). "A Herstory of the #BlackLivesMatter Movement by Alicia Garza." *Feminist Wire*, October 7. www.thefeministwire.com.

Gieryn, T. (2000). "A Place for Space in Sociology." *Annual Review of Sociology* 26: 463–96.

Gladwell, M. (2008). *Outliers: The Story of Success*. New York: Little, Brown.

Gottdiener, M. (1985). *The Social Production of Urban Space*. Austin: University of Texas Press.

———. (2001). *The Theming of America*. Boulder, CO: Westview.

Gottdiener, M., and Hutchinson, R. (2006). *The New Urban Sociology*. 4th ed. Boulder, CO: Westview.

Grazian, D. (2003). *Blue Chicago: The Search for Authenticity in Urban Blues Clubs*. Chicago: University of Chicago Press.

Greenberg, M. (2008). *Branding New York: How a City in Crisis Was Sold to the World*. New York: Routledge.

Hall, S., and Jefferson, T., eds. (1975). *Resistance through Rituals: Youth Subcultures in Postwar Britain*. London: Hutchinson.

Hammersley, M., and Atkinson, P. (2007). *Ethnography: Principles in Practice*. 3rd ed. New York: Routledge.

Harper, D. (2001). "Talking about Pictures: A Case for Photo Elicitation." *Visual Studies* 17 (1): 13–26.

Harvey, D. (1985). *The Urbanization of Capital: Studies in the History and Theory of Capitalist Urbanization*. Baltimore: Johns Hopkins University Press.

Hayward, K. (2004). *City Limits: Crime, Consumer Culture and the Urban Experience.* London: Glasshouse Press.

———. (2012). "Five Spaces of Cultural Criminology." *British Journal of Criminology* 52: 441–62.

Hayward, K., and Presdee, M. (2010). *Framing Crime: Cultural Criminology and the Image.* London: Routledge.

Hebdige, D. (1979). *Subculture: The Meaning of Style.* London: Routledge.

Higgins, M. (2006). "In Board Sports, Insider Status Makes Gear Sell." *New York Times,* November 24. www.nytimes.com.

Hodkinson, P. (2002). *Goth: Identity, Style and Subculture.* Oxford: Berg.

Hou, J. (2010). *Insurgent Public Space: Guerrilla Urbanism and the Remaking of Contemporary Cities.* London: Routledge.

Howell, O. (2001). "The Poetics of Security: Skateboarding, Urban Design, and the New Public Space." http://urbanpolicy.net.

———. (2005). "The 'Creative Class' and the Gentrifying City: Skateboarding in Philadelphia's Love Park." *Journal of Architectural Education* 59 (2): 32–42.

Ilan, J. (2013). "Street Social Capital in the Liquid City." *Ethnography* 14 (1): 3–24.

———. (2015). *Understanding Street Culture: Poverty, Crime, Youth and Cool.* London: Palgrave Macmillan.

Jacobs, J. (1961). *The Death and Life of Great American Cities.* New York: Vintage.

Jerolmack, C. (2013). *The Global Pigeon.* Chicago: University of Chicago Press.

Kelly, D. M., Pomerantz, S., and Currie, D. (2005). "Skater Girlhood and Emphasized Femininity: 'You Can't Land an Ollie Properly in Heels.'" *Gender and Education* 17 (3): 229–48.

Kidder, J. (2011). *Urban Flow: Bike Messengers and the City.* Ithaca, NY: Cornell University Press.

———. (2012). "Parkour, the Affective Appropriation of Urban Space, and the Real/Virtual Dialectic." *City and Community* 11 (3): 229–53.

Klein, N. (2000). *No Logo: Taking Aim at the Brand Bullies.* New York: St. Martin's.

Koerner, B. (2015). "Silicon Valley Has Lost Its Way. Can Skateboarding Legend Rodney Mullen Help It?" *Wired,* January 27. www.wired.com.

Kozol, J. (1991). *Savage Inequalities: Children in America's Schools.* New York: Crown.

Kramer, R. (2011). "Political Elites, 'Broken Windows' and the Commodification of Urban Space." *Critical Criminology* 20: 229–48.

Lefebvre, H. (1991). *The Production of Space.* Oxford: Blackwell.

Lin, J., and Mele, C., eds. (2005). *The Urban Sociology Reader.* New York: Routledge.

Lombard, K.-J. (2010). "Skate and Create/Skate and Destroy: The Commercial and Governmental Incorporation of Skateboarding." *Continuum: Journal of Media and Cultural Studies* 24 (4): 475–88.

Louison, C. (2011). *The Impossible: Rodney Mullen, Ryan Sheckler, and the Fantastic History of Skateboarding.* New York: Lyons Press.

Low, S. (2000). *On the Plaza: The Politics of Public Space and Culture.* Austin: University of Texas Press.

MacDonald, R., and Shildrick, T. (2007). "Street Corner Society: Leisure Careers, Youth (Sub)culture and Social Exclusion." *Leisure Studies* 26 (3): 339–55.

Malone, K. (2002). "Street Life: Youth, Culture and Competing Uses of Public Space." *Environment and Urbanization* 14 (2): 157–68.

Massey, A. (2015). "The Enduring Appeal of a Skater Boi." *New York Magazine*, November 17.

Massey, D., and Denton, N. (1993). *American Apartheid: Segregation and the Making of the Underclass*. Cambridge, MA: Harvard University Press.

McRobbie, A. (1997 [1989]). "Second Hand Dresses and the Role of the Rag Market." In K. Gelder and S. Thornton, eds., *The Subcultures Reader*, 191–99. New York: Routledge.

———. (2002). "Clubs to Companies: Notes on the Decline of Political Culture in Speeded Up Creative Worlds." *Cultural Studies* 16 (4): 516–31.

Mills, C. W. (1956). *The Power Elite*. New York: Oxford University Press.

Mitchell, D. (2003). *The Right to the City: Social Justice and the Fight for Public Space*. New York: Guilford.

Mitchell, D., and Staeheli, L. (2007). *The People's Property: Power, Politics and the Public*. New York: Routledge.

Molotch, H., and Logan, J. (1987). *Urban Fortunes: The Political Economy of Place*. Berkeley: University of California Press.

Muggleton, D. (2000). *Inside Subculture: The Postmodern Meaning of Style*. Oxford: Berg.

Muggleton, D., and Weinzierl, R., eds. (2003). *The Post-subcultures Reader*. Oxford: Berg.

Mullen, R. (2012). "Pop an Ollie and Innovate." TEDxUSC, August 2016. www.youtube.com/watch?v=uEm-wjPkegE.

Mullen, R., and Mortimer, S. (2004). *The Mutt: How to Skateboard and Not Kill Yourself*. New York: Harper-Entertainment.

Nemeth, J. (2006). "Conflict, Exclusion, Relocation: Skateboarding and Public Space." *Journal of Urban Design* 11 (3): 297–318.

Newman, O. (1972). *Defensible Space: Crime Prevention through Urban Design*. New York: Macmillan.

Ocejo, R. (2012). *Ethnography and the City: Readings on Doing Urban Fieldwork*. New York: Routledge.

———. (2014). *Upscaling Downtown: From Bowery Saloons to Cocktail Bars in New York City*. Princeton: Princeton University Press.

Olpin, S., and Irwin, T., directors. (2005). *Freedom of Space: Skateboard Culture and the Public Space*. Fuel TV Experiment.

Park, R. E. (1915). "The City: Suggestions for the Investigation of Human Behavior in the Urban Environment." *American Journal of Sociology* 20 (5): 577–612.

Pena, E. A. (2011). *Performing Piety: Making Space Sacred with the Virgin of Guadalupe*. Berkeley: University of California Press.

Phelps, J. (2006). *Skate and Destroy: The First 25 Years of Thrasher Magazine*. New York: Rizzoli.

———. (2008). *Epic Spots: The Places You Must Skate before You Die*. New York: Universe Press.

Pink, S. (2009). *Doing Sensory Ethnography*. London: Sage.

Pitts, V. (2003). *In the Flesh: The Cultural Politics of Body Modification*. New York: Palgrave.

Polsky, N. (1969). *Hustlers, Beats, and Others*. New York: Anchor Books.

Prashad, V. (2001). *Everybody Was Kung Fu Fighting*. Boston: Beacon.

Rambo-Ronai, C. (1996). "My Mother Is Mentally Retarded." In Ellis and Bochner, *Composing Ethnography*, 109–31.

Redhead, S. (1997). *From Subcultures to Club Cultures*. Oxford: Blackwell.

Rose, A., and Strike, C., eds. (2004). *Beautiful Losers: Contemporary Art and Street Culture*. New York: Iconoclast.

Rose, D. (1987). *Black American Street Life: South Philadelphia, 1969–1971*. Philadelphia: University of Pennsylvania Press.

———. (1990). *Living the Ethnographic Life*. Newbury Park, CA: Sage.

Ross, A., and Rose, T., eds. (1994). *Microphone Fiends: Youth Music and Youth Culture*. New York: Routledge.

Russell, J. S., Kennedy, E., et al. (2002). "Designing for Security: Using Art and Design to Improve Security: Guidelines from the Art Commission of the City of New York." www.designtrust.org.

Sanchez-Jankowski, M. (1991). *Islands in the Street: Gangs and American Urban Society*. Berkeley: University of California Press.

Seymour, W. (2007). "Exhuming the Body: Revisiting the Role of the Visible Body in Ethnographic Research." *Qualitative Health Research* 17 (9): 1188–97.

Shepard, B., and Smithsimon, G. (2011). *The Beach Beneath the Streets: Contesting New York City's Public Spaces*. Albany: State University of New York Press.

Shortell, T. (2016). "Introduction: Walking as Urban Practice and Research Method." In Brown and Shortell, *Walking in Cities*, 1–22.

Snyder, G. (2006). "Graffiti Media and the Perpetuation of Subculture Careers." *Crime, Media, Culture* 2 (1): 93–101.

———. (2009). *Graffiti Lives: Beyond the Tag in New York's Urban Underground*. New York: New York University Press.

———. (2012). "The City and the Subculture Career: Professional Street Skateboarding in LA." *Ethnography* 13 (3): 306–29.

———. (2016). "Long Live the Tag: Representing the Foundations of Graffiti." In Avramidis and Tsilimpounidi, *Graffiti and Street Art*, 264–73.

Soja, E. (1989). *Postmodern Geographies: The Reassertion of Space in Critical Social Theories*. New York: Verso.

———. (2002). "Taking Los Angeles Apart: Some Fragments of a Critical Human Geography." In Dear and Flusty, *Spaces of Postmodernity*, 150–61.

Stratford, E. (2002). "On the Edge: A Tale of Skaters and Urban Governance." *Social and Cultural Geography* 3 (2): 193–206.

Thornton, S. (1996). *Club Cultures: Music, Media and Subcultural Capital.* Middletown, CT: Wesleyan University Press.

Thrasher, F. (1929). *The Gang.* Chicago: University of Chicago Press.

Venkatesh, S. (2008). *Gang Leader for a Day: A Rogue Sociologist Takes to the Streets.* New York: Penguin.

Vivoni, F. (2009). "Spots of Spatial Desire: Skateparks, Skateplazas, and Urban Politics." *Journal of Sport and Social Issues* 33 (2): 130–49.

Wacquant, L. (2004). *Body and Soul: Notes of an Apprentice Boxer.* New York: Oxford University Press.

Wacquant, L., and Wilson, W. J. (1989). "The Cost of Racial and Class Exclusion in the Inner City." *Annals of the American Academy of Political and Social Science* 501 (1): 8–25.

Waldinger, R. (1994). "The Making of an Immigrant Niche." *International Migration Review* 28 (1): 3–30.

———. (1995). "When the Melting Pot Boils Over: The Irish, Jews, Blacks, and Koreans of New York City." In J. Feagin and M. P. Smith, eds., *The Bubbling Cauldron: The New Political Economy of Race and Ethnicity*, 265–81. Minneapolis: University of Minnesota Press.

Weide, R. (2015). "Race War? Inter-racial Conflict between Black and Latino Gang Members in Los Angeles." Unpublished dissertation, New York University.

Weyland, J. (2002). *The Answer Is Never: A Skateboarder's History of the World.* New York: Grove Press.

Whyte, W. (1947). *Street Corner Society.* Chicago: University of Chicago Press.

Willard, M. (1998). "Séance, Tricknowlogy, Skateboarding, and the Space of Youth." In J. Austin and M. Willard, eds., *Generations of Youth: Youth Cultures and History in Twentieth-Century America*, 327–46. New York: New York University Press.

Willis, P. (1990). *Common Culture: Symbolic Work at Play in the Everyday Cultures of the Young.* London: Westview.

———. (2000). *The Ethnographic Imagination.* New York: Polity Press.

Wirth, L. (1938). "Urbanism as a Way of Life." *American Journal of Sociology* 44 (1): 1–24.

Woolley, H., and Johns, R. (2001). "Skateboarding: The City as Playground." *Journal of Urban Design* 6 (2): 211–30.

Wynn, J. (2011). *Tour Guide: Walking and Talking New York.* Chicago: University of Chicago Press.

Young, A. (2014). *Street Art, Public City: Law, Crime and the Urban Imagination.* London: Routledge.

Zitzer, P. (2014). "In Words . . . Nick Tucker." *The Skateboard Mag*, no. 133. www.theskate boardmag.com.

Zukin, S. (1995). *The Cultures of Cities.* New York: Wiley.

———. (2009). *Naked City: The Death and Life of Authentic Urban Places.* New York: Oxford University Press.

INDEX

ABD (already been done), 154, 201, 208, 234

activism, 8, 12, 86–87, 109, 148, 184, 186–87, 195, 205, 215, 222–23, 230, 263n6

Adalpe, Mike, 234

Adidas, 144, 164

Adidas Skateboarding, 152

Adobe Premiere, 161

aerospace industry, 52

aesthetics, 75, 196, 271n27

Airwalk shoes, 101

alcohol, 60, 61

Alien Workshop, 85

Almost Skateboards, 39

already been done. *See* ABD

Alva, 5

amateurs, 38, 153

Anderson, Brian, 12, 51, 56, 113

Anderson, Tim, 150

antiestablishment worldview, 14

antiglobalization, 147

anti-skate devices, 85–86, 130, 184, 185, 208, 209–11, 267n17

Anti-Social Orders, 19

Appleyard, Mark, 120

appropriation, 19, 175

architecture, 9, 18; defensive design, 183–85; DIY, 186; guerilla, 64, 80, 184–86; imagination and, 79; interpretation of, 87, 197; as obstacles, 21, 36, 154; spots and, 27–28, 30, 40, 54, 70; subculture and, 195. *See also* spots

Arguelles, Felix, 137, 139

art, 152, 268n1

Art Worlds (Becker), 152

Asia, 206–7

aspect ratio, 160

Asta, Tom, 183

Atlas, Brian, 132

authenticity, 20

Away Days, 152

backside, 70; bluntslide, to fakie, 250; kickflips, 41, 43, 90, 135, 242; nollie, backside, 180 heelflip, 201; nollie backside flip, 90; nollie heelflip, backside lipslide, to fakie, 139; nollie heelflip, backside nosegrind, nollie heelflip, 118; nollie to backside lipslide, 99; nosegrind, 237; shove it, 43; switch kickflip backside tailslide, 135; tailslides, 1, *8*, 45–47, 69, 80–83, 135; 360 shove it, 41; 270, noseblunt, 139–40; varial heelflips, 42

backwards, 91–92

Bacon, Edmund, 207

bag of tricks, 137

Baker, Lacey, 57, 111, 141–43

Bakerboys Distribution, 164

Baker Skateboards, 39, 44, 164

banks, 64, 67, 135. *See also specific banks*

Barbier, Sal, 156

Barcelona, Spain, 87, 184

The Beach Beneath the Street (Shepard and Smithsimon), 47

Beal, Becky, 20, 171

Beasley, Theotis, 230

the Beatles, 13

Street League Skateboarding: Best Trick,
141; Big Section, 138–39; competition,
7, 103, 132; Control Section, 134, 135,
137, 138; course designs, 141; DC shoes
and, 133; Flow Section, 134, 135; Impact
Section, 134, 138–39; judges, 135–36;
Run section, 141; behind the scenes at,
133–40; scoring, 134–35, 136, 141–42;
Aaron Snyder as judge at, 132, 136–38;
subculture and, 133; Super Crown Finals, 57, 133, 140, 203; women in, 141–42
Streets on Fire, 36, 188
street theater, 87
style, 14, 59–62, 71, 112–13, 128, 201, 266n3
subculture, 10; architecture and, 195; capital,
74, 173, 176, 199; career and, 12, 13–14,
16, 25, 144–48, 152, 166–68, 178–79, 204,
265n35, 268n5; cities and, 166–68; city
and, 166–69; commodification of, 15;
community and, 16; critical mass of,
167; definition of, 55–56, 167; diversity
of, 55; entrepreneurism and, 13–14, 15;
ethnic enclaves, 15–16, 21, 168–70; filmers and, 155; graffiti, 12; history of, 197,
237; identity and, 19, 55–56, 170; impact
of, 145–46; industry, 21; knowledge of,
169; landmarks of, 27; laws and, 200; as
learning network, 101; literature on, 15;
media and, 16, 25, 36–37, 58, 155, 175–77,
200, 236; motivation and, 195; music,
145; norms, 61; outlaw, 103; participation in, 28–29, 58, 172, 179; photographers and, 155; politics of, 12, 58, 195,
209–10; profit and, 200; sports and, 202;
Street League Skateboarding and, 133;
style and, 14; symbolism and, 146–47;
theory, 144; tricks and, 201; types of, 55
"A Subculture Theory of Urbanism," 166
surfers, 35
surveillance, 84, 196, 208
survival, capitalism and, 14
switch, 41; back tailslide, to shove it,
out, 45–47; flips, 42; frontside, 180;

heelflips, 203; frontside bluntslide, 112,
136; frontside blunt slide down the
hubba, 135; frontside nosegrind, 99;
heel, feeble grind on the flat bar,
137–38; heelflips, 116–18; heelflip-switch
manual-switch heelflip, 116–18; hippie
twist, 95; inward heelflip to manual,
121–22, 267n6; kickflip backside
tailslide, 135; kickflip over the bump to
bump, 135; kickflips, 135; smith grind,
99; stance, 42, 92, 95; 360 flip, lip slide,
143; 360 flip, nosegrind, 67
symbolic capital, 173
symbolic creativity, 175
symbolic resistance, 144–45, 171–72
symbolic work, 175
symbolism, 146–47, 197

tailslides, 1, *8*, 43, 45–47, 69, 80–83, 135
talent, 61, 96–97, 105
Tamm, Daniel, 230
The Taxi-Dance Hall (Cressey), 51
Taylor, Grant, 241
Taylor, Mikey, 120, 134
team, 163–65
team managers, 10, 72
Tech Deck, *50, 202*
tech-gnar, 45
technical/risk continuum, 45
technique, risk and, 45
technology, 162, 267n16
tech skaters, 65, 92, 112, 129
teddy boys, 13, 146
TEDxUSC Talk, 74–75
Templeton, Ed, 164
terminology, 22–23
Terpening, Kevin, 190–91
Tershay, Raven, 65, 266n3
Texas Gap, 83–84, *84, 85*
Theme Building, LAX, 215
Thomas, Jamie, 164
Thomas Paine Park, 245
Thornton, Sarah, 74

ABOUT THE AUTHOR

Gregory J. Snyder is a sociologist and ethnographer who studies subcultures. He is currently Associate Professor of Sociology at Baruch College at the City University of New York. His publications include *Graffiti Lives: Beyond the Tag in New York's Urban Underground*, also with NYU Press.

Lightning Source UK Ltd.
Milton Keynes UK
UKOW04f2138281017
311724UK00002B/57/P